C. W. Park

April 7, 2017

Praise for Brand Admiration

The brand admiration model provides a compelling framework (the 3Es) for developing brands that enhance value to customers and companies alike. Such brands connect with customers and meet goals contributing to their happiness by providing meaning, identity, and emotion. This is powerful stuff!

—**JAMES R. BETTMAN**, Burlington Industries Professor, Fuqua School of Business, Duke University

Park, MacInnis, and Eisingerich bring their wealth of experience and insight to offer a thorough, original, and practical view of branding. Comprehensive, concise, and highly actionable, their detailed development of the brand admiration concept is a virtual gold mine for thoughtful practitioners interested in improving the design, implementation, and measurement of their branding strategies.

—**KEVIN L. KELLER**, E. B. Osborn Professor of Marketing, Tuck School of Business, Dartmouth University, and former executive director of the Marketing Science Institute

This book constitutes a rich and insightful addition in the world of brand strategy, as it pinpoints the ins and outs of how to build a beloved brand. For anyone or any company committed to being an admired brand, this book is required.

—**EUI SUN CHUNG**, vice chairman, Hyundai Motor Company

Park, MacInnis, and Eisingerich provide a powerful yet immensely practical perspective on building and managing brand admiration. Solidly grounded in academic research, the book provides an array of actionable tools to curate and measure brand admiration for the short- and long-term success of brands. This book is a must read for senior executives in businesses large and small, as well as for those who are directly involved in managing brand performance.

—**BABA SHIV**, Sanwa Bank, Limited, and Professor of Marketing, Stanford Graduate School of Business

Finally, a book that evolves the discipline of branding with a fresh, comprehensive, and practical approach. This is a must read for business leaders looking to build an enduring brand that will maximize the value of their company.

—**DOREEN IDA**, former division president and marketing director at Nestlé USA

Savvy branders like Apple and Nike know that to win you need to go beyond functionality into emotionality. But how do you execute on making your brand human? Park, MacInnis, and Eisingerich provide an easy-to-use road map grounded in rigorous consumer psychology research. Their enable, entice, enrich framework is logical, intuitive, and timely. This book gives you the conceptual tools to create and sustain brands that are admired.

—**ROHIT DESHPANDÉ**, Sebastian S. Kresge Professor of Marketing, Harvard Business School, and former executive director of the Marketing Science Institute

Brands are social evaluations of organisational vitality. Every leader is looking for ways to enhance his or her brand and reputation in crowded chatter. Park, MacInnis, and Eisingerich offer a practical, research-driven toolbox that unlocks a truly insightful and innovative approach to branding. Must read!

—**GERRY GEORGE**, Dean and Lee Kong Chian Chair Professor of Innovation and Entrepreneurship, Lee Kong Chian School of Business, and Editor, Academy of Management Journal

This book beautifully solidifies why experiential marketing is one of three essential elements that contribute to making a brand admired. The breakthrough integrative framework brilliantly conveys the key issues brand managers must consider when growing their brands.

—**BERND SCHMITT**, Robert D. Calkins Professor of International Business, Columbia University, and faculty director of the Center on Global Brand Leadership

There is much to admire about *Brand Admiration*! The authors present a cutting-edge framework practitioners can use to build valuable brands that consumers trust, love, and respect.

—**DEBORAH ROEDDER-JOHN**, Curtis L. Carlson Chair in Marketing and professor, Carlson School of Business, University of Minnesota

C. Whan Park | Deborah J. MacInnis | Andreas B. Eisingerich

BRAND

ADMIRATION

Building a Business People *Love*

Foreword by Allen Weiss

WILEY

This book is printed on acid-free paper.

Copyright © 2016 by John Wiley & Sons. All rights reserved

Published by John Wiley & Sons, Inc., Hoboken, New Jersey
Published simultaneously in Canada

For general information about our other products and services, please contact our Customer Care Department within the United States at (800) 762-2974, outside the United States at (317) 572-3993 or fax (317) 572-4002.

Wiley publishes in a variety of print and electronic formats and by print-on-demand. Some material included with standard print versions of this book may not be included in e-books or in print-on-demand. If this book refers to media such as a CD or DVD that is not included in the version you purchased, you may download this material at http://booksupport.wiley.com. For more information about Wiley products, visit www.wiley.com.

Library of Congress Cataloging-in-Publication Data is Available

ISBN 9781119308065 (Hardcover)
ISBN 9781119308072 (ePDF)
ISBN 9781119308096 (ePub)

Cover Design: PAUL MCCARTHY
Cover Art: © MAREIKE DRIES / EYEEM / GETTY IMAGES

Printed in the United States of America
10 9 8 7 6 5 4 3 2 1

CONTENTS

LIST OF FIGURES

LIST OF TABLES

ABOUT THE AUTHORS

Dr. C. Whan Park is the Robert E. Brooker Professor of Marketing, University of Southern California. He received a BA in German language and literature from Seoul National University, Korea, in 1967, and an MS and PhD in business administration from the University of Illinois in 1974. Dr. Park has published numerous articles in the *Journal of Marketing Research*, *Journal of Consumer Research*, *Journal of Marketing*, and *Journal of Consumer Psychology*. His works have also appeared in many other journals, including *Organizational Behavior and Human Performance*, the *Harvard Business Review*, and the *Journal of Retailing*. Professor Park coauthored *Marketing Management* (Dryden Press, 1987) with Dr. Gerald Zaltman of Harvard University, and *Handbook of Brand Relationships* (M.E. Sharpe, 2009) with Deborah J. MacInnis and Joseph Priester. In 1987 he was the recipient of the Alpha Kappa Psi award for his article *Strategic Brand Concept-Image Management*, which appeared in the *Journal of Marketing*. He is a fellow of the Society of Consumer Psychology (2012) and the Association for Consumer Research (2015). Dr. Park is a former editor of the *Journal of Consumer Psychology* (2008–2012). He currently serves as director of the Global Branding Center, Marshall School of Business, University of Southern California (2008–present). Dr. Park served as an advisor to Samsung from 1989 to 1998 and as a member of the board of directors for Samsung Corporation from 2001 to 2010. He has been an advisor for Pulmuone Corporation since 1993. He has been directing and teaching a number of marketing executive programs at Marshall since 1998.

Dr. Deborah J. MacInnis is the Charles L. and Ramona I. Hilliard Professor of Business Administration and a professor of marketing at the Marshall School of Business, University of Southern California. She received a BS in psychology from Smith College in 1980 and a PhD in marketing from the University of Pittsburgh in 1986. She is theory development editor at the *Journal of Marketing*, and formerly served as coeditor of the *Journal of Consumer Research* and associate editor of the *Journal of Consumer Research* and *Journal of Consumer Psychology*. She formerly served as treasurer, and president, of the Association for Consumer Research, and is a former vice president of conferences and research for the American Marketing Association's Academic Council. She has received the *Journal of Marketing's* Alpha Kappa Psi Award and its Maynard Award for papers that make the greatest contribution to marketing thought, and the Long-Term Contribution Award from the *Review of*

Marketing Research. Professor MacInnis is coauthor of a leading textbook on consumer behavior (with Wayne Hoyer and Rik Pieters) and coeditor of several volumes on branding (with C. Whan Park and Joseph Priester). She has also served as vice dean of research and strategy and vice dean of the undergraduate program at the Marshall School of Business. She is the winner of local and national teaching awards and is the recipient of USC's Mentoring Award. She is a member of the American Marketing Association and the Association for Consumer Research. Professor MacInnis's research focuses on emotions and branding.

Dr. Andreas B. Eisingerich is the academic programme director of the full-time MBA and professor of marketing at Imperial College Business School, Imperial College, London. He received a BSc degree in management, with a focus on economics, quantitative methods, and psychology, from the London School of Economics in 2003, and a research master's degree (MPhil in management with a focus on marketing) from the University of Cambridge in 2004, where he also earned a PhD in marketing in 2006. He publishes widely in leading academic and practitioner journals, including the *Journal of Consumer Psychology*, *Journal of Marketing*, *Journal of Service Research*, and *Harvard Business Review*, among others. Professor Eisingerich's work focuses on consumer behavior, brand management, and service innovation, and includes collaborations with the Bill & Melinda Gates Foundation, UNAIDS, WHO, WWF, and numerous businesses across industries and markets.

FOREWORD

There are hundreds of books on the market about branding. Almost all talk about how to make your brand more relevant to customers, and maybe gain their trust. But what if there was an overarching framework that could be used to understand how a brand can systematically create value—and ensure that value endures—for both a company and its customers? Researchers C. Whan Park, Deborah J. MacInnis, and Andreas B. Eisingerich have recently introduced such a framework in their book, *Brand Admiration: Building a Business People Love.*

In this breakthrough, integrative, actionable, and research-based book, Professors C. Whan Park, Deborah J. MacInnis, and Andreas B. Eisingerich provide a fresh perspective on branding. The fundamental takeaway is that brand admiration is the ultimate destination point for brands.

Think about a few well-known brands: Nike, Apple, Disney, Google, and Salesforce. What do they have in common? Yes, they're well-known brands with good products or services. But their enduring success can be attributed to the fact that they are admired.

Admired brands are those that customers love, trust, and respect—so much so that they feel some kind of personal connection to the brand. The brand is the first one people think about when they need something in the brand's product category. Customers not only buy an admired brand, they speak well of it (even if they pay a little more for it), and they'll be more forgiving when the brand screws up. Making your brand trusted, loved, *and* respected is critical, because these psychological states exponentially impact how loyal customers will be toward your brand and how much they'll advocate on its behalf.

These customer behaviors *create enormous value for companies* in the form of increased profits, better employee retention, opportunities for partnerships, and more. From the authors' perspective, a brand is more than a mere name that helps to differentiate products or services. It is a value-generating entity relevant to both customers and the brand owner—and the effort required to create an admired brand is worth its weight in gold.

Park, MacInnis, and Eisingerich not only clarify *what brand admiration is*, they show why *every member of the organization* should be intent on creating it. And they clarify *what marketers can do to make their brand admired and keep it so*. Specifically, the most admired brands provide benefits that underlie human happiness: they enable, entice, and enrich customers. This theory is rooted in sound marketing concepts, as well as established psychological theories of human motivations, goals, and needs. In light of the evolving nature of the competitive marketplace, marketers need to not just create, but also sustain brand admiration over time. A sound and actionable set of value-enhancement strategies will give you great insight into how you can continue to best your own brand and outshine competitors.

The authors also make clear recommendations for how marketers can *leverage an admired brand through the strategic use of product and brand extensions*. In this way, admired brands not only become more profitable, they are also more likely to provide *avenues for continued growth*.

As part of their integrative framework, Park, MacInnis, and Eisingerich have also developed a measure of brand equity that can help brand managers and CMOs show the worth of the brand (and of brand investments) to CFOs. Brand managers can also use the dashboard metrics the authors developed to diagnose whether there are any canaries in the coal mine, and if there are, what to do next.

What's more, their framework applies to brands in any type of business and across industries—from B2B and B2C to tech, commodities, celebrities, institutions, nonprofit organizations, and more. It can be applied to new or existing brands with equal success. B2B brands in particular have much to gain by considering this brand admiration perspective. Everyone can learn from this book.

MarketingProfs is so keen on the concept of brand admiration that it has become a focal part of our corporate training program. What we like about this book is that it's not based on fluff or purely on stories. The authors are world-renowned academics who have studied branding for decades. They use their own research and that of other thought leaders in marketing to build their integrative framework. We have yet to see a framework that offers so many new ideas and so much stimulating, action-oriented thinking in a single book.

Allen Weiss
CEO/Founder
MarketingProfs, LLC

PREFACE: WHAT MAKES THIS BOOK DIFFERENT?

The business world does not lack for books on branding. But *Brand Admiration* is different in several game-changing ways.

First, we develop a novel, integrated and overarching perspective on the fundamental goals of brand management and how we achieve them. We call this perspective the brand admiration management system. This system (Figure P.1) provides a *road map* for building, strengthening, and leveraging brand admiration over time, in ways that produce value to customers and companies alike. We regard brand admiration as the most desired state of a brand's health. Unlike other books that primarily provide a set of to do's, we provide an overarching system whose components are connected and integrated. In this way, our book offers the theoretical coherence that makes its set of "to do's" highly compelling.

Second, we directly link brand admiration to the brand's value to companies. Building, strengthening, and leveraging brand admiration is, we argue, the most important and foundational objective of branding. Using decades of research in marketing and psychology, we emphasize three critical classes of benefits that characterize admired brands. Such brands *enable, entice, and enrich* customers. These three classes of benefits, called the 3Es for short, have an *exponential effect* on customers' relationship with a brand. They build brand admiration by enhancing customers' trust in, love of, and respect for the brand. This brand admiration, in turn, provides value to the firm. We describe some important psychological processes in Chapter 3 that explain *why* the 3Es create *value* for customers (and hence companies).

Third, we describe *how* companies can build, strengthen, and leverage this value. Rather than focusing on quick fixes, and tactics to enhance fourth-quarter earnings, we examine forces responsible for efficient short-term competitive advantages that also *build* (Chapters 4, 5, and 6), *strengthen* (Chapter 7), and *leverage* (Chapters 8, 9, and 10) brand admiration over the long term. When a short-term focus and long-term goals are aligned, brands enjoy short-term and long-term success. History is replete with examples of brands that have been market leaders for decades, generations, or even a century or more (Chapter 2).

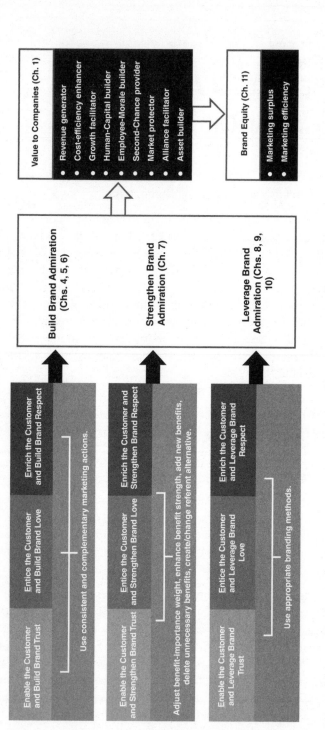

Figure P.1 The Brand Admiration Management System

Fourth, we propose an innovative way of thinking about brand architecture design (Chapter 10). We address how various businesses and products within the company's portfolio are branded to deliver to a company the optimal financial, asset-building, and organizational benefits. We also present a novel and implementable metric for measuring brand equity (Chapter 11) and a set of dashboard metrics that help managers diagnose what's driving (or not driving) successful brand performance (Chapter 12).

Fifth, our framework is not based on mere assertions. Nor is it based purely on a particular brand example. Instead, it is grounded in decades of *theoretical and empirical* research from us and other academics in marketing and psychology. In particular, our framework derives from research on fundamental human needs, goals, emotions, and motivations, as well as in empirical research that supports needs, goals, emotions, and motivations as drivers of brand admiration.

Finally, our framework is *generalizable. It is equally applicable* to the introduction of new brands and the management of existing brands. It is appropriate for brands in different industries and for both B2B and B2C brands. Brand managers, CMOs, CEOs, and employees who work for product brands, service brands, celebrity brands, country brands, institution brands, and NGO brands can all use our framework.

We hope you will see that the ideas in this book are novel, actionable, and strong—indeed, game changing in driving the value of your brand to your customers and your company.

SECTION 1

THE BIG PICTURE

CHAPTER 1

Why Brand Admiration?

A dmired brands create blockbuster value for companies and customers alike.

INTRODUCTION

Yes, we have heard about it and seen it with our own eyes, but it is still hard to fully grasp Apple's miraculous comeback during the first 16 years of the 21st century. In 1999, Microsoft's stock was at a record high, with its market capitalization close to $620 billion. Apple was teetering on bankruptcy. The notion that Apple would ever match Microsoft's financial firepower, let alone surpass it, was unthinkable. In a 1998 *Vanity Fair* interview, Bill Gates "couldn't imagine a situation in which Apple would ever be bigger and more profitable than Microsoft." Nearly 17 years later, Apple's market capitalization stands at $683 billion, more than double that of Microsoft's. Sales of the iPhone 6s have been phenomenal, and more than 48 million iPhone 6 and 6s units were sold during the last quarter of 2015 alone.[1] Indeed, in July of 2015 Microsoft's chief executive Satya Nadelia stated that if Microsoft is to compete with Apple, Google, and others, Windows must become *desired*. Microsoft's Windows operating system has endured as a must-have work tool, not because it's an object that customers *love*. From his perspective, making customers love Windows was the critical objective.[2]

We don't know what will happen to Apple five or 20 years from now. But the answers to two important questions might help Apple strengthen its success over time. The first asks how Apple turned itself around. The second asks what Apple must do to ensure continuous growth and prosperity. As to the first question, we've heard a lot about the things that Apple did right when it introduced the iMac, iPod, and iPhone. However, we do not understand *how* these and other factors created the powerful Apple brand. Knowing a list of factors is one thing. Understanding how they work together to produce such a strong impact on customers is another. Unless we can answer the first question, it is hard to answer the second.

Microsoft needs to ask why it failed to make people love Windows, despite its must-have usefulness. It also needs to ask whether creating brand love is the ultimate and true destination point to which Microsoft should aspire. We think the answer is no. While important for developing prosperous customer relationships, love alone is limited in its power to sustain customer relationships over time. To create prosperous and sustainable customer relationships, Windows needs to *go beyond brand love*. Like the world's most successful brands, it needs to *become admired*. A fundamental goal of this book is to discuss what admired brands are, how to develop them, how to strengthen them, and how to leverage them over time so that they reap maximal benefits for customers and the company alike. Why does this matter? Let's explore the brand's value to companies and customers alike.

THE VALUE OF A BRAND

The American Marketing Association defines a *brand* as a name, term, symbol, and/or design that's intended to *identify* the goods and services of one seller or a group of sellers and to *differentiate* them from those of the competition.[3] However, we argue that a brand is more than a mere name that helps with identification and differentiation. Identifying a brand and differentiating it from competing brands only makes sense when the brand offers *value*. We define a *brand* as *a value-generating entity (name) relevant to both customers* and *the brand owner*. If no one wants to buy the brand, the name doesn't have much market relevance. Such a brand fails to provide value to either the company or customers. But what does it mean to say that a brand offers value to customers and companies? Let's first consider what we mean by *brand value to companies*.

Value to Companies

Surprisingly, we have paid so much attention to brands as identifiers and marketplace differentiators that we have not paid much attention to the substantial, real, and strategic benefits that brands can provide to companies. But these benefits are numerous and significant, as Table 1.1 (and Figure 1.1, later in the chapter) suggests.

Revenue Generator

An admired brand increases customer loyalty and attracts new customers. These twin outcomes enhance a brand's revenue. Although

Table 1.1 Value of an Admired Brand to a Company

Types of Value	What an Admired Brand Does
Revenue Generator	An admired brand increases customer loyalty and attracts new customers.
Cost-Efficiency Enhancer	An admired brand is in demand, which allows the company to take advantage of economies of scale and allows the company to enjoy cost-saving customer brand loyalty and brand advocacy behaviors.
Growth Facilitator	An admired brand facilitates the introduction and success of its extensions to other markets and other products.
Human-Capital Builder	An admired brand helps recruit and retain talented people who will ultimately determine the company's success in the market place.
Employee-Morale Booster	An admired brand motivates employees to protect and strengthen the brand.
Second-Chance Provider	An admired brand enhances customers' willingness to forgive mistakes made by a company.
Market Protector	An admired brand serves as a barrier to entry to future competitors.
Alliance Facilitator	An admired brand facilitates alliances with desirable and powerful external partners.
Asset Builder	An admired brand enhances the company's marketplace value, and also allows it to demand a premium price in a brand-selling situation.

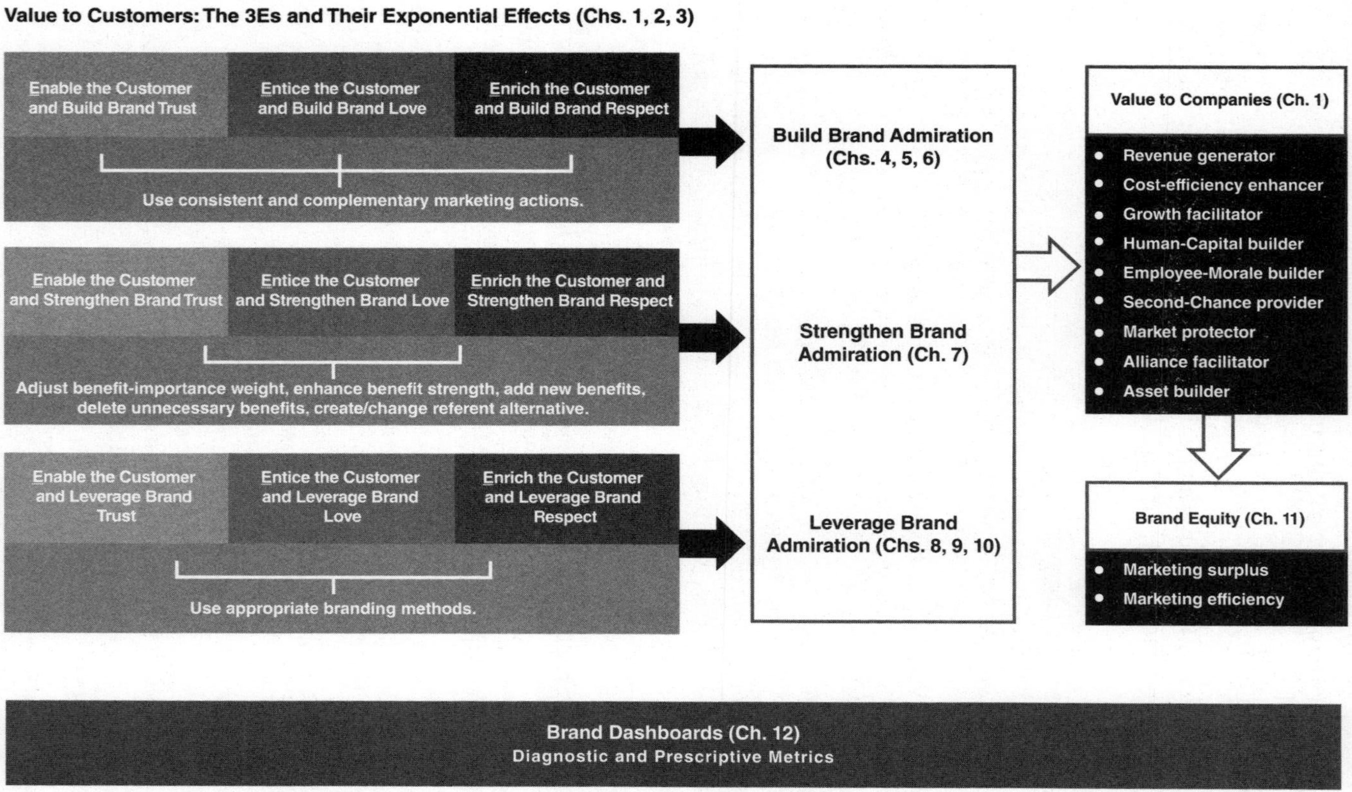

Value to Customers: The 3Es and Their Exponential Effects (Chs. 1, 2, 3)

Enable the Customer and Build Brand Trust	Entice the Customer and Build Brand Love	Enrich the Customer and Build Brand Respect
Use consistent and complementary marketing actions.		

Enable the Customer and Strengthen Brand Trust	Entice the Customer and Strengthen Brand Love	Enrich the Customer and Strengthen Brand Respect
Adjust benefit-importance weight, enhance benefit strength, add new benefits, delete unnecessary benefits, create/change referent alternative.		

Enable the Customer and Leverage Brand Trust	Entice the Customer and Leverage Brand Love	Enrich the Customer and Leverage Brand Respect
Use appropriate branding methods.		

Build Brand Admiration (Chs. 4, 5, 6)

Strengthen Brand Admiration (Ch. 7)

Leverage Brand Admiration (Chs. 8, 9, 10)

Value to Companies (Ch. 1)
- Revenue generator
- Cost-efficiency enhancer
- Growth facilitator
- Human-Capital builder
- Employee-Morale builder
- Second-Chance provider
- Market protector
- Alliance facilitator
- Asset builder

Brand Equity (Ch. 11)
- Marketing surplus
- Marketing efficiency

Brand Dashboards (Ch. 12)
Diagnostic and Prescriptive Metrics

Figure 1.1   The Brand Admiration Management System

6

producing a soft drink is not rocket science, new entrants find it incredibly hard to compete in this market, since most customers have a strong and long-standing preference for a particular soft drink brand. And this holds true worldwide! A strong brand also increases revenue by making customers less price sensitive, allowing companies to charge a higher per-unit price. Think about the price premium brands such as McKinsey and Goldman Sachs can charge in the marketplace.

Cost-Efficiency Enhancer

An admired brand is in demand, which allows the company to take advantage of economies of scale. Strong brands also create favorable word of mouth (WOM) and customer evangelists who further contribute to marketing efficiency by lowering marketing costs. In fact, some brands became marketplace successes purely through WOM. Trader Joe's is an example. Think about the stories customers relate about the unique products they can get only at Trader Joe's. China's Xiaomi, a tech company, relies entirely on brand communities and WOM from its fans for publicity and brand-promoting activities. Or consider the pride customers take in their durable Patagonia jackets and the stories they share about them. Since advertising and promotion costs often eat up a substantial portion of companies' budgets, enormous cost efficiencies are realized by fan-based WOM.

Growth Facilitator

An admired brand can be leveraged and extended, creating growth (and revenue) from new product or market categories. An admired brand makes it easier for companies to grow and grow efficiently, through product and brand extensions that use the brand name. Such extensions help the company's overall growth. Oracle grew by extending its brand to a portfolio of cloud and mobile solutions. Apple's extensions have allowed it to grow from $19.3 billion in 2006 to $234 billion in December of 2015.[4]

Human-Capital Builder

An admired brand helps recruit and retain talented people who will ultimately determine the company's marketplace success. Talent is the most difficult core competency for competitors to copy. Think about Google and Tesla's abilities to attract top talent. Admired brands attract top talent at all levels of the organization.

Employee-Morale Booster

An admired brand also motivates employees to protect and strengthen the brand. Employees of admired brands are more committed to nurturing customers than are employees working for brands with no discernable equity. Why? Because they believe in the brand and are proud of what they do to help it flourish.[5] Costco, which can be called an admired brand, has higher employee morale than competitor companies in the same industry. Employees who work for companies ranked as most admired in their industries take pride in the company's success, and they work harder to protect and strengthen the company's reputation. Executives who manage admired brands are even willing to accept lower pay for the opportunity to work for the brand.[6]

Second-Chance Provider

An admired brand also enhances customers' willingness to forgive unfortunate mistakes made by a company, giving it another chance to redeem itself.[7] Martha Stewart, Paula Deen, Toyota, Nike, and Harley-Davidson, to name just a few, have all fallen victim to brand gaffes and disasters. Yet the strength of their brands, the loyalty of their customer bases, and their customers' willingness to see brand mistakes as rare and unusual events have helped them to recover.

Market Protector

An admired brand protects companies by serving as a barrier to competitive brand entry. Customers are reluctant to switch from an admired brand to a new one unless the benefits of the new brand are sufficiently compelling to motivate switching. Customers' familiarity with admired brands provides comfort via what they know and have experienced. Their affection for a brand they know and admire makes them unwilling to invest in a new and untried brand. History shows that while many companies can produce athletic clothing, toys, and databases, they can't simply compete with the likes of Nike, Lego, and IBM.

Alliance Facilitator

An admired brand can facilitate alliances with desirable and powerful external partners. Such alliances can both leverage brand admiration and enhance it further. Alliances allow companies to build additional revenue and markets without making costly investments in areas in which they lack expertise. The ability of Apple and Samsung to attract partners serves as a testament to how much other companies admire these brands. Recent alliances between BMW and Louis Vuitton, Apple Pay and MasterCard, and Spotify and Uber also illustrate this point.[8]

Asset Builder

Finally, an admired brand generates greater shareholder return because investors take notice of admired brands when making their investment decisions.[9] This in turn makes a company's marketplace value substantially higher than its book value. That explains why Wanda Group paid $650 million to acquire the Ironman brand, which organizes, promotes, and licenses triathlons around the world, including the signature Ironman event that consists of a 2.4-mile swim, a 112-mile bicycle ride, and a 26.2-mile (a full marathon) run. As a sign of "having made it", some participants tattoo the Ironman logo on their bodies upon completing this hellish and grueling event.

The critical question is this: If an admired brand offers value to companies on so many dimensions, *how can companies develop an admired brand*? The answer to this question is both simple and deceptively complex. The simple answer is that companies can't reap the benefits of these myriad and significant sources of value unless they also provide value to customers. The deceptively complex answer is that the field of marketing has yet to develop a compelling perspective on what customers actually do value. Our brand admiration framework aims to provide this perspective.

Value to Customers

In order to provide value to companies, brands must first provide value to customers. But how do companies make their brands valuable to customers?

Value from Product Innovations?

Several scholars claim that brand success hinges on creating an uncontested market space. Or sometime we hear people say it is all about creating a "killer application". But what is a killer application? The argument goes that in today's information-rich economy, customers have full access to information about products. As such, brands can only compete on product quality and price. Accordingly, customers' relationships with brands are based on an economic calculus where what one gets (brand quality) is commensurate with what is given (the price paid). The idea goes that due to this excessive product quality and price comparison trend, companies must focus on product innovations that reshape industry boundaries and create new competitive opportunities.[10] This argument has merit. Clearly product innovations are crucial to a brand's success in today's markets.

Value from Benefits That Provide Happiness (the 3Es)

However, having an innovative product is just part of the solution for achieving competitive success. Decades of research on customer behavior show that a buying decision is not based purely on an economic calculus. Brand choices are largely driven by perceptions of what brands *do for customers*. In other words, rather than competing on purely economic terms, brands compete based on the degree to which their benefits make customers happy. Clearly, customers will not invest in brands that are not worth the money. But what they are looking for, more than a quality product at the right price, is a brand whose benefits *help them to do what they need and want to do*, in a way that is experientially gratifying to them and that makes them feel good about themselves as people. Whether it's in a personal or a professional context, brands that provide these benefits make customers happy.

Brand benefits refer not to the *features* the product has, but rather the outcomes from brand acquisition or use that meet customers' *needs, wants, and goals*, as human beings. This holds true regardless of whether these humans are occupying the role of B2B customers, B2C customers, sports and/or celebrity fans, or targets of nonprofit marketers.[11] Our perspective on customer value is both novel and parsimonious. Specifically, we identify three broad classes of benefits

Table 1.2   Value of an Admired Brand to Customers

Brand Benefits (the 3Es)	Emotional and Motivational Effects on Customers
Enablement Benefits	An admired brand enables customers by offering solutions to problems and challenges (large and small) and conserving customers' limited resources (time, money, psychological capacity, physical capacity). When enabled, customers feel empowered, secure, safe, relieved, and confident.
Enticement Benefits	An admired brand entices customers by engaging customers' senses (touch, sight, sound, smell, and taste), their thoughts, and their hearts. When enticed, customers feel gratified, stimulated, engaged, and warmhearted.
Enrichment Benefits	An admired brand enriches customers by resonating with their beliefs and their sense of self (who they are, who they were, and who they want to be). When enriched, customers feel inspired, proud, connected, and validated.

that underlie human happiness: benefits that enable, benefits that entice, and benefits that enrich customers (see Table 1.2).

Benefits That Enable Customers

Customers find value in brands that *enable* them. Such brands solve customers' problems. They remove barriers, eliminate frustrations, assuage anxieties, and reduce fear. They provide peace of mind. Benefits that enable customers offer solutions to nagging problems (both large and small): for example, *how do I avoid this acid reflux, how can I protect my home from burglars*, and *how can we get one IT system to talk to another*. With the brand as a solution, customers feel empowered to take on challenges in their personal and professional lives. Knowing that they can count on (and trust) the brand to solve problems reduces anxiety and allows the customer to get on with other aspects of their lives. Fear and anxiety are replaced with feelings of empower-ment, confidence, and security.

Sometimes both problems (and solutions) relate to resources, such as money, time, and physical and psychic energy. Brands can also enable customers when they help customers conserve the scarce resources they have or help them acquire the resources they want. Schwab helps customers plan for secure retirements: people feel more confident about dealing with the future when they have a safety net to protect them from life's unexpected curveballs. SAP helps organizations to streamline their processes, cut waste, and run simple for greater agility and growth. Waze maps the most efficient route from where one is to where one wants to go.

Brands that solve problems and conserve resources make cus-tomers feel empowered, secure, confident, relieved, and safe, and they provide peace of mind. In short, customers desperately want products and services whose benefits enable them. They want to feel that they can live with more security and efficacy and with fewer complications and stressors.

Benefits That Entice Customers

Customers also seek benefits that *entice* them.[12] Enticement benefits stimulate customers' minds, their senses, and their hearts. They replace work with play, lack of pleasure with gratification, boredom with excite-ment, and sadness with feelings of warmth and amusement. Customers, whether in a B2B or B2C environment, want to feel gratified, engaged, excited, playful, grateful, and warmhearted. For example, they like marketing materials and web sites that are interesting and visually pleasing, and ads that are emotionally evocative. They want to feel cared for and taken care of by the brand and its employees. They want corporate offices and retail spaces to be warm, comforting, and inviting. They want to interact with employees who are friendly and helpful.

Disneyland epitomizes these sensory and heartwarming benefits. Disneyland creates magic for millions of kids (and adults) every day. Park guests experience these benefits through the beauty of the Magic Kingdom, the thrill of the rides, the joy of meeting Mickey and Pluto, and the vivid fireworks show and parade. Enticing benefits also seem to explain the success of the Hello Kitty brand. How else can we explain how a seemingly deformed and mouthless cat commands such strong loyalty from children, let alone fully grown adults? Hello Kitty offers sense-pleasing and heartwarming benefits that are difficult to explain. Devotees can't stay away from the brand. In the 40 years since its introduction, more than 50,000 product items have been introduced under the Hello Kitty brand name. Interest in and affection toward this brand are still high.

Benefits That Enrich Customers

Finally, customers seek benefits that *enrich* them and their sense of who they are as people. Customers want to feel as if they are good people who are doing good things in the world. They want to act in ways that are consistent with their beliefs and hopes. They want to feel as if they're part of a group in which others accept and respect them. They want to be inspired to be the best people they can be, now and in the future. They want to feel proud of their identities and where they came from. Enriching benefits provide meaning to life. Without meaning people feel at a loss and regard their lives as pointless.[13] Benefits that enrich customers make them feel inspired, proud, connected, and validated. They motivate people to act with good intentions and with honor and courage, and to be their authentic selves.

Salesforce.com isn't just a cloud computing company with technologies that serve all manner of companies in an easy and visually pleasing way. It's also a company designed to make the world a better place. It supports nonprofits and higher-education customers, and it has donated more than $53 million in grants. Salesforce employees have donated more than a million hours of their time to charitable organizations.[14] Customers know that by using Salesforce products, they too are contributing to make the world a better place, both locally and globally.

Exponential Impact of the 3Es

We call benefits that enable, entice, and enrich customers the 3Es for short. Combined, these three types of benefits have an exponential effect on enhancing customers' happiness. We argue that the most

Table 1.3   The Exponential Impact of the 3Es

The Powerful Difference between Additive and Multiplicative Relationships	
Additive Relationship	$8 + 8 + 8 = 24$
Multiplicative Relationship	$8 \times 8 \times 8 = 512$

admired brands enhance customers' happiness by offering all three types of benefits. Such brands make customers happier than other brands do. These three types of benefits relate directly to all theories of human motivation and to a large body of research on positive emotions. A key finding from our research is that the superior performance of one E cannot fully compensate for deficiencies in the other two Es. The upshot is that the 3Es have an exponential (multiplicative versus additive) effect on enhancing brand admiration. The interactive (or exponential) effects of the 3Es simply cannot be underestimated (see Table 1.3).

Let's illustrate the power of these 3Es. Undoubtedly, Harley-Davidson customers believe that the brand offers a good quality product at a fair price. But that logic can't describe how the brand *resonates* with them. Harley buyers invest time, money, and their own reputation in this brand because it makes them happy, and it does so on multiple levels. Its machinery produces an *exciting and thrilling* ride (enticing benefits). Customers feel *protected and in control* while riding their Harleys (enabling benefits). Product accouterments, such as Harley jackets, symbolize membership in the Harley community, allowing customers to feel *pride in membership* in this brother- or sisterhood. Involvement in the Harley Owners Group gives customers a sense of being *connected* to others, allowing customers the opportunity to gain increasing *respect* from others as they move from novice to expert status. The fact that the brand symbolizes *independence, autonomy, and freedom* inspires customers and makes them feel as if they are *getting in touch with their authentic selves and who they are as people* (enrichment benefits). Chapter 2 describes other examples of brands that have created value for customers over extended periods of time by offering benefits that map onto these 3Es.

THE BRAND ADMIRATION MANAGEMENT SYSTEM

The perspectives on the value of admired brands to companies and customers provide the foundation for the brand admiration management system shown in Figure 1.1.

The 3Es and Brand Admiration

Let's start with the assumption that admired brands provide *value to companies* by producing the outcomes noted on the right-hand side of Figure 1.1. Companies can enjoy these outcomes when their brands offer *value to customers*; that is, benefits that enable, entice, *and* enrich customers. When brands provide these three types of benefits and empower, gratify, and inspire customers, customers *want* to establish a long-term relationship with the brand. When a brand provides these three benefits, customers come to trust, love, and respect the brand; in short, they *admire* it. Chapter 3 discusses the 3Es and brand admiration in greater detail, and formally defines this concept. As we show in that chapter, creating brand admiration isn't all about creating brand love. It's about creating brand love, brand trust, *and* brand respect. These three components emanate from the 3Es, and they work interactively to affect brand admiration. They are the keys to driving long-term brand relationships.

Building Brand Admiration

A new brand needs to establish itself on the market by building brand admiration; that is, by offering benefits that *enable, entice, and enrich customers*. Providing these benefits fosters the three conditions that characterize brand admiration: brand trust, brand love, and brand respect. Chapter 4 suggests that building brand admiration with customers starts with building brand admiration among employees. As critical intermediaries between the company and the marketplace, employees (internal customers) need to embody the brand's mission, embody the 3Es, and feel enabled, enticed, and enriched themselves. Chapter 5 considers strategic decisions companies must make in building brand admiration among external customers, particularly as it applies to developing a positioning statement that involves communicating and delivering the brand's identity to target customers. Chapter 6 pushes these ideas further by showing how certain marketing decisions can accelerate the process of building brand admiration by enhancing top-of-mind brand recall.

Strengthening Brand Admiration

Building a brand that customers admire is a huge achievement. However, the marketplace is continually evolving. The company's resources that have been spent on achieving this success would be difficult to recover if brand admiration begins to wane. To create long-term value for companies and customers, brands should not only build brand admiration but also *strengthen* brand admiration over time. The competitiveness of the marketplace dictates that brand managers must continuously identify opportunities to best their own brands. A brand must continue to improve on its attempts to enable, entice, and enrich customers. By doing so, customers recognize and appreciate the brand's continual commitment to making them happy. Chapter 7 describes various strategies that companies can use to strengthen brand admiration. Companies can (1) enhance the current benefit strength, (2) add new benefits, (3) delete unnecessary benefits, (4) adjust the current benefit-importance weight, and/or (5) create/change the referent alternative to which the brand is compared.

Leveraging Brand Admiration

The more brand holders are able to cultivate brand admiration, the better able they will be to leverage brand admiration and efficiently grow the brand through product and brand extensions. By leveraging brand admiration, we mean seeking efficient brand growth through product and brand extensions. By using the brand name on new products (i.e., by using extensions), the brand can grow efficiently. Growth is efficient because customers are more accepting of a new product from an admired brand. They also see more ways in which the brand is relevant to their personal and professional lives. This expansion of the brand's relevance strengthens brand admiration even further. Chapters 8 and 9 present innovative ideas about how companies can leverage an admired brand and what they should consider when using product and brand extensions.

Brand Architecture Design

Also relevant to leveraging brand admiration is the issue of brand architecture design; that is, the process of ensuring that the various products and businesses associated with the company provide a coherent face to the marketplace. Chapter 10 presents a theoretically driven structure of brand architecture design. That structure identifies five different levels of a brand hierarchy and illustrates eight different branding options. This structure and three key evaluation criteria serve as a basis for which a company can assess and choose an optimal brand architecture design.

Brand Equity

The value of the brand to the company is revealed in the brand's equity. Brand equity is a financial measure that reflects the economic value of the brand to the brand holder (the company), based on its efforts to build, strengthen, and leverage customer brand admiration. Chapter 11 provides a novel, useable, and informative measure of brand equity. The brand equity measure is based on three key variables that reflect the strength of customers' brand admiration and marketers' efforts to build (strengthen or leverage) the brand: (1) the brand's unit price, (2) its sales volume, and (3) the marketing costs expended to generate its total revenue. This measure is theoretically grounded, reliable, and easy to implement. It also allows comparison of the brand's equity with other (competing or non-directly competing) brands and with one's own brand over time.

Brand Admiration Dashboard Metrics

Finally, our brand admiration management system articulates additional metrics about how to measure brand success, regardless of whether a company is building, strengthening, or leveraging brand admiration. Without effective metrics, it's difficult to assess how well a brand is doing overall and vis-à-vis its competitors and understand what's driving current brand equity. Metrics allow companies to diagnose where critical problems are arising and how they may be rectified. As such, a critical aspect of the brand admiration management system involves using an insight-oriented *brand admiration dashboard*. This dashboard, which is linked to each component of the brand admiration management system, is discussed in Chapter 12. Data relevant to the brand admiration dashboard is easy to collect. Moreover, data from the dashboard provides clear insight into how the brand is doing right now, what's contributing to good or poor performance, and what should be done next. As such, we are confident that brand managers will find the dashboard to be extremely useful in understanding why their brands are or are not providing value to their customers and companies. Ultimately, building, strengthening, and leveraging brand admiration is a journey on which we invite you to embark.

Let's begin this journey now.

NOTES

1. Sarah Buhr, "48 Million in iPhone Sales Leads Apple's Q4 2015 Earnings," TechCrunch, October 27, 2015, www.techcrunch.com/2015/10/27/48-million-in-iphone-sales-leads-apples-q4-2015-earnings.
2. James B. Stewart, "How, and Why, Apple Overtook Microsoft," *New York Times*, January 29, 2015, www.nytimes.com/2015/01/30/business/how-and-why-apple-overtook-microsoft.html?_r=0.
3. American Marketing Association dictionary, accessed April 9, 2016, www.ama.org/resources/Pages/Dictionary.aspx?dLetter=B.
4. "Apple Reports Record Fourth Quarter Results," Apple Press Info, accessed April 9, 2016, www.apple.com/pr/library/2015/10/27Apple-Reports-Record-Fourth-Quarter-Results.html.
5. Douglas E. Hughes and Michael Ahearne, "Energizing the Reseller's Sales Force: The Power of Brand Identification," *Journal of Marketing* 74, no. 4 (2010): 81–96; Fortune.com, "100 Best Companies to Work For," *Fortune*, http://fortune.com/best-companies.
6. Nader T. Tavassoli, Alina Sorescu, and Rajesh Chandy, "Employee-Based Brand Equity: Why Firms with Strong Brands Pay Their Executives Less," *Journal of Marketing Research* 51, no. 6 (2014): 676–690.
7. Jenny Van Doorn and Peter C. Verhoef, "Critical Incidents and the Impact of Satisfaction on Customer Share," *Journal of Marketing* 72, no. 4 (2008): 123–142; Leigh Anne Novak Donovan, Joseph Priester, Deborah J. MacInnis, and C. Whan Park, "Brand Forgiveness: How Close Brand Relationships Influence Forgiveness," in *Customer-Brand Relationships: Theories and Applications*, eds. Susan Fournier, Michael

Braezeale, and Marc Fetscherin (New York: Routledge, 2012), 184–203; Rohini Ahluwalia, Robert E. Burnkrant, and H. Rao Unnava, "Consumer Response to Negative Publicity: The Moderating Role of Commitment," *Journal of Marketing Research* 37, no. 2 (2000): 203–214.

8. Michelle Greenwald, "11 of the Best Strategic Brand Partnerships in 2014," *Forbes*, December 11, 2014, www.forbes.com/sites/michellegreenwald/2014/12/11/11-of-the-bestsmartestmost-interesting-strategic-brand-partnerships-of-2014/#5c8d73041d52.

9. Sundar G. Bharadwaj, Kapil R. Tuli, and Andre Bonfrer, "The Impact of Brand Quality on Shareholder Wealth," *Journal of Marketing* 75, no. 5 (2011): 88–104; Christian Schulze, Bernd Skiera, and Thorsten Wiesel, "Linking Customer and Financial Metrics to Shareholder Value: The Leverage Effect in Customer-Based Evaluation," *Journal of Marketing* 76, no. 2 (2004): 7–32.

10. Chan W. Kim and Renée Mauborgne, *Blue Ocean Strategy: How to Create Uncontested Market Space and Make Competition Irrelevant* (Boston: HBS Publishing, 2005).

11. C. Whan Park, Bernard J. Jaworski, and Deborah J. MacInnis, "Strategic Brand Concept-Image Management," *Journal of Marketing* 50, no. 4 (1986): 135–145.

12. Morris B. Holbrook and Elizabeth C. Hirschman, "The Experiential Aspects of Consumption: Consumer Fantasies, Feelings, and Fun," *Journal of Consumer Research* 9, no. 2 (1982): 132–140.

13. Viktor Frankl, *Man's Search for Meaning* (Boston: Beacon Press, 1959).

14. Marc Benioff and Carlye Adler, *Behind the Cloud: The Untold Story of How Salesforce.com Went from Idea to Billion-Dollar Company and Revolutionized an Industry* (San Francisco: Jossey-Bass, 2009).

CHAPTER 2

Living Examples of Admired Brands

B randing is deceptively commonsensical, but it is incredibly nonintuitive.

INTRODUCTION

As a fashion and sports brand, Nike competes with ordinary apparel in the same way that Coke competes with water. Yet, since its founding in 1964, Nike has become one of the world's most admired and highly valued brands. It is trusted, loved, and respected, making customers willing to incorporate Nike not just into their athletic endeavors but also into their lives in general. Without a doubt, Nike's efforts have resulted in tremendous brand equity. Indeed, Nike has realized all of the components of brand value to companies noted in the brand admiration management system (see Figure 2.1). With worldwide sales estimated to be over $30 billion, Nike enjoys a market capitalization exceeding $100 billion.[1] Nike attracts top talent, whose dedication to the brand spills over into enthusiasm in product innovations and toward customer support in stores and on the web. Nike's uplifting mission statement is: "To bring inspiration and innovation to every athlete in the world."[2] Although it is no stranger to brand crises, such as past claims of reliance on sweatshop labor, Nike has been able to bounce back strongly from these corporate transgressions.

Nike's growth is explained not only by its ability to *build and strengthen admiration* of its core product—athletic performance shoes—but also by its ability to *leverage* brand admiration through introducing other products with the Nike brand name. Bill Bowerman, cofounder

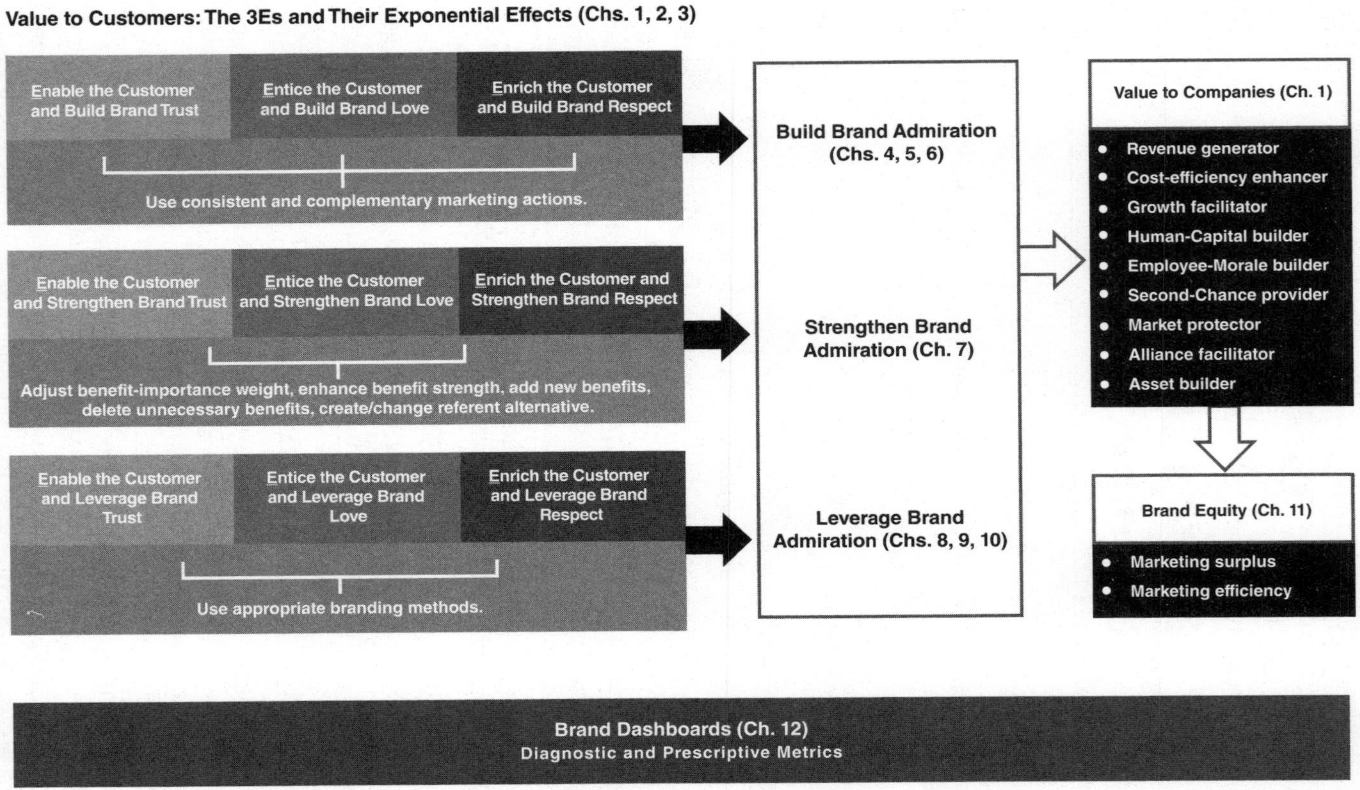

Value to Customers: The 3Es and Their Exponential Effects (Chs. 1, 2, 3)

		Value to Companies (Ch. 1)
		• Revenue generator
		• Cost-efficiency enhancer
		• Growth facilitator
		• Human-Capital builder
		• Employee-Morale builder
		• Second-Chance provider
		• Market protector
		• Alliance facilitator
		• Asset builder

Brand Equity (Ch. 11)
• Marketing surplus
• Marketing efficiency

Build Brand Admiration (Chs. 4, 5, 6)

Strengthen Brand Admiration (Ch. 7)

Leverage Brand Admiration (Chs. 8, 9, 10)

Enable the Customer and Build Brand Trust

Entice the Customer and Build Brand Love

Enrich the Customer and Build Brand Respect

Use consistent and complementary marketing actions.

Enable the Customer and Strengthen Brand Trust

Entice the Customer and Strengthen Brand Love

Enrich the Customer and Strengthen Brand Respect

Adjust benefit-importance weight, enhance benefit strength, add new benefits, delete unnecessary benefits, create/change referent alternative.

Enable the Customer and Leverage Brand Trust

Entice the Customer and Leverage Brand Love

Enrich the Customer and Leverage Brand Respect

Use appropriate branding methods.

Brand Dashboards (Ch. 12)
Diagnostic and Prescriptive Metrics

Figure 2.1   The Brand Admiration Management System

of Nike, once defined an athlete as "anyone who has a body." This expansive view of the target market has made Nike highly relevant to any type of athletic experience (running, tennis, golf, cricket, and more) and any type of athletic gear (clothes, bags, eyewear, digital devices, and more). Indeed, Nike has become so embedded in the lives of "anyone who has a body" that the brand's relevance extends beyond the sports domain to everyday life (casual wear, accessories, and even work life). As an admired brand with strong brand equity, Nike has also grown through its alliances with other powerful brands, such as Michael Jordan, Apple, and Japan's fashion brand, Sacai.

At a fundamental level, however, the financial value of Nike's brand can be attributed to the value it provides to customers. Customers admire the brand because it provides enabling, enticing, and enriching benefits that make them trust, love, and respect it. These benefits, and the emotions they produce, are central to the brand admiration management system.

From an *enablement perspective*, Nike aids customers in the pursuit of functional benefits and is relentless in its pursuit of innovations that enhance athletic performance. Serious and casual athletes alike feel that they can trust Nike to consistently and reliably maximize their athletic performance. Different shoes and clothing for different athletic events ensure that the brand has the versatility to offer athletic benefits regardless of the sport. Nike's research-driven products reassure customers. They know that products are engineered to protect them from injury or discomfort. Nike products help them perform to the top of their athletic skills with the greatest degree of support and with minimal loss of physical energy. Because they know they can trust the brand across time and context, consumers feel empowered when using Nike products.

From an *enticement perspective*, consumers love Nike products because they look good and feel comfortable. The bright, cheerful colors and the comfort that is engineered into Nike products bring experiential pleasure and emotional vibrancy to myriad athletic endeavors. Nike embodies fun, physical comfort, and true love for sports and exercise in general.[3] Fabrics are designed to feel soft and cool to the body. Its distinctive logo is eye-catching and pleasing. And enticement doesn't stop with Nike products. Nike stores are experiences in their own right. Nike's pod allows store visitors to dance or jump around while tracking their movements on a wall of pixels. Nike is also known for its heartwarming commercials (e.g., the RE2PECT campaign) that celebrate the supporters and mentors who have helped great athletes reach their potential.

From an *enrichment perspective*, consumers respect Nike in part because it's so inspirational. Nike's tagline and logo inspire athletes to Just Do It, and to not procrastinate or overcomplicate things and simply "get on with it". Using the world's greatest athletes (Michael Jordan, Serena Williams, Rory McIlroy), Nike inspires customers to literally walk in the shoe of athletes they admire and aspire to be like. Finally, Nike has made significant strides in bonding people with one another, making them feel part of a larger community that values sports, athletics, and health. Community-driven membership is fostered through apps that allow users to track and compare their performance with a community of others, and to feel proud of how well they've done.

It's no wonder that Steve Jobs labeled Nike as "the best example of all, and one of the greatest jobs of marketing that the universe has ever seen."

OVERVIEW

Chapter 1 introduced the brand admiration management system, which suggests that a brand's value to companies is maximized when the brand offers strong value to customers. Companies realize such value over the long term by building, strengthening, and leveraging brand admiration. Brand admiration is realized by continual efforts to enable, entice, and enrich customers, building their trust in, love of, and respect for the brand. Chapter 2 builds on these ideas in several ways. First, we show that the framework in Figure 2.1 is not specific to certain brands. Rather, it is generalizable. It is equally applicable to brands in B2C (Nike) *and* B2B markets (Caterpillar), nonprofit (service) markets (the US Marines), and international markets (Pulmuone in Korea). Of course, we will show myriad other examples throughout the book, but we discuss these examples here just to clarify the applicability of the brand admiration management system to all kinds of brands. We focus on long-lived brands, some of which have been around for close to a century or more. We do so to show that the brand admiration management system can help explain why certain brands fade into obscurity while others survive the test of time. Each of the brands discussed in this chapter has enjoyed long-run success and commanded tremendous value for their companies. We also illustrate how these brands have enhanced value to customers through the 3Es, and how companies have built, strengthened, and leveraged brand admiration over time.

ADMIRED BRAND IN THE B2B MARKET

Through its focus on benefits that enable, entice, and enrich customers (and by creating brand trust, love, and respect) the brand admiration management system is clearly relevant to B2C markets. But is it equally relevant in the B2B domain? Some branding experts argue that B2B markets are different from B2C markets in a number of ways (e.g., number of customers, purchasing-decision process, the level of customers' product knowledge, etc.), and hence a different approach to branding is needed. We disagree. Yes, the two markets require many different methods and tactics, but the foundational principles that guide the strategies of each are not different. All customers are humans, after all. Business customers should be just as likely as customers in consumer markets to want to buy goods and services that make them feel empowered, gratified, and inspired. Regardless of how many or how few customers a company has, each customer wants to be happy. Each wants benefits that enable, entice, and enrich their lives. Each wants to patronize those companies that they trust, love, and respect. Let's talk about a brand that has limited entry in the consumer market and largely competes in a B2B environment: namely, Caterpillar.

Now celebrating its ninetieth birthday, and with products in more than 180 countries, Caterpillar stands out as a world leader in the manufacture of construction and mining equipment, industrial gas turbines, diesel-electric locomotives, and more. Its success is remarkable, particularly considering the cutthroat price-competition Caterpillar faces internationally. Yet Caterpillar has done several things that set it apart from the competition.

First, it provides some of the best and most durable/functional products in the industry. Products with such enabling benefits are critical to end users (e.g., construction companies) that need dependable, reliable equipment that they can trust. Caterpillar also provides highly efficient after-sales service and support (e.g., minimizing downtime on the part of end users). Most importantly, it never bypasses dealers by selling to end users directly. In this sense, Caterpillar has provided a solid and high-quality product with a transparent and trust-based selling process that enables and empowers end users and dealers.

But Caterpillar has also enabled its independent dealers to profitably run their own businesses. The company's dealer advisory group fosters two-way communication between dealers and the company, providing suggestions and advice to Caterpillar about how to run its business for the better. This makes dealers feel empowered. Signifying its trusting relationship with the dealers, the company developed a short, three-page contract with no expiration date—quite a contrast from the lengthy legalese-based contracts that typify dealer agreements. The documents allowed dealers to terminate their relationship with Caterpillar without cause, specifying only 90 days advanced notice. Imagine how empowered and secure such an arrangement makes dealers feel!

Caterpillar also offers enticing benefits that dealers find very gratifying. A pressing issue for independent dealers is that they are often family owned, so dealers are concerned about the future of their businesses to their families. Caterpillar addresses these concerns head-on by organizing conferences and networking events to introduce the children of dealership owners to Caterpillar. These events are designed to get dealers' children excited about the business, with the hope that dealers' children might one day take over these businesses. This creates a tremendously heartwarming benefit for the Caterpillar dealers, who want to see their business continue and passed on to the next generation.

Dealers can meet with Caterpillar's CEO anytime they choose to, which serves as a powerful sign of who the bosses are.

Finally, Caterpillar offers enriching benefits by fostering strong camaraderie among dealers around the world. Dealers feel part of a tight-knit community that does good work for the world. Caterpillar and its dealers make and sell great machines that literally make the world work. Dealers' identities are thus partially built around their involvement with Caterpillar. Caterpillar fosters a camaraderie and a connectedness that are inspiring to dealers. Dealers can respect a brand that's trying to do well by them, and one that tries to make the world a better place.

Caterpillar has established and strengthened brand admiration for 90 years. But it's also been able to leverage that equity. Today, Caterpillar's brand extensions include Cat Financial (which offers financing and services during the purchase, management, and reselling stages of Caterpillar products) and Cat Reman (which provides parts restoration, giving dealers and end users more options for repair while also being environmentally friendly). The key benefits noted in the brand admiration management system are relevant to B2B brands beyond Caterpillar.

Think about Navistar, a leading manufacturer of trucks and buses. The 3Es characterize how the company thought about its big-rig trucks. In addition to being a truck, a big rig is a small home with a cabin above the cab where the driver can eat, sleep, change clothes, do work, and relax. Most trucks offer bare-bones, unappealing spaces, which contributes to high driver turnover. Navistar does things differently. It makes its cabin highly pleasing to drivers. It uses chrome (which many truckers love) in as many places as possible. Its living space has hardwood flooring. The cabin is also equipped with a seven-speaker Monsoon sound system and TV. Beyond these enticing benefits, Navistar offers enablement benefits. It has highly comfortable and efficient interior features, such as a Murphy bed, a kitchenette with food storage, a microwave and refrigerator, and overhead storage. It also provides enrichment benefits. Navistar truckers feel that they are part of a brotherhood or community of drivers that values these special trucks. Belonging to such a community makes truckers feel proud of their identity as trucking professionals.

ADMIRED BRAND IN THE NONPROFIT (SERVICE) MARKET

So far we've discussed for-profit brands. A brand that's quite different from those described above is the United States Marine Corps (USMC), a nonprofit brand that offers a service to the nation. Many young men and women aspire to join the Marine Corps. Like the brands we've just described, the USMC is an admired brand by virtue of its ability to provide enablement, enticement, and enrichment benefits.

Since its founding in 1775, the USMC's mission has been constant: serve the country, fight for independence, protect the United States from harm, and defend its freedom. The Marine Corps offers powerful *enablement benefits* to those who consider joining the military. Recruits know that the Marines go through the most rigorous training possible to prepare them for and protect them from the ravages of war and social upheaval. The Marines' use of the most advanced and technologically sophisticated equipment in the world reduces anxiety and provides assurance that the USMC supports recruits physically. The USMC also provides other enablement benefits, including medical, housing, and educational benefits that extend beyond a tour of duty. In this way, the USMC funds the highest expenditure categories faced by average Americans (health, housing, and education). These benefits make recruits feel empowered to do what they need to do on the battlefield and in life.

From an *enticing benefit* standpoint, the USMC emblem of the golden Eagle, Globe, and Anchor provides striking visual gratification. The Marine uniform has been in service longer than those of the other military services and is also distinct from them. Dress Blues (or simply Blues) is a visually sophisticated and formal uniform. It is the equivalent of civilian black tie dress. As a Marine, one is entitled to 30 days of paid vacation each year. Additional enticing benefits include exciting opportunities to travel the world, taking on assignments at American embassies and consulates, and experiencing cultures across the globe. The Marines' enticing benefits further recruits' love for the brand.

As an elite group, the USMC offers the opportunity for considerable enrichment benefits. Membership is limited to those who are willing and able to undergo painful training and to risk their lives, and who take pride in their service to the nation. The USMC motto—The Few. The Proud. The Marines—embodies the sense of strong self-esteem that comes from being a member of the Corps. This theme deeply resonates with young men and women in this country and provides strong inspiration. The rigorous training that Marines receive has a transformational effect on recruits. Once trained, recruits have a sense of having made it. They also have a sense of being unique, strong, and brave enough to overcome their own fears and weaknesses in order to keep on fighting. Recruits are different people coming out of training than they were going in. Post training, they are the elite: capable, fearless, strong, and Semper Fidelis—Latin for Always Faithful. These qualities differentiate the Marine Corps from other military service organizations. The marine's uniform is the only military uniform to include all three colors of the American flag. It symbolically conveys feelings of pride, patriotism, and capability. There is genuine inspiration and pride that young men and women feel in being part of the U.S. Marines.

ADMIRED BRAND IN THE INTERNATIONAL MARKET

The brand admiration management system is equally applicable to brands in international markets. For example, Koreans love, trust, and respect an unusual food company called Pulmuone (referred to as PMO hereafter). At a time when the term *organic* was unfamiliar to Koreans (and Americans), PMO introduced organic foods. Its steady focus on organic products made it one of the most trusted, loved, and respected brands among all Korean food manufacturers (many of which are powerful global food companies). Since it was founded in 1984, PMO has focused on living in harmony with nature by marketing organic and natural foods. Its corporate mission aims to make consumers feel proud of making the "right" food choices. Spear-headed by Chairman Seung-Woo Nam and managed by President Hyo Youl Lee, PMO has instituted a series of innovative benefits that enable, entice, and enrich Korean consumers, fueling positive feelings in customers and building brand trust, love, and respect.

The company refuses to use artificial or chemical ingredients, such as taste-enhancing or decay-prevention chemicals and artificial colors. Instead, it honors seven "right food principles." It keeps products fresh through the point of purchase using its refrigerated distribution system. In 2007, PMO adopted a new policy that disallowed GMO-based ingredients in its products. Eggs are purchased from animal welfare–certified sources. Recently, PMO introduced a supply-chain tracking system that allows consumers to find the origin of key product ingredients. These enabling benefits make customers feel more secure and confident in what they are putting in their bodies, and they build brand trust. Its product and package designs and its corporate logo are distinctive and enticing, while its advertising and publicity materials are impeccable and clearly convey the brand's clean, fresh, and natural identity. Executive Director Kim, Hyun-Joong recently developed a children's song and a dance for its Right Food slogan. This song and dance combination is remarkably popular and enticing to Korean consumers. Rarely has a company cause-related song been accepted by children with so much interest and enthusiasm. These enticing benefits are emotionally gratifying and they build brand love. Finally, its slogan "Feed the family with the right foods" serves as a philosophy for employees, and it incorporates values of keeping one's family in good health; values with which Koreans identify. These enriching benefits inspire parents to do what's best for their families. They create a strong sense that the brand's values align with customers' values, which builds brand respect.

TYPES OF BRANDS

Brand admiration isn't an all-or-nothing state. It's something a brand holds to varying degrees. The ultimate goal is to make your brand as highly admired as possible, but at a minimum you want to be more highly admired than you are now, and clearly you want to be

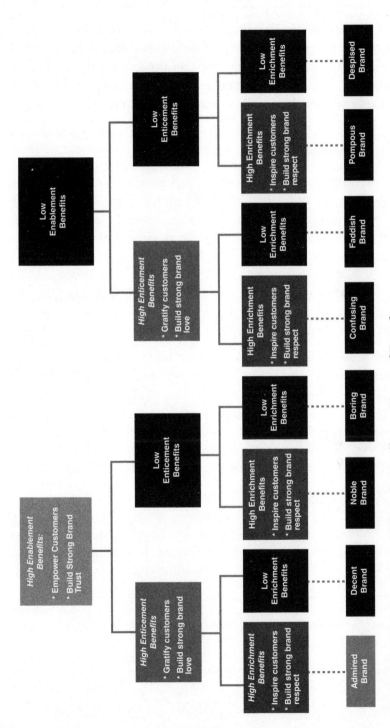

Figure 2.2   Different Types of Benefits, Different Types of Brands

more highly admired than competitors' brands. We use Figure 2.2 to reinforce the idea that the more a brand offers enabling, enticing, and enriching benefits, the more it generates powerful positive emotions in customers, and the more trusted, loved, and respected it becomes. All three benefit types contribute exponentially to brand admiration.

Admired Brands

The more your brand enables, entices, and enriches customers, evoking their positive emotions and building their trust, love, and respect, the more highly admired it will be. An admired brand offers the greatest opportunity for enduring and profitable growth. When your brand is seen as lacking in even one of the three components of brand admiration, it will not be regarded as strongly admired. As discussed in Chapter 1, Apple is clearly one of the most successful brands in recent history and it has become an admired brand by providing benefits that enable, entice, and enrich customers.

First, Apple is a clear leader in providing enablement benefits. Its technology, while not simple, makes learning and using Apple products easy. Its famous one-touch solution and intuitive interface took what was otherwise an intimidating product category and made it user friendly. Apple products "speak" to one another by virtue of their common operating system, making it easy for consumers to move seamlessly from one Apple product (e.g., a Mac) to another (e.g., an iPhone).

Second, Apple products are different from other technological products in their enticement benefits—specifically, through their design. Indeed, for Steve Jobs visual design elements were on equal footing with technological advances in product development. The design of the buttons and screen and even the partially bitten apple logo itself makes customers gravitate toward Apple's products. The visual simplicity and clean lines of Apple retail stores make for a warm and inviting environment where customers can play with any Apple product on the market.

Finally, Apple offers strong enrichment benefits. It speaks to consumers' sense of self, asking them to Think different. Apple products were a status marker at one time, with people defining themselves as

Mac, rather than PC, users. Users saw themselves as cool, and they felt proud of being Apple fans. Mac users felt more open minded, younger, and hipper. Apple's Think different commercial showcased iconoclastic thinkers (e.g., Mahatma Gandhi, Albert Einstein, Muhammad Ali, and John Lennon). It inspired consumers to think that they, too, could one day change the world. No other products have become so embedded and respected in every aspect of our daily lives as have Apple products.

Nonadmired Brands

Customers consider nonadmired brands differently. As Figure 2.2 shows, these brands might be called *decent*, *noble*, *boring*, *confusing*, *faddish*, *pompous*, or even *despised*. These brands are lacking in their ability to offer one or more of the enablement, enticement, and enrichment benefits. They just can't command the trust, love, and respect that admired brands do. Despised brands are the opposite of admired ones. Customers aren't just indifferent to them; they actively avoid them or speak poorly of them. We're not suggesting that a brand that's not admired can't be profitable. Even a despised brand can be profitable in the short term with great manufacturing and other operational efficiencies, particularly if customers have no other choice but to buy it. But it's unlikely to survive the test of time, grow into new markets, and have strong equity unless it delivers on the things that are important to customers and make them happy.[4]

KEY TAKEAWAYS

1. Across highly diverse industries, admired brands are similar in their ability to provide enabling, enticing, and enriching benefits that yield positive customer emotions and build brand trust, love, and esteem.

2. Such brands have been able to build, strengthen, and leverage their admiration over the long term by their continual efforts to best themselves and their competitors in the benefits (and hence value) they provide to customers.

3. Benefits that enable customers to solve their problems and conserve their scarce resources leave customers feeling

empowered, in control, secure, confident, and relieved. Customers trust brands that they can consistently rely on to solve their problems and conserve their resources.

4. Benefits that entice customers stimulate their senses, their minds, and/or their hearts. The brand's benefits leave customers feeling gratified, engaged, entertained, upbeat, and/or warmhearted. The more the brand provides these benefits, the more customers will come to love the brand.

5. Benefits that enrich customers reflect their beliefs and hopes for a better future. They can also symbolize aspects of who one is, the status or respect one commands from others, and the groups of which one is a part. The brand's benefits make customers feel inspired, proud, connected, validated, and influential. Customers respect brands whose beliefs and hopes are congruent with their own. They respect brands that help them connect with others who support them.

6. Brands that have emphasized these benefits relentlessly over time have managed to thrive over decades, generations, and even a century or more.

WHAT ABOUT YOUR BRAND?

1. Is your brand focused on a specific type of benefit, or on enablement, enticement, *and* enrichment benefits? How well is it performing on each benefit type? If you think it's difficult to differentiate your brand from others, take heed of the lessons from brands such as Nike and Caterpillar.

2. If your brand is fully differentiated from competing brands, does this differentiation have anything to do with types of benefits and the emotions that result from their provision? How would your brand stack up relative to competitors if you tried to differentiate it with the 3Es in mind?

3. How would customers describe your brand? Is it admired? Is it faddish? Is it decent?

Notes

1. "Nike Market Capitalization," YCharts, accessed April 15, 2016, https://ycharts.com/companies/NKE/market_cap.
2. "Nike Mission Statement," Nike, accessed April 20, 2016, http://help-en-us.nike.com/app/answers/detail/a_id/113/~/nike-mission-statement.
3. Susan Fournier, Michael R. Solomon, and Basil G. Englis, "When Brands Resonate," in *Handbook of Brand and Experience Management*, eds. Bernd H. Schmitt and David L. Rogers (Cheltenham, UK: Edward Elgar, 2008), 35–57.
4. Creating brand admiration involves the task of creating brand awareness and making it personally relevant to customers through the 3Es. In addition to the brand types shown in Figure 2.2, there may be others such as *hidden*, *lost*, *dead*, and so on—that is, brands that customers are not aware of or don't care about.

Chapter 3

The Science behind Brand Admiration

T he secret is to understand *how* to make your brand admired.

Introduction

The *Star Wars* brand is skilled in the art of building and sustaining strong relationships with customers. The original *Star Wars* movie, launched in 1977, was as captivating as it was heartwarming in *enticing* moviegoers. The film's vivid sights, sounds, and special effects astounded viewers, taking them to a fantastic world replete with unusual creatures, planets, and spaceships. Cute droids such as R2D2 and funny alien creatures added humor to an otherwise dark story. The movie's hero, Luke Skywalker, *enriched* audiences by reinforcing the inspiring beliefs and hopes of adherence to good versus evil, and to loyalty, bravery, justice, freedom, and staying true to one's dreams. Luke spoke to the hero inside of all of us, and reinforced our individual and collective desires to do what is good and right. On Luke's side was his sage mentor and Jedi Master Obi-Wan Kenobi, who *enabled* Luke, reinforcing the idea that continual hard work pays off in efforts to master challenging tasks and overcome difficult obstacles. Luke embodied that part of us that strives to have the power to take on new challenges and make our world a safer and better place.

Overview

We've seen brands that are wildly successful, with devoted fans who spend their time, money, and reputation in the service of the brands they admire. Caterpillar's independent dealers have developed such a strong relationship with the brand that they stay with Caterpillar an average of more than 50 years! Customers have spent hours in line waiting to buy the newest (and premium priced) iPhone or Samsung Galaxy. Moreover, some customers gladly work on behalf of their brands as brand champions. College football fans not only watch their alma mater's games, they also commune at tailgates, develop team-specific rituals and cheers, wear team colors, defend their team against rivals, buy season tickets, and, in some cases, donate substantial portions of their personal wealth to the team's school. We call brands that create this intense and positive brand-self relationship *admired brands*. This chapter takes a deep dive into what we mean by brand admiration and what are its key drivers. We call this chapter "The Science behind Brand Admiration" because the material it presents is consistent with considerable research that we[1] and many colleagues[2] in the fields of marketing and psychology have conducted. Let's begin by describing what we mean by brand admiration.

THE THEORY BEHIND BRAND ADMIRATION

We define brand admiration as the degree to which customers have a salient, personal connection with the brand, emanating from their trust in, love of, and respect for the brand.[3] When brand admiration is strong, customers have a strong relationship with the brand; they use it repeatedly and loyally, and they talk to others about it as often as they can. As such, the brand is often top of mind.

Connection with the Brand

When customers admire a brand, they feel a personal connection between the brand and themselves. Admired brands are part of who customers are, what they do, and what makes their worlds work. An admired brand provides a meaningful connection to customers' needs, goals, and wants in some aspect of their personal or professional lives. Admired brands resonate with customers' personal, social, cultural, and organizational lives. Customers' sense of who I am, what I like, what I do, and what makes my world work includes not just themselves but also the brand. When there's a connection between customers and a brand, customers think about themselves in *terms of the brand*. For example, many customers who use a Mac (versus a PC) consider themselves to be "Mac people."

Salient/Top of Mind

Perhaps because admired brands are strongly connected to the self, they're also salient, or top of mind (TOM) in memory and easily recalled. Consumers' autobiographical memories include the brand, and they think about the brand frequently. For these reasons, admired brands are often the first ones that customers think of when someone mentions the product category that the brand competes in.

Brand admiration (and also brand-self connections and TOM brand recall) becomes stronger as customers' relationship with the brand deepens and grows more positive. Because customers have such a strong personal connection to the brands they admire, they also feel great distress at the prospect of losing their brands. Think about the incredible outpour of sadness people experienced at the death of celebrities such as Prince or Whitney Houston, or at the discontinuation of a favorite brand or TV show. We feel that our lives would simply not be the same without these brands.

Brand Admiration's Effects on Customer Behavior

Brand admiration matters because it affects sets of behaviors that make the brand valuable to the company: (1) brand-loyalty behaviors, and (2) brand-advocacy behaviors.

Brand-Loyalty Behaviors

When customers admire a brand, they purchase it consistently over time, rather than buying competing brands. And they're willing to pay a price premium for it. They're also more likely to wait to buy an admired brand (versus opting for a competitive brand) if the brand is out of stock or being updated. And if the brand messes up, loyal customers are more likely to forgive it, discount the severity of its transgression, and/or find sympathetic reasons as to what happened and why.

Brand-Advocacy Behaviors

When customers admire a brand, they often become brand advocates. They might display the brand name publicly on items that they own (e.g., car bumper stickers, apparel with the brand's logo, or—in extreme cases—on their bodies in the form of tattoos!). They willingly recommend the brand to others, and they actively defend the admired brand if others talk poorly about it. They might also trash-talk a competitor's brand. Finally, they want to connect with others like them who feel the same way about the brand. Customers who admire the same brand can develop brand communities, rituals, blogs, and web sites that showcase their brand devotion.

Brand loyalty and brand advocacy behaviors are interesting because some of them take a lot of time, money, or reputational resources to enact. Another way of saying this is that *the more customers admire a brand, the more willing they are to devote their time, money, and reputation to support the brand.*

One reason why is that they admire the brand so much that they're willing to take unusual steps to support it. Another reason is that because the brand is so tightly connected to customers (who they are, and what makes their world work), they see the brand as part of themselves. Spending time, money and other resources on the brand means supporting not just the brand, but the customer too.

Brand Admiration and Value to the Company

Brand loyalty and advocacy behaviors create value for the company. When customers are loyal to a brand, and when they advocate on its behalf, companies should realize greater revenue (from customers and from those to whom they advocate). They should also achieve that revenue at a lower cost since brand advocates (versus marketing communications) more persuasively convince others to buy the brand. Together, *these two types of behaviors serve as a theoretical link between brand admiration and brand profitability.* Customers who are loyal to the company and advocate on its behalf also produce some of the other benefits that Figure 1.1 linked with admired brands (e.g., growth facilitator, second-chance provider, human-capital builder). We return to these benefits in Chapter 11, when we discuss brand equity.

Critically, *brand admiration is what connects the brand's benefits (the 3Es) to the value of the brand to the company*. Customers want to buy and use admired brands because these brands (more so than other brands) provide benefits that contribute to customers' happiness. Companies want customers to admire their brands because admired brands foster strategically important outcomes to companies. Brand admiration is not an all-or-nothing state. Instead, customers admire brands to greater or lesser degrees. All companies should want to enhance the *extent* to which their brands are admired, so that they can reap the benefits in Figure 3.1 to greater degrees.

BRAND TRUST, LOVE, AND RESPECT

Our research shows that brand admiration and its effects on brand loyalty and advocacy behaviors are greatest when the brand is trusted, loved, *and* respected. Brand trust is defined as the degree to which customers can count on the brand to be there for them. When customers trust a brand, they believe it will act in their best interests, now and in the future. Customers who trust a brand are willing to put themselves in situations that might otherwise be risky for them. They do so because they believe they can depend on the brand to do what it's supposed to do. Brand love is defined as the degree to which customers have a strong degree of affection toward the brand. Customers who love a brand adore it and want to be near it at all times because of how much it pleases their senses, minds, and hearts. Brand respect is defined as the degree to which customers look up to the brand and hold it in high regard. Customers applaud what the brand does. They commend it for what it stands for, feel that the brand speaks to who they are as people (including their beliefs and hopes), and they idolize it for its aspirational impact.

It is the *combined effect* of brand trust, love, and respect that explains why brand admiration produces the brand loyalty and brand advocacy behaviors shown in Figure 3.1. Our research shows that brand love taps into customers' motivation to approach the brand and their desire to explore more about it. Brand trust provides directional focus by influencing customers' desires to own and use the brand because they can count on it. Finally, brand respect produces energy

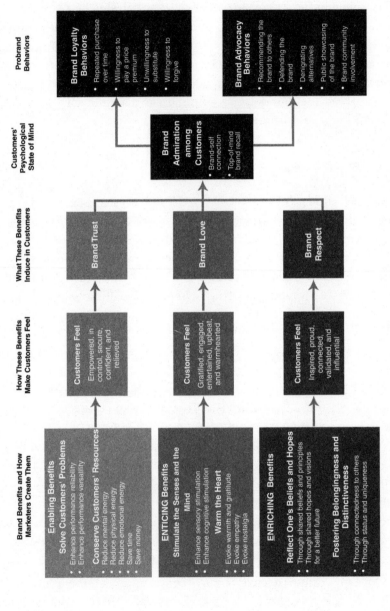

Figure 3.1 Brand Admiration Model: Drivers and Consequences

that motivates customers to overcome barriers that could otherwise interfere with buying or using the brand (e.g., price, physical distance, and the time it takes to have a brand delivered). Brand respect sustains the customer-brand relationship when external shocks occur (e.g., when a low-priced competitor enters the market). Brand respect is perhaps the most potent motivational force that bridges the gap between customers' intentions to buy the brand and their actual purchasing behavior over time.

HOW TO BUILD BRAND ADMIRATION: THE 3ES

So how can companies enhance brand trust, love, and respect (and as a result, brand admiration)? Chapters 1 and 2 suggested that brands that enable, entice, and enrich customers make them happy. Why? As Figure 3.1 shows, enabling, enticing, and enriching benefits create different types of positive feelings that lift our moods, make us feel better, and in general contribute to our happiness and overall sense of well-being. Let's explain how and why.

Theoretical Grounding of the 3Es

In our work, we've spent a lot of time looking at psychological research on people's needs, goals, and motives. In the process we've discovered a number of typologies of human needs, goals, and motives that can explain how and why customers use (and come to admire) brands. Importantly, these typologies can be subsumed within the higher-order categories that we call the 3Es (for enabling, enticing, and enriching). For example, Ford and Nichols identified 24 goal categories that reflect the 3Es. Among them include enabling goals like the need for mastery, management, material gain, and safety. Also included are enticing goals, like task creativity and artistic expression, as well as enriching goals like needs for individuality and superiority. Likewise Murray's list of needs includes needs regarding enablement (e.g., harm avoidance), enticement (e.g., need for play, sex), and enrichment (e.g., affiliation, achievement, autonomy). Kahle and colleague's 1986 List of Values includes values related to enablement (security), enticement (excitement, fun, enjoyment), and enrichment (sense of belonging, self-fulfillment, self-respect, being respected by others). Many other typologies of needs, motivations, and goals can similarly map onto the 3Es.[4]

Positive Feelings from the 3Es

When a brand's benefits make customers feel enabled, enticed, and enriched, the brand naturally evokes positive feelings (see Figure 3.1). To illustrate: when brands enable them, customers *feel empowered* to do what they need to do in the easiest way possible. They feel secure, in control, confident, and relieved. Feeling empowered and in control has been noted as a critical driver of a sense of self-efficacy and optimism; feelings that ward off depression and make people feel as if they have the power to do what they need to do in their lives.

When brands entice customers, customers *feel gratified* by the sense-pleasing, thought-pleasing, and heartwarming benefits inherent in the brand. Much recent research in marketing shows the power that marketers can realize when they consider brand benefits that stimulate customers' senses, thoughts, and hearts.[5] Enticing benefits can make us feel not only gratified, but also engaged, entertained, upbeat, and/or warmhearted. Brands with these benefits stave off feelings of boredom, making purely functional products much more interesting, engaging, and exciting.

Enriching benefits are fundamental to theories that incorporate needs such as belongingness, self-actualization, and self-esteem, and needs for relatedness versus autonomy. We feel enriched when we believe that we are acting in a way that is consistent with our beliefs and hopes, and as such are doing what we believe is right for ourselves, for others, and for society. We feel inspired as people by brands that reflect our deepest beliefs and hopes. We also feel connected, proud, validated, and influential when brands provide benefits that connect us to others or make us feel special.

Let's briefly describe *how* marketers can enable, entice, and enrich customers so as to build brand trust, love and respect, and with it, brand admiration.

How to Provide Enabling Benefits?

Figure 3.1 shows two ways in which brands can provide enabling benefits. They can (1) solve customers' problems, and/or (2) conserve customers' resources. A brand that provides these enabling benefits makes customers feel empowered, in control, secure, confident, and/or relieved. When a brand helps to resolve customers' problems and/or conserve their resources, customers feel that the maker of the brand recognizes the constraints customers are under (their problems and their limited resources), and that it can be trusted to help them deal with these constraints.

Enabling by Problem Resolution

Brands can empower customers and give them a greater sense of control over their environments by helping customers solve their problems—large and small, at work or at home, in their business relationships or their personal relationships. Need to upgrade your marketing skills? Try an online course from MarketingProfs. Can't get your various software systems to talk to one another? See if Salesforce's integrative cloud-computing products can help. Gaining control over our environments (in part through the brands we use) provides relief through problems being solved and feelings of protection and security from future threats. Enabling benefits thus solve customers' problems, offering physical, social, psychological, and economic protection and avoiding negative future harm.

When it comes to enabling customers, what's critical is not only that the brand solves problems but also that it can be counted on to do so *reliably* over time. Tesla, for example, has designed a software system through which vehicles in need of repair can immediately and automatically download corrective software. Brand benefits can also be enabling when brand use is expanded to cover additional usage occasions. Marketers can enhance product *versatility* by affecting when, where, how, and why (for what reasons) the brand's use can be expanded. For example, the iPhone has become indispensable in usage contexts that include communication through e-mail and text, taking pictures, playing games, finding directions, and much more.

Interestingly, while it is still called a phone, making phone calls is becoming the least frequently used function on the iPhone. What resonates with customers is the iPhone's versatility.

Enabling by Conserving Resources

Benefits can also enable customers in a different way: by how much they help customers conserve scarce time, monetary, psychological, and physical resources. A brand that conserves scarce resources and/or allows customers to acquire them (e.g., by earning more money via better investment options, or gaining physical energy from sleeping on a supportive mattress) makes customers feel less mentally taxed, less physically tired, and less emotionally anxious. A brand can also conserve scarce resources by minimizing the time or money customers must spend to own and use the brand. Uber and Lyft have wreaked havoc on the taxi industry because they do a better job than regular taxi companies in minimizing the resources customers must exert to get a ride and pay for it. Supermarket brands Aldi and Lidl have created upheaval for traditional supermarket brands by offering a simpler, more convenient, frugal shopping experience. Brands that conserve (or save) scarce resources provide comfort, security, and convenience. Customers feel more empowered, safe, and more relieved when their resources are not taxed.

Enabling Benefits and Brand Trust

When customers can count on a reliable and versatile brand to address their problems consistently and over time, they feel that they can depend on it. They trust it to be there for them when they need it. Trust enhances feelings of security, lowers anxiety, and enhances confidence in the brand as a relationship partner. Customers are more willing to establish a connection between the self and the brand because they know they can depend on (trust) the brand. Conserving customers' scarce resources also fosters brand trust. When a brand helps customers save time, money, and physical/ psychological energy, customers believe that the brand is acting in their best interests. It's helping them do more with less. The brand maker recognizes the constraints customers are under and it is being responsive to these constraints. Feeling that the brand is acting on the customer's behalf fosters trust.

Enticing Benefits

Figure 3.1 shows two ways in which brands can provide enticing benefits. They can provide sensory or cognitive stimulation, activating customers' thoughts and senses in ways that make customers feel good. They can also speak to customers in ways that arouse sentimentality, humor, empathy, gratitude, and/or nostalgia. A brand that provides these enticing benefits makes customers feel gratified, engaged, entertained, upbeat, and warmhearted. These positive feelings foster brand love.[6]

Enticing by Pleasing the Mind and Senses

Brands can please the senses when they provide cognitive stimulation (arousing curiosity and imagination, making people think) and/or sensory stimulation (activating pleasant sights, sounds, tastes, smells, and tactile sensations). Enticing benefits encompass the term *experiential marketing* and the concept of *design* that today differentiates the truly great brands from mediocre ones. Popular online video games offer strong cognitive stimulation. In League of Legends, for example, players control a range of characters called champions and try to unlock their champion's unique abilities and augment them by making the right decisions in the game. Four Seasons hotel brand epitomizes sensory stimulation in the hotel industry. From its visually stunning décor, beautiful locations, gourmet meals, and golf and other entertainment options to the most luxurious bedding, and amenities like Jacuzzi tubs and soft robes and slippers, Four Seasons' customers want for nothing. IMAX Theatres' 3D technology is so realistic, viewers feel as if they are actually immersed in and part of the movie. Think about the alluring fragrance of Chanel No 5, the adorable Hello Kitty, Justin Bieber's hairstyle, and the rich taste of Godiva chocolates. These brands all offer sense-pleasing benefits.

Enticing by Warming the Heart

Customers also feel enticed when the brand offers heartwarming benefits. Brands can offer heartwarming benefits in several ways. They can evoke heartwarming emotions such as humor, excitement, and gratitude. They can evoke empathy[7] and/or create nostalgia.[8] Hallmark warms the heart in each of these ways. It does so through its conviction that Life Is a Special Occasion. Hallmark cards, whether delivered electronically or via mail, warm the heart by messages that celebrate all manner of occasions with sentiments that card recipients appreciate. To mark and remember special events, Hallmark produces Keepsake Ornaments and personalized books. Hallmark is also known for entertainment, with its Hallmark Channel and Hall of Fame TV programming. As of 2015, "the series has earned 81 Emmys, nine Golden Globes, 11 Peabody Awards, 28 Christopher Awards, and four Humanitas Prizes."[9] Some brands warm the heart through nostalgia (think about the Slinky toy, the similar theme songs and gameplay mechanics shared by Nintendo's various Supermario and Pokemon games over the years, and the TV show *The Wonder Years*). A simple, sincere smile, a gentle reminder about our childhoods, a fun and engaging way of interacting with customers, or an act of kindness as part of service delivery all go a long way in warming customers' hearts.

Benefits that stimulate the mind, senses, and heart are just as important in a B2B environment as in a B2C one. Unfortunately, many B2B marketers (and a fair number of B2C marketers) often do an inadequate job of considering how they might enhance their brand's relevance through enticing benefits. Navistar, described in Chapter 2, focused extensively on enticing benefits when developing new models of their trucks. The psychological impact of these enticing benefits clearly had a tremendous effect on truckers.

Enticing Benefits and Brand Love

Whereas enabling benefits foster one of the critical drivers of brand admiration (brand trust), enticing benefits foster a second driver of brand admiration, specifically brand love (see Figure 3.1). Enticing benefits, and the brand love that follows from them, create an approach response toward the brand, making customers want to explore and be around these brands for the consistent gratification they can provide. Enticing benefits thus attract our attention to and interest in the brand. We feel more inclined to approach the brand and see what else it has in store for us.

Enriching Benefits

Figure 3.1 shows two ways in which brands can provide enriching benefits: (1) by reflecting personal beliefs and hopes, and (2) by fostering belongingness and distinctiveness.[10] A brand that provides these enriching benefits makes customers feel inspired, proud, connected, validated, and/or influential. These feelings enhance customers' brand respect.

Enriching by Reflecting Personal Beliefs and Hopes

We all want to feel that we are good people. We want to make a positive difference somehow, or in some way. Being a good person builds an internal sense of pride, which bolsters self-esteem. Customers feel enriched when the brands they buy and use have principles that align with their personal or professional hopes and their beliefs about what is moral, good, just, and right. Customers feel true to themselves (authentic) when the brands they buy and use have principles that converge with their own.

The shoe brand Camper abhors the rush of modern life. It emphasizes walking as a valued goal. Camper promotes walking as a way of appreciating and taking in the wonderful world that surrounds us. The brand reinforces the value of the environment and the joys that going for a walk can bring. Camper's customers hold similar beliefs and principles, so there is a congruity between the brand and the self. Brands can also inspire people to become better persons, to eat more healthfully, to exercise, to be better parents or employees, and to look better. In addition, brands can inspire by speaking to and supporting critical social challenges. For example, Shell Oil believes that the world needs more experts who can address the world's energy challenges. To inspire others to help in this challenge, Shell supports Shell Ideas360, a competition that encourages students to think in innovative ways about energy. Shell's GameChanger nurtures and supports ideas from entrepreneurs and innovators. The company's commitment to making the world a better place inspires others who feel similarly, elevating customers' respect for Shell.

Enriching by Fostering Belongingness and Distinctiveness

Belongingness. Customers also like to feel accepted by and connected to others. They want to feel like they belong to a family, group, or community who accepts them. Feelings of belongingness provide meaning to life. Marketers can enrich customers by boosting their *sense of belongingness as a member of a group.* This can be accomplished by referencing customers' roots, their ancestors, their places of origin, and the close and distant families they have. The importance of one's roots and personal history explains customers' historical tendencies to document (and present idealized images of) moments of their own lives as lived with the people that they care about. It also explains consumers' interest in ancestry search, documenting their lives and the lives of their families, colleagues, and friends through pictures and movies, engaging in Facebook activities, and wearing clothes that symbolize the group(s) that they are a part of. Being a member of a community of like-minded people (whether virtual or face-to-face) can help people feel accepted and appreciated for who they are.

Many successful marketers have aligned their brands with specific groups, which serves as badges of belonging to a particular group. Facebook's success is tied, in part, to its ability to connect people with family, friends, and colleagues. The American Girl retail store fosters belongingness: in this case, intergenerational connectedness. It's a place where mothers, grandmothers, and daughters can enjoy each other's company over lunch, take photos with the dolls, and visit the salons together. Porsche has introduced its GTS Community, which invites members to collect and share spectacular driving routes all over the world with other community members. Being part of the Porsche family means something to its members.

Distinctiveness. People also want to convey to others that they are *distinctive and special in some way.*[11] Sometimes this distinctiveness is related to *status*. People would like to believe that others evaluate and look up to them for who they are (e.g., their style, their beauty, their knowledge) or what they've accomplished (e.g., their wealth, professional successes, musical talents, athletic accomplishments). Indeed, the use of brands to signal distinctiveness has long been recognized.[12] Brands signal one's status and the groups one belongs to, with the effect that others can immediately infer something about users—their characteristics, beliefs, and preferences—merely by the brands they use. This signaling value is important for luxury brands, which are differentiated from other brands by virtue of their prestige, exclusivity, and price. Making certain customers signature clients or VIPs, and providing options that are limited to a privileged few, are examples of ways in which marketers can enrich customers through distinctiveness related to status.[13]

Also related to distinctiveness, is customers' use of brands that signal their *uniqueness* relative to others.[14] Customers want to believe that they have independent minds, their own personal styles, and a sense of autonomy. This desire for uniqueness has given rise to a movement in product customization, in which customers are allowed to create versions of a brand that perfectly fit their unique personalities or situations. Nike has been on board with this movement by allowing customers to design the colors and patterns of their own shoes. What's considered cool is often not related to what everyone is doing, but rather what only a few people are doing.

Enriching Benefits and Brand Respect

Our research finds some very important insights into enriching benefits. Although enabling and enticing benefits build brand admiration through their impact on brand trust and brand love, enriching benefits have the greatest impact on brand admiration through their impact on brand respect.[15] Enabling and enticing benefits enhance brand admiration only to a certain degree. Indeed, our research suggests that enriching benefits may be the most critical E for building, strengthening, and sustaining brand admiration. This is so for several reasons.

First, individuals' beliefs, hopes, sense of belongingness, and sense of distinctiveness are frequently challenged in daily life. People are frequently reminded that they are not the people they aspire to be. They often find themselves behaving in values-inconsistent ways (using disposable diapers even though one values being "green"). They might feel rejected and left out of groups to which they wish to belong, or feel that there is nothing that stands out to make them distinctive and special.[16] As a result, people are highly sensitive to enriching benefits.

Second technological advances often allow brands to capably offer enabling benefits, and the enabling benefits of many top brands are often quite similar. Additionally, people take enabling benefits for granted after some time. When was the last time you truly appreciated the fact that your refrigerator works reliably? Moreover, there has been increasing attention to the role of aesthetics and consumer experiences in differentiating brands from others in the market (enticing benefits). However, it is easy for people to get bored with enticing benefits and not gain pleasure from them after a time. We may love the design of our smartphone, only to replace it with the next thin, slick smartphone that comes out the next year. Yet, inspiring consumers by speaking to their beliefs and hopes, their sense of belongingness and distinctiveness has a powerful effect on consumers. It speaks to their sense of self and the meaning of life.

Brands have tremendous opportunities to capitalize on the power of enriching benefits as a way of differentiating their brands. Once customers understand the brand's enriching benefits it can be very difficult for them to switch to other brands because enriching benefits speak to our sense of identity and the beliefs they hold. The importance of enriching benefits in building brand admiration cannot be overemphasized. Many brands fail to speak to their customers in ways that enrich their customers' lives.

Importantly though, our research clearly shows that enriching benefits alone may not be sufficient to truly make a brand admired. Instead, brand admiration is greatest when brands enable, entice, *and* enrich customers. Together, these three classes of benefits offer *exponential power* in driving brand admiration.

KEY TAKEAWAYS

1. Brand admiration is the most critical destination point for marketers.

2. Strong brand admiration makes customers more likely to engage in brand loyalty and advocacy behaviors, which enhance the equity of the brand (and the company that makes it).

3. Brand trust, brand love, and brand respect drive brand admiration. Because brand trust, brand love, and brand respect have a multiplicative effect on brand admiration, the greatest degree of brand admiration comes from marketing efforts that create all three.

4. Brands make customers happy by activating what will (1) enable, entice, and enrich them, (2) build brand trust, love, and respect, and consequently (3) enhance brand admiration.

5. Feelings of empowerment from benefits that enable customers (solving their problems and conserving their resources) foster brand trust, and with it brand admiration.

6. Feelings of gratification from benefits that entice customers (stimulating their thoughts/senses and warming their hearts) foster brand love, and with it brand admiration.

7. Feelings of inspiration from benefits that enrich customers (reflecting hopes/beliefs and fostering belongingness and status) create brand respect, and with it brand admiration.

8. Brand admiration is greatest when brands offer benefits that enable, entice, *and* enrich customers' lives.

9. As Figure 1.1 shows, companies not only need to build admiration (see Chapters 4 through 6), they need to sustain (Chapter 7) and leverage brand admiration over time (see Chapters 8 through 10). We turn to these issues in subsequent chapters.

WHAT ABOUT YOUR BRAND?

1. How much do customers currently admire your brand? How extensively do your customers engage in brand loyalty and brand advocacy behaviors? What can you do to create stronger brand loyalty and advocacy behaviors?

2. Is your brand trusted, loved, and respected? If not, why not? How can you improve in these areas?

3. To what extent does your brand currently offer benefits that enable, entice, and enrich customers? Where are

you doing an excellent job? In what ways can your brand improve?

NOTES

1. C. Whan Park, Deborah J. MacInnis, Joseph Priester, Andreas B. Eisingerich, and Dawn Iacobucci, "Brand Attachment and Brand Attitude Strength: Conceptual and Empirical Differentiation of Two Critical Brand Equity Drivers," *Journal of Marketing* 74, no. 6 (2010): 1–17; C. Whan Park, Andreas B. Eisingerich, and Jason Whan Park, "Attachment–Aversion (AA) Model of Customer-Brand Relationships," *Journal of Consumer Psychology* 23, no. 2 (2013): 229–248; Leigh Anne Novak, Joseph Priester, Deborah J. MacInnis, and C. Whan Park, "Brand Forgiveness: How Close Brand Relationships Influence Forgiveness," in *Customer-Brand Relationships: Theories and Applications*, eds. Susan Fournier, Michael Braezeale, and Marc Fetscherin (New York: Routledge, 2012), 184–203; Matthew Thomson, Deborah J. MacInnis, and C. Whan Park, "The Ties That Bind: Measuring the Strength of Consumers' Emotional Attachments to Brands," *Journal of Consumer Psychology* 15, no. 1 (2005): 77–91; Alexander Fedorikhin, C. Whan Park, and Matthew Thomson, "Beyond Fit and Attitude: The Effect of Emotional Attachment on Consumer Responses to Brand Extensions," *Journal of Consumer Psychology* 18, no. 4 (2008): 281–291.

2. Others whose work has inspired our thinking include (but is not limited to) Joseph W. Alba and Elanor F. Williams, "Pleasure Principles: A Review of Research on Hedonic Consumption," *Journal of Consumer Psychology* 23, no. 1 (2013): 2–18; Rajeev Batra, Aaron Ahuvia, and Richard P. Bagozzi, "Brand Love," *Journal of Marketing* 76, no. 2 (2012): 1–16; Russell W. Belk, "Possessions and the Extended Self," *Journal of Consumer Research* 15, no. 2 (1988): 139–168; Russell W. Belk, "Extended Self in a Digital World," *Journal of Consumer Research* 40, no. 3 (2013): 477–500; Lan Nguyen Chaplin and Deborah Roedder John, "The Development of Self-Brand Connections in Children and Adolescents," *Journal of Consumer Research* 32, no. 1 (2005): 119–129; Arjun Chaudhuri and Morris B. Holbrook, "The Chain of Effects from Brand Trust and Brand Affect to Brand Performance: The Role of Brand Loyalty," *Journal of Marketing* 65, no. 2 (2001): 81–93; Jennifer Edson Escalas and James R. Bettman, "Self-Construal, Reference Groups, and Brand Meaning," *Journal of Consumer Research* 32, no. 3 (2005): 378–389; Jennifer Edson Escalas and James R. Bettman, "You Are What They

Eat: The Influence of Reference Groups on Consumers' Connections to Brands," *Journal of Consumer Psychology* 13, no. 3 (2003): 339–348; Susan Fournier, Michael Solomon, and Basil Englis, "When Brands Resonate," in *Handbook of Brand and Experience Management*, eds. Bernd H. Schmitt and David Rogers (Northampton, MA: Edward Elgar, 2008), 35–57; Morris B. Holbrook and Elizabeth C. Hirschman, "The Experiential Aspects of Consumption: Consumer Fantasies, Feelings, and Fun," *Journal of Consumer Research* 9, no. 2 (1982): 132–140; Kevin L. Keller, "Understanding the Richness of Brand Relationships: Research Dialogue on Brands as Intentional Agents," *Journal of Consumer Psychology* 22, no. 2 (2012): 186–190; Aradhna Krishna, "An Integrative Review of Sensory Marketing: Engaging the Senses to Affect Perception, Judgment and Behavior," *Journal of Consumer Psychology* 22, no. 3 (2012): 332–351; James H. McAlexander, John W. Schouten, and Harold F. Koenig, "Building Brand Community," *Journal of Marketing* 66, no. 1 (2002): 38–54; Joann Peck and Terry L. Childers, "Sensory Factors and Consumer Behavior," in *Handbook of Consumer Psychology*, eds. Curtis P. Haugtvedt, Paul M. Herr, and Frank R. Kardes (New York: Taylor and Francis, 2008), 193–219; Martin Reimann and Arthur Aron, "Self-Expansion Motivation and Inclusion of Brands in Self," in *Handbook of Brand Relationships*, eds. Deborah J. MacInnis, C. Whan Park, and Joseph R. Priester (New York: M.E. Sharpe, 2009), 65–81; Julie A. Ruth, "Promoting a Brand's Emotion Benefits: The Influence of Emotion Categorization Processes on Consumer Evaluations," *Journal of Consumer Psychology* 11, no. 2 (2001): 99–113; Bernd H. Schmitt, *Experiential Marketing: How to Get Customers to Sense, Feel, Think, Act, Relate* (New York: Simon and Schuster, 2000); Matthew Thomson, "Human Brands: Investigating Antecedents to Consumers' Strong Attachments to Celebrities," *Journal of Marketing* 70, no. 3 (2006): 104–119.

3. In our past research, we used the term brand attachment instead of brand admiration. However, our current research leads us to believe that brand admiration best characterizes what we describe in this book. The term brand admiration is also more appropriate than brand attachment in describing B2B customers' brand experiences.

4. Abraham H. Maslow, "A Theory of Human Motivation," *Psychological Review* 50, no. 4 (1943): 370; Louis Tay and Ed Diener, "Needs and Subjective Well-Being Around the World," *Journal of Personality and Social Psychology* 101, no. 2 (2011): 354–365; Ada S. Chulef, Stephen J. Read, and David A. Walsh, "A Hierarchical Taxonomy of Human Goals," *Motivation and Emotion* 25, no. 3 (2001): 191–232; Martin E.

Ford, and C. W. Nichols, "A Taxonomy of Human Goals and Some Possible Applications," in *Humans as Self-Constructing Living Systems: Putting the Framework to Work*, eds. Martin E. Ford and Donald H. Ford (Mahwah, NJ: Lawrence Erlbaum Associates, 1987), 289–311; Valerie A. Braithwaite and H. G. Law, "Structure of Human Values: Testing the Adequacy of the Rokeach Value Survey," *Journal of Personality and Social Psychology* 49, no. 1 (1985): 250–263; Edward Deci and Richard M. Ryan, "Self-Determination Research: Reflections and Future Directions," *Handbook of Self-Determination Research* (NY: University of Rochester Press, 2002), 431–441; Lynn Kahle, Sharon E. Beatty, and Pamela M. Homer, "Alternative Measurement Approaches to Consumer Values: The List of Values (LOV) and Values and Life Style (VALS)," *Journal of Consumer Research* 13, no. 3 (1986): 405–409; Bernd Schmitt, "The Consumer Psychology of Brands," *Journal of Consumer Psychology* 22, no. 1 (2012): 7–17; Michel Tuan Pham, "On Consumption of Happiness: A Research Dialogue," *Journal of Consumer Psychology* 25, no. 1 (2015): 150–151. Murray, H. A. (1938), Explorations in Personality, NY: Oxford University Press.

5. Peck and Childers, "Sensory Factors"; Krishna, "An Integrative Review of Sensory Marketing"; Schmitt, *Experiential Marketing*.

6. We offer a more narrow definition of love than do some other researchers.

7. Jennifer Edson Escalas and Barbara B. Stern, "Sympathy and Empathy: Emotional Responses to Advertising Dramas," *Journal of Consumer Research* 29, no. 4 (2003): 566–578.

8. Morris B. Holbrook, "Nostalgia and Consumption Preferences: Some Emerging Patterns of Consumer Tastes," *Journal of Consumer Research* 20, no. 2 (1993): 245–256; Robert M. Schindler and Morris B. Holbrook, "Nostalgia for Early Experience as a Determinant of Consumer Preferences," *Psychology & Marketing* 20, no. 4 (2003): 275–302.

9. "Hallmark Hall of Fame," Hallmark, accessed April 22, 2016, http://corporate.hallmark.com/OurBrand/Hallmark-Hall-of-Fame.

10. Sidney J. Levy, "Symbols for Sale," *Harvard Business Review* 37, no. 4 (1959): 117–124; Joseph M. Sirgy, "Self-Concept in Consumer Behavior: A Critical Review," *Journal of Consumer Research* 9, no. 3 (1982): 287–300; Hazel Markus and Paula Nurius, "Possible Selves," *American Psychologist* 41, no. 9 (1986): 954–969; Americus Reed, "Activating the Self-Importance of Consumer Selves: Exploring Identity Salience Effects on Judgments," *Journal of Consumer Research* 31, no. 2 (2004): 286–295; Nicole Verrochi Coleman and Patti Williams, "Looking for My Self: Identity-Driven Attention Allocation," *Journal of Consumer Psychology* 25, no. 3 (2015): 504–511; Sharon Shavitt, Carlos J. Torelli, and Jimmy

Wong, "Identity-Based Motivation: Constraints and Opportunities in Consumer Research," *Journal of Consumer Psychology* 19, no. 3 (2009): 261–266; Daphna Oyserman, "Identity-Based Motivation: Implications for Action-Readiness, Procedural-Readiness, and Consumer Behavior," *Journal of Consumer Psychology* 19, no. 3 (2009): 250–260.

11. Jonah Berger and Chip Heath, "Where Consumers Diverge from Others: Identity Signaling and Product Domains," *Journal of Consumer Research* 34, no. 2 (2007): 121–134.

12. Levy, "Symbols for Sale."

13. Joseph C. Nunes, Xavier Drèze, and Young Jee Han, "Conspicuous Consumption in a Recession: Toning It Down or Turning It Up?," *Journal of Consumer Psychology* 21, no. 2 (2011): 199–205; Silvia Bellezza and Anat Keinan, "Brand Tourists: How Non-Core Users Enhance the Brand Image by Eliciting Pride," *Journal of Consumer Research* 41, no. 2 (2014): 397–417.

14. Berger and Heath, "Where Consumers Diverge"; Cindy Chan, Jonah Berger, and Leif van Boven, "Identifiable but Not Identical: Combining Social Identity and Uniqueness Motives in Choice," *Journal of Consumer Research* 39, no. 3 (2012): 561–573.

15. Park, Eisingerich, and Park, "Attachment–Aversion."

16. Katherine White and Jennifer J. Argo, "Social Identity Threat and Consumer Preferences," *Journal of Consumer Psychology* 19, no. 3 (2009): 313–325; Katherine White, Jennifer J. Argo, and Jaideep Sengupta, "Dissociative versus Associative Responses to Social Identity Threat: The Role of Consumer Self-Construal," *Journal of Consumer Research* 39, no. 4 (2012): 704–719; Leilei Gao, Christian Wheeler, and Baba Shiv, "The 'Shaken Self': Product Choices as a Means of Restoring Self-View Confidence," *Journal of Consumer Research* 36, no. 1 (2009): 29–38.

BUILDING ADMIRED BRANDS

CHAPTER 4

Building Admiration from the Inside

T he world's most admired brands have the world's most devoted employees.

INTRODUCTION

The Mayo Clinic, the world's largest nonprofit medical group practice, states its mission simply: "Providing the best care to every patient. We live and work together in a community that welcomes and respects everyone ... a community of richly diverse people contributing their unique ideas."[1] Notably, the Mayo Clinic's mission acts as its compass. It articulates both *what* the Mayo Clinic aims to do and *how* it plans to do it. That is, having the best patient care requires contributions from a diverse set of employees so as to leverage the strengths that each brings to the table. This diversity matters because it accelerates innovation, enhances problem solving, and fosters productivity. The Mayo Clinic's employees themselves embrace the Clinic's mission, not because of glossy brochures or posters, but because its employee programs (and its treatment of customers) embody its mission. As a result, employees can be authentic in their passion for the brand. The Clinic invests heavily in continual professional development. It has built programs focused on cultural and linguistic competence and mentoring for staff to ensure culturally sensitive patient care and behavior. These programs enable employees by helping them perform their daily jobs. They foster *trust* that the organization is behind its mission and employees' professional development. They contribute to a strong sense of warmth, openness, and inclusion, which enhances employees' *love* for the Clinic. Ultimately, they create a sense of connectedness, and they build pride in being part of a community where employees can have an impact, thereby fostering brand *respect*.

OVERVIEW

It seems obvious that developing successful relationships with customers requires strong and successful relationships with those inside the company. Strikingly, though, many companies ignore employees in their branding efforts. Indeed, brands that focus on creating brand admiration from the inside are often the exception, not the rule. Yet if the people who represent the brand and deliver its promise to the outside world don't themselves admire the brand, how can they credibly and authentically convince customers to do the same? Customers and other stakeholders often see employees and employees' actions as synonymous with the brand.[2] As such, it's essential that companies build brand admiration among employees, a topic we explore in this chapter.

EMPLOYEES AS BRAND-BUILDING RESOURCES

It's easy to see how *enhancing brand admiration among employees helps a company to realize its value*. Employee brand admiration activates probrand employee behaviors, including employee brand-loyalty. Employees who admire the brand (1) want to work for the brand and are loathe to leave it. (2) They have a sense of ownership in the brand, taking personal responsibility for its achievement and success. (3) They are more forgiving of organizational mistakes. When employees admire the brand, (4) it plays a role in their lives even outside of work (e.g., at home), and (5) they are vigilant about competitor actions deemed threatening to the brand.

Employees who admire the brand are also brand advocates. (1) They are strong and authentic brand champions. (2) They go beyond their prescribed roles for the well-being of customers and the brand. (3) They participate in various brand community-related events. (4) They recommend the brand to friends. (5) They defend the brand from criticism. (6) They also encourage other employees to focus on the brand (versus focusing on internal politics or other negative company behaviors). (7) They also publically display their association with the brand (e.g., on T-shirts, branded gear, tattoos, etc.). Beyond contributing to employee morale, these outcomes should also reduce employee acquisition and retention costs and enhance employee and knowledge retention.

Recognizing the power of internal customers, Herb Kelleher, founder of Southwest Airlines, once noted the importance of treating employees like customers.[3] He apparently succeeded at this effort. When Kelleher retired after 37 years at Southwest Airlines, the company's pilots and flight attendants took out a full-page ad in the *USA Today* newspaper to thank him for his service to the company. By way of contrast, the very same day American Airlines pilots and flight attendants went on strike and picketed during American Airlines' annual meeting.

As with customers, marketers can create brand admiration and its drivers by finding ways to enable, entice, and enrich employees. We call this process *internal branding* (see Figure 4.1). As we suggest shortly, the mission statement serves as the guidepost for employees' feelings, thoughts, and probrand actions. Hence, we define internal branding as a set of processes that enable, entice, and enrich employees so they can deliver on the brand's mission in a consistent and credible way.

Cultivating brand admiration starts with the mission statement and its features. Specifically, *building trust, love, and respect among employees is possible only when a brand's mission statement has enabling, enticing, and enriching features, and when the company offers enabling, enticing, and enriching benefits to employees.* These combined outcomes boost employee brand admiration, enhancing employees' brand loyalty and advocacy behaviors. What's important to realize here is that by creating these effects, the company develops internal brand admirers who consistently deliver on the brand promise and help to set it apart from competitors. But before going further, let's first discuss a few issues regarding the company's mission statement.

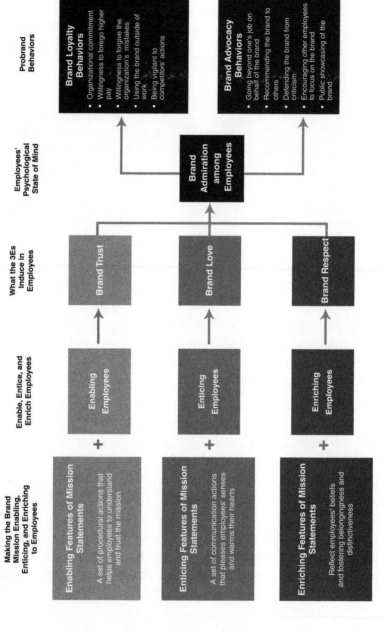

Figure 4.1 Building Employee Brand Admiration

CREATING A MEANINGFUL MISSION STATEMENT

The company's *mission statement* plays an important role in creating employee brand admiration. When the company is new and it has a single brand, the mission is closely aligned with the brand's positioning in the marketplace (which we discuss in detail in Chapter 5). When companies become larger and have a portfolio of distinct brands, the company's mission can become more abstract so as to accommodate the various brands that it makes. Each brand's positioning may well be somewhat different. But the mission statement is important because it represents a global perspective on what the company (and each of its brands) stands for. It provides a broader description of the company's identity, based on the brands it markets. Thus, the company's mission and brand positioning statements should be aligned (or at least not inconsistent) with each other.

When thinking about the mission, consider the following quote from Starbucks' CEO Howard Schultz: "People want to be part of something larger than themselves. They want to be part of something they're really proud of, that they'll fight for, sacrifice for, that they trust."[4] As human beings, we want to have a sense of belonging and distinctiveness, and we take pride in what we do. Employees are no different. The mission statement can encapsulate this belief, such that employees are inspired to have faith in it and make it happen. But if a mission is to contribute to employees' behavior, it must be meaningful. *A meaningful mission statement should describe the brand's purpose and goals and answer the following questions: (1) what benefits should be offered, (2) to whom, and (3) how should they be delivered.*

Table 4.1 describes some mission statements that address these questions. The decision about what benefits to offer gets at *what core customer needs* have yet to be addressed in the marketplace (an issue we explore in Chapter 5). Employees are frustrated when they lack clarity on what the brand is supposed to do for customers. Employees must understand what the brand (and by extension, they themselves) is expected to deliver to customers. A clear promise (i.e., an articulation of *what benefits the brand offers*) makes it easier for employees to deliver on that promise.

Table 4.1   Company Mission Statements

Mission Statement	What Benefits to Offer	To Whom the Benefits are Offered	How to Deliver the Benefits
Google: To organize the world's information and make it universally accessible and useful.	To organize the world's information (the *what*)	and make it universally (the *whom*)	accessible and useful (the *how*)
McKinsey: Our mission is to help our clients make distinctive, lasting, and substantial improvements in their performance and to build a great firm that attracts, develops, excites, and retains exceptional people.	To help...make distinctive, lasting, and substantial improvements in their performance (the *what*)	our clients (the *whom*)	to build a great firm that attracts, develops, excites, and retains exceptional people (the *how*)

The *for whom* question asks *which target customers* are most likely to appreciate the brand's benefits. If employees know what benefits to deliver but they lack knowledge about who the real target customer is, they are less capable and effective in communicating these benefits. Without clarity on the core target market, employees end up using their resources inefficiently—by targeting the wrong customer group(s)—or even worse, inadvertently damaging the brand.

Finally, the *how* question describes the *means or strategies by which a brand plans to respond to target customers' needs*. Answering the *how* question gives employees guidance and clarity on what needs to be done to satisfy customers' needs, particularly as it pertains to employees' own roles and responsibilities. A mission statement that addresses these questions acts as a compass for employees. It gives them a sense of direction and it reassures them of the path taken to get there. Consider, for example, Google's mission "to organize the world's information (the *what*) and make it universally (the *whom*) accessible and useful (the *how*)" (see Table 4.1).[5] Such a sense of purpose and direction helps to build employee brand trust, love, and respect.

Whereas it's helpful for a company to have a mission statement, employees must also accept and embody it to make it meaningful. Unfortunately, some internal branding experts suggest that over 50 percent of employees don't believe in their company's mission statement, or don't think they have the knowledge, skills, and training to deliver on it.[6] Thus, beyond stating a mission statement, internal branding needs to focus on making that mission come to life for employees.

ENABLING, ENTICING, AND ENRICHING FEATURES THAT MAKE THE MISSION STATEMENT COME TO LIFE

The first step in building admiration from the inside is to ensure that employees trust, love, and respect the brand mission itself. To do so, employees should find their company's mission statement or its embodiment enabling, enticing, and enriching.

Enabling Features That Foster Trust

Several important enabling features foster employees' trust of the mission.

Involvement in the Mission's Development

Employees are more likely to support and trust a mission that they have had a voice in developing. A mission statement that's been thrust upon them is not likely to create the same degree of brand admiration. Involving employees in the mission statement's development provides a strong sense of ownership. To whatever extent possible, brand holders should proactively invite employees to be part of the mission's formulation process. In this way, brands *actively manage the mission-statement experience.* By involving employees in developing and communicating the company's mission, employees are better enabled to craft it, endorse it, act on it, and share it wholeheartedly with (other internal and) external customers.

Stating the Mission in a Memorable Way

The mission statement is particularly memorable, and it resonates well with employees when it can be restated in a simple way. For example, the Ritz-Carlton's credo about being the gold standard of service is communicated in its "Ladies and gentlemen serving ladies and gentlemen" statement. Another example is Goldman Sachs, whose list of business principles starts with "Our clients' interests always come first."[7] Or consider McKinsey's to-the-point statement: "We believe we will be successful if our clients are successful."[8] A shortened version of the mission keeps it clear and top of mind.

Making the Mission Concrete

Employees are enabled to act on the mission when they are given specific guideposts that make it concrete. This is particularly important for new hires, for whom the mission statement might be somewhat abstract and unfamiliar. To illustrate, consider that the Ritz-Carlton's tenet ("We are ladies and gentlemen serving ladies and gentlemen") translates into three concrete behaviors that employees can enact in a mission-consistent way: (1) provide a warm and sincere greeting that uses the guest's name, (2) anticipate and fulfill the guest's needs, and (3) wish the guest a warm goodbye, again using the guest's name. These concrete "steps of service" clarify mission-consistent actions, and they empower employees to create their own unique, memorable guest experiences.[9]

Providing Consistency

Enabling employees to understand and live the mission is not a one-time deal. Employees should see the mission as part of their onboarding process, and the mission should be continually referenced and reinforced throughout employees' tenure. Unfortunately, employees aren't always made aware of the mission and why it's important to their jobs. Sometimes the company's actions are inconsistent, making employees question the company's commitment to its mission. Lack of consistency and frequent changes in policies and procedures used to implement it, create confusion and make employees feel less secure in enacting the mission.[10] Even worse, lack of consistency reduces employees' commitment to the brand and ultimately negatively affects financial performance.[11] When missions do change, employees should be closely involved in the change process. Through employee involvement, problems with the current mission and how the organization embodies it can be identified, new ideas can be generated, and ownership in the new message can be established.

Enticing Features That Foster Love

Most people genuinely *want to* love their work and the brand they work for. Hence, it's important that companies make the brand mission enticing in their internal marketing efforts. Both sense-pleasing and/or heartwarming actions can enhance employees' love for the brand's mission.

Enticing through Sensory Appeals

The visual, auditory, and/or tactile appeal associated with a brand's mission statement matters in influencing how quickly and readily employees understand and accept the mission, and how interesting it appears to them. Consider Porsche Consulting's operational excellence mission: "For something to run smoothly, obstacles must be ironed out. We make you become the Porsche of your industry."[12] Porsche Consulting visually and tangibly expresses its mission to employees by having Porsche consultants wear technician's clothes. This is highly unusual for consultants, who typically wear expensive, polished designer suits. But the technician's clothes remind Porsche employees that consultants are humble master craftspersons who must roll up their sleeves in the service of the brand. They must get on with a job in a factory or wherever need be. The mission thus is communicated in ways beyond a mere statement; it literally is worn on employees' bodies. As such, the mission is tangible. Employees not only see the mission, they *feel* it too.

Enticing through Heartwarming Appeals

A mission statement may also become enticing to employees through heartwarming appeals that make the mission come to life. Notre Dame's football team has placed a sign that reads "Play Like a Champion Today" in a stairwell between the team locker room and the tunnel to Notre Dame Stadium. This inspiring message (which is enriching to players) is made concrete through an emotional ritual where the players and staff touch the sign before running onto the field, in the hopes that they can "play like a champion today." The ritual is emotionally evocative. By physically touching the sign players make this sign's meaning personal and intimate.

One way to make the mission interesting and heartwarming to employees is through storytelling.[13] Storytelling inspires brand beliefs and connections with the mission. Employees can tell their own mission-congruent stories and personal experiences. Beyond storytelling, company missions can be communicated through personal contact (as opposed to via memos, e-mails, or documents) and communicated in a nonwork-related setting or at company retreats (e.g., a fireside chat in a forest or by the ocean on a Hawaiian beach). Brand biographies, which are stories of how the brand went from its humble origins to its current state of success, are extremely appealing to employees and customers alike. This is particularly true when the brand biography depicts that brand as an underdog who has overcome serious obstacles in its efforts to succeed.[14]

The following three points are worth mentioning about sharing a brand's mission through storytelling. First, storytelling provides emotional touchstones for employees. Storytelling can motivate employees to feel psychologically closer to the brand and its mission. Sharing mission-consistent stories immerses employees in the mission. They also have a greater sense of ownership over the brand story because they themselves are spreading the word and acting as brand missionaries. Second, stories can make the brand's beliefs and principles more visible and tangible. When shared, stories emotionally engage employees in ways that go beyond mere knowledge of and memory for the mission statement. Third, storytelling cuts across cultures. It's part of our DNA as humans. We bond with others through the stories we tell.

When employees share brand stories they feel more emotionally connected to the brand and to each other.

Enriching Features That Foster Respect

A mission statement that's enabling and enticing to employees is a good start. But these features won't guarantee that employees feel inspired by it. A mission statement that is merely familiar may not come to mind automatically or create a sense of emotional resonance. Indeed, as the saying goes, "familiarity breeds contempt." To enhance employees' respect for the mission, it must inspire them and reflect their core beliefs and principles. A company can make the mission statement inspiring by proving a strong connection between a brand's mission and beliefs and the principles of employees. Figure 4.2 notes Starbuck's mission and the four beliefs/principles that it subsumes. A glance at that mission shows how beliefs endorsed by and subsumed within the mission can inspire employees.

Starbucks mission is "To inspire and nurture (the *what*) the human spirit (the *for whom*)—one person, one cup, and one neighborhood at a time (the *how*)."[15] The four beliefs subsumed in its mission are (1) "Delivering our very best in all we do; holding ourselves accountable for results," (2) "Creating a playful organizational culture; being present; connecting with transparency, dignity, and respect,"

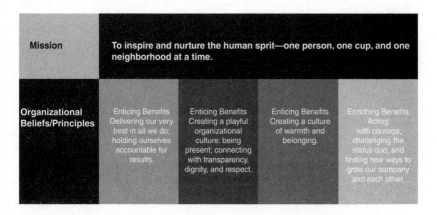

Figure 4.2   Beliefs/Principles Subsumed in Starbucks' Mission

(3) "Creating a culture of warmth and belonging," and (4) "Acting with courage, challenging the status quo, and finding new ways to grow our company and each other."

These are inspiring beliefs/principles. Employees can see their own personal beliefs in the brand ethos. These statements eloquently capture how employees should conduct themselves in the organization, what the organization and employees themselves want to be, and what type of a work environment they want to create together, as an organization. Combined, these statements enrich and inspire employees, drawing them closer to the brand and to each other. Indeed, a recent study shows that businesses that have inspiring beliefs that are centered on improving people's lives grew three times faster than their competitors did.[16]

A mission statement should be developed and embodied through enabling, enticing, and enriching features and must be tightly aligned with a company's own conduct. Practices that are inconsistent with the mission statement undermine employees' trust for, love of, and respect for the company and the mission that guides it.

ENABLING, ENTICING, AND ENRICHING EMPLOYEES AS PEOPLE

In the previous section we discussed how to make the *company's mission statement* enabling, enticing, and enriching for employees so that they deeply understand and can embody it. In this section we focus on how to enable, entice, and enrich *employees themselves*, motivating them to act on the brand mission in ways that benefit the brand. Employees are most motivated to act on behalf of the brand they work for when the brand is seen as doing something for them—*as people*. Hence (as Figure 4.1 suggests), whereas enabling, enticing, and enriching features of a brand mission are important, it's also important for a brand to create benefits that make employees happy people.

Companies can enable, entice, and enrich employees in ways similar to those described in Chapter 3. Specifically, they can do so through (1) enabling problem resolution and fostering resource conservation, (2) enticing employees through using sensory, cognitive, and heartwarming appeals, and (3) enriching them by reflecting their beliefs and hopes and fostering belongingness and distinctiveness. Such activities empower, gratify, and inspire employees. They build brand trust, love, respect, and ultimately admiration from the inside by making employees happy. Note that while we examine various methods for focusing on individual Es, a given method could have multiple effects—enabling, enticing, *and* enriching employees.

Enabling Employees as People

Empowering customers can build their brand admiration by enabling them to do what they need to do in their lives. So too can enabling employees play a powerful role in building their trust in and admiration for the brand.

Through Problem Solving

Employees need to feel enabled and empowered to do their work. For example, Starbucks' employees receive considerable training. The Barista Basics Training Program gives newly hired employees the essential knowledge required to prepare a great cup of coffee. The program enhances employees' competence, which also boosts their confidence. When employees first come on board, they are given the *Green Apron Book*, which explicitly details what they need to do to be successful at Starbucks. Employees also receive a dedicated Coffee Passport, which provides extensive information on coffee. Such guidance enables employees, making them knowledgeable about the product and the company. As a consequence, employees feel that Starbucks is investing in them and setting them up to be successful. This information should assuage anxiety about whether the company is acting in their employees' best interests. It should also build a sense of self-efficacy in employees and enhance their trust that the brand cares about them.

Micromanaging is inefficient and it erodes trust. To avoid micromanaging and distrust, employees should be encouraged to do what they think is in the best interests of the customer. Starbucks employees know that when things get tough, they have the tools, support, and autonomy to do what needs to be done to make customers happy—even if it's outside the script of what they normally do. Moreover, Starbucks employees are actively encouraged to share information about their experiences with each other: for example, the *Green Apron Book* encourages employees to "catch one another doing something right" and to *recognize* and *thank* each other for it.

Let's look at another example. Aman is an iconic and globally acclaimed luxury resort. Its mission is built on four pillars: (1) keeping the resorts noninstitutional, (2) providing guests with a luxury private home, not a merely a hotel, (3) offering guests a holistic holiday experience by combining luxury with the unique heritage and culture of the resort location, and (4) maintaining a very high level of exclusivity. Right from the start, Aman aimed to be as far from a typical commercial resort chain as possible.[17] Staff members are consistently urged to be innovative and creative in their efforts to provide guests with excellent personalized service and to create memorable service encounters. Managers and staff are asked to run the resorts as if they were their *own* companies. This unique work culture has enabled Aman's employees to continue to delight its high-paying guests in ways that seem genuine and that make sense.

Through Resource Conservation

Employees can also be enabled in another way. Starbucks helps employees conserve their own financial resources. By paying employees' tuition to get an undergraduate degree at Arizona State University, the organization enables employees to learn and improve themselves. Employees also feel enabled when the workplace is flexible, allowing them to work from home or schedule their own hours. Employees feel less stressed because they can schedule other aspects of their life along with their work. Working from home can also save time, one of our most precious assets. Google employees aren't required to work from the office all the time. However, its flexible approach does not mean employees don't work hard; quite the opposite is true.

Companies can also offer perks like emergency babysitting services or counseling services that make employees feel less stressed and resource constrained. In consideration of the dangers of sleep deprivation on health and worker productivity, a few companies (including Goldman Sachs and Johnson & Johnson) have offered employees programs to battle insomnia. Salesforce offers mindfulness meditation workshops, yoga, and/or exercises to help battle stress and improve decision making.[18] Recognizing that everyone is different, Google, Deutsche Bank, Oracle, and other brands provide a sense of efficacy and empowerment by allowing employees to design a benefits package that best works for them, given their personal circumstances.

Enticing Employees as People

Workplace environments have a powerful effect on employees' sense of gratification, and the extent to which they love coming to work and admire the brand. There are a number of things that organizations can do to entice employees as people and make them feel that being at work is exciting, fun, cognitively stimulating, and emotionally pleasing.

Through Sense-Pleasing Benefits

Many brand touchpoints (e.g., the building's exterior and interior design, the ambience of the office, the brand logo, and the uniform employees wear) have a conscious and subconscious impact on employees. A visually pleasing exterior design of an office building and its interior design offer employees more sensory pleasure than we may initially think. Employees are exposed to these workplace environments every minute that they spend at work. Office ambiance has a huge impact on how employees feel. Google employees have kitchens and coffee bars, Lego play areas, sunny outdoor terraces with chaises, and Broadway-themed conference rooms. Each element is consistent with Google's philosophy, which is "to create the happiest, most productive workplace in the world."[19] Other sense-pleasing benefits offered by Google include weekly eyebrow shaping, yoga and Pilates classes, and live interviews with Jimmy Fallon and Justin Bieber—all for free. Wearing a visually pleasing and comfortable uniform can also entice employees. Being exposed to other colleagues' eye-pleasing uniforms on a daily basis should positively influence one's own perceptual pleasure of the brand. In contrast, some employee uniforms degrade employees and make them feel uncomfortable.

Through Heartwarming Benefits

Employees' hearts are also warmed by the respect, affection, and care they get from polite and supportive colleagues. In its set of principles, McKinsey invites its employees to "create an unrivaled environment for exceptional people" by (1) being "nonhierarchical and inclusive," (2) sustaining "a caring meritocracy," and (3) developing "one another through apprenticeship and mentoring."[20] Creating an environment where people *want* to contribute matters. If employees are stressed out by their own colleagues, what are the chances that they'll come up with novel, impactful solutions for clients? Other heartwarming perks can include special gifts to employees who reach personal or professional milestones or paid time off for personal events involving grief and the loss of significant others.

Enriching Employees as People

Finally, there are a number of ways that companies can enhance employees' respect for the company and brand admiration by providing enriching benefits that inspire them.

Through Benefits Consistent with Beliefs and Principles

While the beliefs and principles embedded in the brand's mission statement may look inspiring, employees must internalize these beliefs. To inspire its employees, Stryker Medical Products encourages employees to observe surgeries and listen to patients' stories about their recoveries. As one employee observed, "I see the face of someone who is alive because of our product, and that's amazing."[21] These kinds of opportunities are highly inspirational because they let employees witness firsthand the impact of their work.

Many companies engage in corporate social-responsibility programs that aim to do good in the world. These programs can inspire employees who believe in these programs and the company's commitment to them.[22] Some companies actively encourage employees to volunteer their time so as to make a difference outside of work. Some companies even provide paid time off for volunteer work. These outside activities not only help employees feel that they have time to do good in the world: the time they spend on these activities can have a burnishing effect on the company and its identity.

Through Belongingness and Distinctiveness

Companies can also engage in actions that enrich employees by making them *feel connected* to others or *distinctive* from others because of their status or uniqueness. Starbucks employees are encouraged to recognize and appreciate others and comment on their contributions. Hearing praise and recognition of one's work is highly validating. Employees report that when they have friends at work, their job is more fun, enjoyable, worthwhile, and satisfying.[23] People with a best friend at work are seven times more likely to engage fully in their work. Building camaraderie among employees is about more than just having fun (which is an enriching benefit). Camaraderie creates a common sense of purpose and the mentality that we are in it together. It makes employees proud of being on the same team when they mutually reinforce one another's contribution to the organization. Companies like Zappos, Google, Dropbox, CAPiTA Snowboarding, and Southwest are known for fostering camaraderie at work. Camaraderie at work can create a powerful esprit de corps, which includes mutual respect, a sense of identity and compassion—for example, rooting for each other during promotion rounds, consoling each other about mistakes, giving advice, and providing support in personal situations.

Employees often yearn to *be distinctive* through recognition of their status or accomplishments. McKinsey's ethos that "solving the hardest problems requires the best people," together with its belief that "the best people will be drawn to the opportunity to work on the hardest problems," instills tremendous pride in McKinsey employees.[24] This kind of recognition bestowed by the company on employees certainly creates pride, fostering employees' respect for the company. It also reflects employees' desired beliefs (contributing to difficult challenges) and identity (being one of the best). McKinsey further instills a sense of community through its active alumni and informal networking events for current and former McKinsey employees.

Consider that employees who work at the counter at Starbucks are given the title of barista. Such titles provide a sense of dignity and respect, helping them *validate themselves* and develop respect toward the company. For example, have you noticed that some Starbucks baristas wear black aprons instead of the usual green ones? These individuals have been awarded the title of Coffee Master and have been trained to be the best of the best. Anyone from the organization can receive special training and an assessment to earn the title of Coffee Master. Those employees who are passionate and diligent enough—those who "want to breathe, sleep, and dream coffee"—must pass five rigorous tests and are even invited to speak at the annual Starbucks conference.

Employees can also feel distinctive because of their association with the brand. Earlier, we noted that uniforms can be sense pleasing. They can also signal employees' association with a brand. We want employees to wear their uniforms with pride, signaling their association with a brand in terms of who they are and what they do. In Korea, for example, people often notice Asiana Airlines attendants as they wear their uniforms on the street, at bus terminals, or at the airport. The USMC's distinctive formal Blue Dress uniform lets others know that the wearer is among the "few and the proud."

Many brands also give their employees the chance to apply for a corporate credit card, which not only makes it easier for employees to track and handle work-related expenses, but also can signal their association and status with a brand to the public. Or think about brand-themed license plates that some employees use on their cars, or tattoos they get on their bodies to show their affiliation with a brand.

KEY TAKEAWAYS

1. Whereas managing relationships with customers is commonly considered to be what marketing is all about, brands must also focus on marketing to their own employees, a process called internal branding.

2. Employees can play a powerful role in helping the company realize outcomes that contribute to its value (enhanced revenue, reduced costs, brand advocacy, employee acquisition and retention, employee morale, etc.).

3. Building admiration from the inside starts with the brand's mission. Good mission statements should specify *what* benefits the brand offers, *to whom*, and *how* it offers these benefits. To be effective brand ambassadors, employees need to understand and relate to each of these components of the brand's mission.

4. The company mission serves as a critical guidepost in internal branding. Good missions and how they are embodied enable, entice, and enrich employees.

5. A brand should also create employee brand admiration by enabling, enticing, and enriching employees as people.

WHAT ABOUT YOUR BRAND?

1. How would you assess your brand's mission statement? Does it specify the three requirements that make up good mission statements: *what* benefits, delivered to *whom* and *how*?

2. In making your mission statement personally relevant to and connected with employees, have you considered incorporating each of the 3Es?

3. How have you shared your brand's mission statement with your employees? Is it clearly stated, concrete, and consistent over time?

4. Is your brand's mission statement communicated to employees with sensory and heartwarming appeals?

5. Does your brand's mission statement have inspiring beliefs and principles?

6. What enabling, enticing, enriching benefits does your brand offer to employees as people?

NOTES

1. "About Mayo Clinic," Mayo Clinic, accessed April 12, 2016, www.mayoclinic.org/about-mayo-clinic.

2. Valerie S. Folkes and Vanessa M. Patrick, "The Positivity Effect in Perceptions of Services: Seen One, Seen them All?," *Journal of Consumer Research* 30, no. 1 (2003): 125–137; Christopher Groening, Vikas Mittal, and Yan Anthea Zhang, "Cross-Validation of Customer and Employee Signals and Firm Valuation," *Journal of Marketing Research* 53, no. 1 (2016): 61–76; Douglas E. Hughes and Michael Ahearne, "Energizing the Reseller's Sales Force: The Power of Brand Identification," *Journal of Marketing* 74, no. 4 (2010): 81–96; Christine Porath, Deborah J. MacInnis, and Valerie Folkes, "Witnessing Incivility Among Employees: Effects on Consumer Anger and Negative Inferences about Companies," *Journal of Consumer Research* 37, no. 2 (2010): 292–303.

3. Tom Peters, "Leadership: American vs. Southwest," www.Youtube.com/watch?v=PpVpRLrq8Jg

4. Joseph A. Michelli, *The Starbucks Experience* (New York: McGraw Hill, 2007), 38. This excellent book also serves as the source of many additional Starbucks examples provided in this chapter.

5. "Company Overview," Google Company, accessed April 10, 2016, https://www.google.com/about/company/; "Our Mission and Values," McKinsey&Company, www.mckinsey.com/about-us/what-we-do/our-mission-and-values.

6. John F. Marshall, "How Starbucks, Walmart and IBM Launch Brands Internally and What You can Learn From Them," *Forbes*, April 9, 2013, www.forbes.com/sites/onmarketing/2013/04/09/how-starbucks-walmart-and-ibm-launch-brands-internally-and-what-you-can-learn-from-them/#365b587d1355.

7. "Business Principles and Standards," Goldman Sachs, Who We Are, accessed March 10, 2016, www.goldmansachs.com/who-we-are/business-standards/business-principles.

8. "Our Mission and Values," McKinsey & Company, About Us, accessed April 12, 2016, www.mckinsey.com/about-us/what-we-do/our-mission-and-values.

9. "Gold Standards," Ritz Carlton, accessed March 18, 2016, www.ritzcarlton.com/en/about/gold-standards.

10. Felicitas M. Morhart, Walter Herzog, and Torsten Tomczak, "Brand-Specific Leadership: Turning Employees into Brand Champions," *Journal of Marketing* 73, no. 5 (2009): 122–142.

11. Christopher K. Bart, Nick Bontis, and Simon Taggar, "A Model of the Impact of Mission Statements on Firm Performance," *Management Decision* 39, no. 1 (2001): 19–35.

12. "Mission and Brand," Porsche Consulting, accessed April 7, 2016, www.porsche-consulting.com/en/company/mission-and-brand.

13. Arch G. Woodside, Suresh Sood, and Kenneth E. Miller, "When Consumers and Brands Talk: Storytelling Theory and Research in Psychology and Marketing," *Psychology & Marketing* 25, no. 2 (2008): 97–145.

14. Neeru Paharia, Anat Keinan, Jill Avery, and Juliet B. Schor, "The Underdog Effect: The Marketing of Disadvantage and Determination through Brand Biography," *Journal of Consumer Research* 37, no. 5 (2011): 775–790.

15. "Our Mission," Starbucks, accessed March 8, 2016, www.starbucks.com/about-us/company-information/mission-statement.

16. Jim Stengel, *Grow: How Ideals Power Growth and Profit at the World's Greatest Companies* (New York: Random House, 2011).

17. Martin Roll, *Asian Brand Strategy* (New York: Palgrave Macmillan, 2015).

18. Eugene Kim, "Salesforce Put a Meditation Room on Every Floor of Its New Tower Because of Buddhist Monks," *Business Insider*, March 7, 2016, www.businessinsider.com/salesforce-put-a-meditation-room-on-every-floor-of-its-new-tower-2016-3.

19. James B. Stewart, "Looking for a Lesson in Google's Perks," *New York Times*, March 15, 2013, www.nytimes.com/2013/03/16/business/at-google-a-place-to-work-and-play.html.

20. Kimmy Wa Chan and Echo Wen Wan, "How Can Stressed Employees Deliver Better Customer Service? The Underlying Self-Regulation Depletion Mechanism," *Journal of Marketing* 76, no. 1 (2012): 119–137; Christine Pearson and Christine Porath, *The Cost of Bad Behavior: How Incivility Is Damaging Your Business and What to Do About It* (New York: Penguin, 2009).

21. Fortune Editors, "Human Capital 30: Companies That Put Employees Front and Center," *Fortune*, March 8, 2016, http://fortune.com/2016/03/08/human-capital-30.

22. Todd Donavan, Tom J. Brown, and John C. Mowen, "Internal Benefits of Service-Worker Customer Orientation: Job Satisfaction, Commitment, and Organizational Citizenship Behaviors," *Journal of Marketing* 68, no. 1 (2004): 128–146.

23. Christine M. Riordan, "We All Need Friends at Work," *Harvard Business Review*, July 3, 2013, https://hbr.org/2013/07/we-all-need-friends-at-work.

24. "Our Mission and Values," McKinsey&Company, accessed April 12, 2016, www.mckinsey.com/about-us/what-we-do/our-mission-and-values.

CHAPTER 5

Building Brand Admiration among Customers

T he best brands make customers' lives easier, more gratifying, and more meaningful.

INTRODUCTION

Many people love to vacation by taking a cruise. But it wasn't always that way. In the early 2000s, Royal Caribbean (RC) discovered that noncruisers thought three types of people went on cruises: (1) the newly wed (honeymooners), (2) the overfed (sedentary people), and (3) the almost dead (retired people)! Many people didn't perceive themselves as belonging to any of these categories. But in fact, there was a large market of people who wanted excitement, adventure, fun, and opportunities to see different places—benefits that were not typical of the cruise experience at the time. This untapped market of active adults was big and reachable through advertising and social media. Competitors weren't targeting this group, and even if they had been, they were unlikely to outcompete RC. Tapping this new market also fit RC's goal of becoming a leader in the cruise industry, and RC had the resources and competence to cater to it. A new RC target market was borne. To attract these customers, RC made innovative design changes to its ships and added features like rock-climbing walls and ice-skating rinks. On-board and off-board activities emphasized what these users wanted. For example, its European cruise featured an off-board excursion to the Sistine Chapel, with reminders to customers to visit the on-board spa after a day of sightseeing.[1]

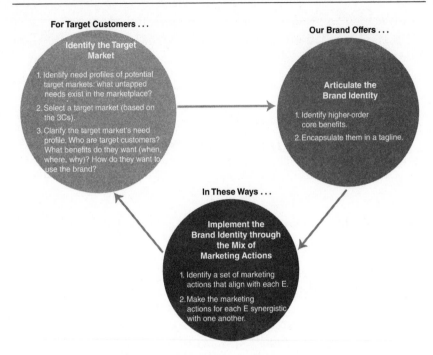

Figure 5.1   Strategic Decisions Underlying the Brand-Positioning Statement

OVERVIEW

The preceding short vignette illustrates the core strategy issues considered in Chapter 5: specifically, building brand admiration by creating solid positioning for a new brand. In this chapter we describe the characteristics of a positioning statement and three strategic decisions that underlie its development (see Figure 5.1, the overarching framework for this chapter). We propose a novel approach to the task of building brand admiration.

THE BRAND-POSITIONING STATEMENT

A positioning statement and a mission statement are very similar. The major difference is that a positioning statement is directed at external customers while the mission statement is directed at employees. The mission statement is also more abstract. It's not specific enough to guide how the brand is *positioned to external customers*. It doesn't specify which set of marketing actions and tactics will bring the brand's identity to life. When it comes to targeting external customers, the brand's positioning statement serves as the guiding tool.

Components of a Positioning Statement

A positioning statement is a short, internal document that distills what is known about the target market, the benefits its members seek, and ways to communicate and deliver these benefits. A positioning statement is the *distillation* of three strategic decisions, as shown in Figure 5.1. A positioning statement specifies:

1. The target market being pursued. It begins with the phrase *"For target customers"* followed by a description of the target market.

2. The brand's identity, meaning the higher-order (abstracted) summary of core benefits that the brand offers. It begins with the phrase *"Our brand offers"* followed by a description of the higher-order summary of core benefits offered by the brand, including a tagline.

3. The marketing actions that make the brand identity real in the minds of target customers. It begins with the statement *"In these ways."*

Good positioning statements help employees understand what the brand is and does, and why it should be attractive to customers. In short, they specify how brands can build brand trust, love, and respect (and brand admiration) among customers.

Sample Positioning Statements

Table 5.1 illustrates a potential positioning statement for Petco. It describes the target market *(for target customers ...)*, the brand's identity *(our brand offers ...)*, and how the brand's identity is implemented *(in these ways ...)*. *This final implementation element is an often-neglected*

Table 5.1   Sample Positioning Statement

Petco Target Market	For people who respect animal rights and love their pets as much as they do their children.
Petco Brand Identity	Petco nurtures pet health and happiness more completely throughout the life of one's pet than the leading competitors (as captured by its tagline "The Power of Together").
Petco Identity Implementation	(1) Enabling benefits: Offering nutritionally balanced pet foods with natural ingredients at affordable prices that contribute to the nourishment and health of pets throughout their lives (thus making the "power of together" sustainable).
	(2) Enticing benefits: Offering communication, promotional events, and vivid packaging/logo elements that underscore the sense-pleasing and/or heartwarming appeal of "the power of together."
	(3) Enriching benefits: Building on "the power of together" by reflecting how pets have the ability to connect all living souls.

but critical component of a good positioning statement. Without considering this implementation element, employees are less clear about their roles and responsibilities in building brand admiration among customers. The implementation described in this sample positioning statement does not include all the specific marketing activities that Petco may pursue for each of enabling, enticing, and enriching benefits.

STRATEGIC DECISIONS FOR DEVELOPING A POSITIONING STATEMENT

Positioning statements require strategic thinking about each of the three decisions shown in Figure 5.1: the target market, the brand identity, and the implementation. The strategic thinking involves the task of addressing customers' needs more quickly and efficiently than competitors, thereby building brand admiration among customers.

Identifying the Target Market

When identifying the target market, brand managers should consider the three elements shown in the first circle of Figure 5.1: (1) identifying need profiles of potential target markets, (2) choosing a target market, and (3) clarifying the chosen target market's need profile.

Identifying Need Profiles of Potential Target Markets

Potential markets are untapped markets whose needs are not fully met by existing brands. Customers' needs can be described in terms of any of the four factors shown next. We use the term *need profile* to describe the target market's needs on all four factors.

1. *What* benefits customers want from a product and *why* they want these benefits. Specifying not just the benefits customers are looking for but also why they want them is important because a given benefit can be linked to different customer needs. Customers may want a noncalorie soft drink because they want to avoid health problems, or because they don't want to add calories to their diets, or because they believe that aspartame tastes bad. Specifying *why* customers want a particular benefit helps internal employees understand the mind-set of target customers and what motivates their purchases.

2. *When* they want these benefits. It's possible that customers want certain benefits because they're useful in specific situations. For example, customers might want a sports watch that allows them to listen to music *when running*. They may want automobile tires with a special grip for *when it snows in winter*.

3. *Where* they seek these benefits. For example, there might be an untapped market that wants a café-type cappuccino *at home*. They may want a bicycle that they can ride *to the office*. They may want to access and analyze critical data *from anywhere*.

4. *How* they want to use or experience benefits. For example, they may want to use medicine *without having to struggle to*

open the bottle, drink coffee *from a tetra pack* rather than sitting down in a coffeehouse, or complete an MBA *online* rather than going to classes on campus.

When we specify customers' need profiles based on each of the four factors, we are most likely to identify multiple potential target markets. Some might be combined to form a large and more inclusive potential market. Others may be dropped quickly from further consideration, due to their impracticality. RC found an untapped market by considering these unmet benefits. In terms of *what benefits*, a sizable market wanted to feel enticed through action. They wanted fun and adventure. They wanted to learn something new (cognitive stimulation). They wanted to feel enriched by a status-enhancing trip that offered intellectual pursuits, fine dining, a spa, and the opportunity to connect with others in their general social circle. From the standpoint of *when* and *where*, they wanted these benefits during times of the year that might be different from those of the typical family traveler (enabling benefits). From the standpoint of *how*, they wanted benefits that would be delivered in a way that provided excitement and adventure (enticing benefit). Addressing these four factors helped RC identify a wholly distinctive, underserved, and large potential target market.

Selecting a Target Market Using the 3Cs

Companies can use the 3Cs (customers, competitors, and the company) as screening criteria to assess the viability of one or more potential target markets (see Table 5.2).

A new market is promising when (1) *customers* are highly responsive to the new brand's benefits, (2) there are a large enough number of these customers to make economic sense, (3) target customers can be easily reached, and (4) there is no serious cannibalization of an existing market. A product opportunity is promising when *competitors* currently offer different benefits from those the new market wants, and/or they operate in such a different manner that they don't pose a threat (e.g., their benefits are weak). Finally, from a *company perspective*, an opportunity is promising when the company has the human, financial, and technological resources and competence to deliver the benefits, and

Table 5.2   The 3Cs: Criteria for Choosing a Target Market

Customers	Competitors	Company
Will customers be responsive to these benefits?	Would we offer a product in a different way from that of competitors?	Do we have the resources and competence to deliver these benefits?
Is the market sizable?	Could we outstrip the competition on quality?	Are these benefits consistent with the brand's mission and vision?
Is the market accessible? Will the market cannibalize the existing market?		

when serving these customers fits with the company's mission (see Chapter 4).

RC identified a target market whose needs (e.g., excitement and adventure) were substantially different from those of both its existing target markets and those of competitors. This target complemented (versus cannibalized) its existing product lines. Other competitors were not targeting this market, and they were not likely to pose a threat given RC's experience, investments, and credibility in the cruise industry. RC also had the resources and competence to deliver these benefits given its prior investments in the cruise industry. Emphasizing excitement and adventure were also consistent with RC's vision, as stated on its website: "Generating superior returns for our shareholders by empowering and enabling our employees to *deliver the best vacation experience* and enhancing the well-being of our communities."

Clarifying the Target Market's Need Profile

After selecting the target market, we need to clarify who the customers in this target market are: the better we understand who the customers in the target market are, the more guidance we'll have in articulating and implementing the brand's identity (see Figure 5.1).

Often target markets are described in terms of demographics or psychographics. While helpful in understanding how to reach customers, this information can be limiting. For example, Facebook did not have a particular gender in mind when developing its branding strategy, nor did Red Bull or SAP. Demographics and psychographics alone don't tell us how to be competitive in the marketplace, nor will they tell us what will resonate with customers. A target market description is much more informative if it includes the target market's need profile. The Petco target market description (see Table 5.1) contains the need profile of customers on "what," "how," and "who." RC's target market can be described accordingly:

- *Who they are*. Active adults (demographics and psychographics may be helpful in articulating the characteristics of the target market).

- *Their need profile*. Specifically:

  - *What they need and want and why. Fun, learning*, and *excitement* so that they can feel fulfilled by having new life experiences.

  - *When these needs arise*. At times other than honeymoons or retirement occasions.

  - *Where these needs arise*. In novel and exotic places.

  - *How customers want to use the brand to satisfy these needs*. By enjoying adventurous activities on- and off-board.

Articulating the Brand Identity

Choosing a target market and clarifying the need profile of target customers form the basis for articulating the brand's identity. As was the case with RC, managers should identify the *core enabling, enticing*, and *enriching benefits* from the need profile that reflect what target customers really want.

A brand's identity is the foundation of branding strategy. It is the face of a brand, and it reflects the brand's key promise to customers. It is a higher-order summary of the core benefits identified in the customers' need profile. The higher-order summary may pertain to any one enabling, enticing, or enriching benefit. Or it may be sufficiently inclusive to cover all three benefit types. For example, Red Bull's brand identity reflects more of the enabling benefit (i.e., an energy drink). In contrast, Nike's brand identity is highly abstract ("To bring inspiration and innovation to every athlete in the world"), and seems to encompass enabling, enticing, and enriching benefits. Once the brand's identity is articulated, marketing actions can clarify and deliver on the identity in such a way that the identity (and the enabling, enticing, and enriching benefits that comprise it) is clearly understood and validated. Thus, marketing actions must be aligned with the identity, and they should reinforce each other such that the identity (and its underlying 3Es) come to life, are clear, compelling, and differentiating.

Articulating a brand's identity is critical, because as the brand's central promise (e.g., to enable, entice, and enrich its customers), the identity of a brand is the key factor that causes customers to choose that brand over others. Customers should be motivated to choose the brand because its higher-order benefits both resonate with their (what, why, when, where, and how) needs and cannot be found in other brands. Yet brand managers often fail to clearly articulate their brand's identities.

A brand identity should be relevant, differentiating, and compelling. So brand managers should ask themselves (1) how much do the core benefits expressed by brand identity *resonate* with customers, (2) how *differentiating* is the identity from other product/services—that is, how fresh and unique it is, and (3) whether customers will *believe it*. We consider these questions and how to address them below and in the next section.

Encapsulating Core Benefits in a Tagline

Communicating these higher-order and more abstract meanings of a brand is easier when its identity is cast in customer-friendly language, as in the brand's slogan or tagline. Brand identity and the brand tagline are closely related but distinct concepts. For instance, Aldi's brand identity is "We do everything possible, from our carts to checkout to energy-saving stores, to give you incredibly high quality at impossibly low prices." Its more memorable, succinct, and user-friendly tagline is "We cut prices, not corners."

Whereas the brand identity stated in the positioning statement is more fleshed out so as to *guide employees* in their marketing actions, the brand's tagline captures the essence of this identity in an attention-getting, appealing, and memorable phrase *for customers*. Memorable taglines, such as BMW's "The ultimate driving machine," "Red Bull gives you wings," AT&T's "Reach out and touch someone," and SAP's "Run simple," help customers visualize the brand identity in ways that map into their own personal experiences. The powerful effect of taglines is also clear in many legendary public service announcements, such as "Only you can prevent forest fires," "A mind is a terrible thing to waste," and "Friends don't let friends drive drunk." In today's hypercompetitive markets, having a short but powerful tagline that communicates core brand benefits to external customers is a necessity.

Implementing the Brand Identity through Marketing Actions

The critical task in implementing the brand's identity involves identifying marketing actions for each E that are most synergistic in communicating and delivering on that identity. By *marketing actions*, we mean any marketing activities that a company uses to communicate and implement the brand's identity. They include but expand upon the marketing actions typically associated with the 4Ps (product, place, price, and promotion).

Creating Synergy in Marketing Actions for Each E

To make marketing actions synergistic in communicating and delivering on the brand's identity, brand managers should first identify marketing actions in each E. They should then ensure that the identified marketing actions in each E communicate and deliver the brand identity as a whole.

Consistency and Complementarity of Marketing Actions

Creating this synergy in marketing actions comes from identifying the marketing actions associated with each E and selecting those that are most consistent with the brand's identity and that best complement one another in making the identity real. *Consistency* means that the marketing actions employed to deliver each *E* are congruent and aligned with the brand's identity. They should thus *reflect* the brand's identity. Spending money on marketing actions that do not directly reflect the brand's identity is an unacceptable mistake and a waste of resources. *Complementarity* means that the selected marketing actions support one another as much as possible in communicating and delivering on each *E*, thereby making their impact stronger.

The more consistent a specific marketing action associated with each E is with the brand's identity, the more accurately and quickly customers will understand and appreciate the brand's identity. The more marketing actions complement each other in communicating and delivering on benefits associated *with each E*, the more powerful their effects will be. Put in a different way, consistent and complementary marketing actions communicate and deliver on the brand's identity in a more synergistic manner.

To illustrate: In-N-Out Burger has enjoyed great success in an industry characterized by fierce competition and negative press about fast food and health. In-N-Out's tagline is "The quality that you can taste." This identity is communicated and delivered through several marketing actions relevant to each E. Customers can understand that In-N-Out offers functionally enabling benefits because its drive-through layout promotes easy access to the menu. The burger assembly process is efficient, in part due to the restaurant's simple menu. Long lines clear quickly. Burger ingredients are all fresh. The restaurant's red and yellow store sign and distinctive logo are easily recognized. By virtue of these brand identity–consistent and mutually complementary (synergistic) activities, consumers quickly understand In-N-Out Burger's identity and *trust* the brand.

Analogously, consumers can understand that In-N-Out offers enticing benefits because In-N-Out's marketing actions offer several enticement benefits that underscore "quality you can taste." They include the in-store aroma (the fresh smell that is highly consistent with quality), the smiling staff, and the mobile truck that attracts long lines of excited customers (with quality burgers). These actions are aligned. They're not seen as a set of discrete parts, but rather a clear, global, holistic entity, with each action reinforcing the other. These brand identity–consistent and mutually complementary (synergistic) actions make customers readily understand its brand identity and facilitate their *love of* the brand.

Similarly, the effective mix of marketing actions that evoke enriching benefits allows the brand to readily become respected in the eyes of customers. Its community atmosphere, which fosters belongingness, and the brand's faithful devotion to the values and principles of its founder (e.g., stories written about the brand and its founder) are consistent with and reflect the quality taste of its burgers. These benefits are printed on In-N-Out cups, placemats, and other communication devices. These mutually complementary enrichment benefits resonate with In-N-Out Burger customers. Synergy among multiple enriching marketing actions facilitates both customers' understanding of the brand's identity and their *respect* for the brand. By using marketing actions synergistically, customers gain a clearer sense of the brand's identity, and their experience will map onto that identify. Because each E is important to customers and its implementation is synergistic, brand trust, love, and respect will be created most powerfully and efficiently. This perspective toward the mix of marketing actions differs significantly from a traditional four Ps marketing-mix approach in the following ways:

- All marketing actions are grounded in the brand's identity.

- All marketing actions are based on the goal of building or enhancing brand admiration through the 3Es.

- Marketing actions are synergistic to the extent that they are based on the consistency and complementarity principles.

- The outcome of synergy is specified in terms of the time taken and resources spent in developing brand admiration.

Note that the In-N-Out example describes marketing actions pertinent to each E separately. However, as we show in the Singapore Airlines and Caterpillar cases described next, the same marketing action (e.g., stellar in-flight entertainment system; a dealer advisory group) can sometimes influence customers' perceptions of several Es. When the same marketing action influences more than one E, its impact on customers should be both powerful and cost efficient.

Case in Point: Singapore Airlines

Consider Singapore Airlines (SIA), one of the most admired brands in the airline industry.[2] Widely regarded as an industry leader and a trendsetter, customers love, trust, and respect this brand because of the exemplary quality of its service. SIA truly controls the brand's identity through every interaction and experience with customers. SIA was Asia's first and the world's third airline accredited by the IATA (International Air Transport Association) with the IOSA (IATA Operations Safety Audit). Its brand identity, which is reflected in its tagline ("A Great Way to Fly"), is communicated and delivered to customers by a set of synergistic marketing actions that focused on service and quality excellence.

As Figure 5.2 shows, in 2007 SIA became the first airline in the world to fly the Airbus A-380, the world's largest airplane. SIA has also been a pioneer in many in-flight service and entertainment innovations, such as offering meal choices, free beverages, free headphones, hot scented towels, personal entertainment systems, and video on demand in all cabins. SIA recognizes that innovation is an important part of the brand. As such, it also maintains the youngest fleet and the best safety record of all major air carriers.

These benefits enable customers, making flying less stressful. They are consistent with the brand's overarching identity, "A Great Way to Fly." Moreover, the actions are strongly complementary; each reinforces the other such that their combined impact is stronger. Being the first airline to fly the Airbus A-380 *and* having the world's youngest fleet of aircraft *and* having an excellent safety record help one another in reinforcing the brand's identity. The presence of only one action in the absence of the others would communicate these enabling benefits less powerfully and credibly. These complementary actions also help to reduce customers' anxiety and stress during the flight, meaning fewer physical and mental resources are required.

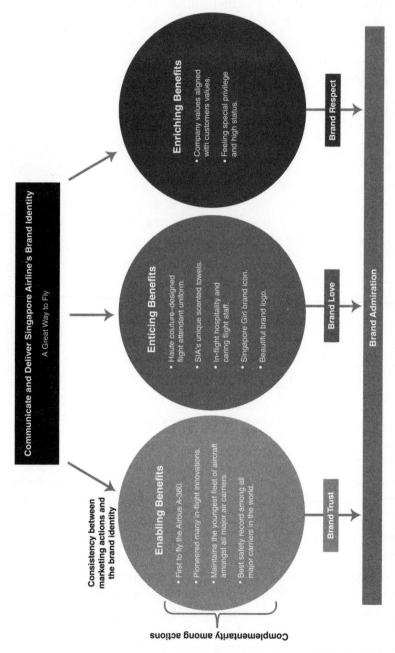

Figure 5.2 Communicating Brand Identity: Singapore Airlines

From the standpoint of enticing benefits, SIA had French haute-couture designer Pierre Balmain design a special version of the Malay sarong-kebaya for the uniform worn by flight attendants. Today this uniform is a recognized visual signature of the airline. SIA also provides hot scented towels, an outstanding array of entertainment choices, and other in-flight experiences that elevate the brand experience. The Singapore Girls are truly genuine and heartwarming in performing their in-flight service duties. SIA's striking and colorful bird logo is noteworthy. In 2010, SIA launched Above and Beyond, a collection of recipes from SIA's International Culinary Panel, clearly reinforcing its "great in-flight food" identity. SIA's International Wine Panel ensures that fine wine will accompany in-flight food. SIA's in-flight entertainment is recognized as among the best in the world. Each action is consistent with the brand's identity and each complements the other. Combined, these seemingly small marketing actions are highly synergistic in communicating and implementing the brand's "A Great Way to Fly" identity.

What about enriching benefits? The first time SIA flew the Airbus A-380 between Singapore and Australia in 2007, it held a ceremony the next day in Sydney, where it announced that it would donate all revenue from those 455 first-flight passengers to three charities. This socially responsible action likely resonated well with the customers' values and the principles they identified with. SIA also offers undergraduate college scholarships to promising students who it hopes might one day join the company. In 2008 SIA became the first airline to operate an all-business-class service from Singapore to New York and then Singapore to Los Angeles. Passengers felt special and high in status. Moreover, in addition to booking first-class and business-class tickets, passengers can also book private airline suites. Also conveying status and prestige, SIA's PPS Club provides preferential treatment and luxury, with special attention given to passengers. Benefits include personalized service focusing on passenger comfort, an increased in-baggage allowance, priority standby at check-in, and worldwide lounge access. Only first-class, business-class, and suites-class travelers are eligible for these special privileges. To solidify pride in being Singaporean, SIA offers a set of delectable mooncakes during the country's Mid-Autumn Festival. These actions are also consistent with the brand's "A Great

Way to Fly" identity, and they complement one another in communicating this enriching aspect of its identity.

Case in Point: Caterpillar

Let's illustrate how a completely different brand (Caterpillar) applied these same consistency and complementarity principles to create synergy in its marketing actions.

Caterpillar uses a number of identity-consistent marketing actions that convey the brand's enabling benefits (see Figure 5.3) and support the brand's identity (*Caterpillar as a partner that dealers want to work with*). Caterpillar's products are high in quality and they command a high resale value. Dealers likely regard Caterpillar as a highly reliable and versatile brand based on its high quality, high resale-value products, its exclusive distribution methods, and dealers' opportunities to make product and marketing suggestions. Such active participation by dealers not only accelerates time to market but also binds dealers more closely to the company.[3] Because Caterpillar sells its products *only* through its exclusive dealer networks, dealers can profitably run their own businesses without worrying that Caterpillar will bypass them. Caterpillar also provides efficient after-sales service and support, which minimizes end users' downtime. Caterpillar enables dealers who buy its solid and high-quality products with a clear-cut, easy-to-navigate, and trust-based selling process. Caterpillar's dealer advisory group actively seeks dealers' voices and opinions, and this input is reflected in Caterpillar's product development and market-support system. Signifying that dealers are equal partners, the company developed a short partnership contract with no expiration date. The document allows dealers to terminate their relationship with Caterpillar without cause, requiring only 90 days advanced notice. These benefits enable dealers and are consistent with the brand's overarching identity. These marketing actions motivate dealers to trust Caterpillar and to integrate their own operations into Caterpillar's system. Moreover, the actions support one another in delivering these enabling benefits. They are strongly complementary: one reinforces the other such that their combined impact on brand trust is stronger. Complementary enabling actions can minimize customers' expenditure of scarce

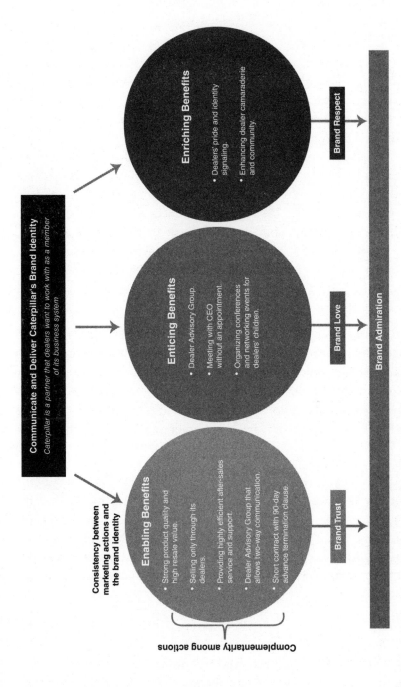

Communicate and Deliver Caterpillar's Brand Identity
Caterpillar is a partner that dealers want to work with as a member of its business system

Consistency between marketing actions and the brand identity

Enabling Benefits
- Strong product quality and high resale value.
- Selling only through its dealers.
- Providing highly efficient after-sales service and support.
- Dealer Advisory Group that allows two-way communication.
- Short contract with 90-day advance termination clause.

Complementarity among actions

Brand Trust

Enticing Benefits
- Dealer Advisory Group.
- Meeting with CEO without an appointment.
- Organizing conferences and networking events for dealers' children.

Brand Love

Enriching Benefits
- Dealers' pride and identity signaling.
- Enhancing dealer camaraderie and community.

Brand Respect

Brand Admiration

Figure 5.3   Communicating Brand Identity: Caterpillar

99

resources. The actions that Caterpillar uses to enable dealers clearly complement one another in reducing dealers' expended stress, time, and energy.

Caterpillar's enticing heartwarming benefits also support its identity. In terms of specific marketing actions, Caterpillar's dealer advisory group makes dealers feel good about their role in improving Caterpillar's operations. Dealers can meet with Caterpillar's CEO at any time. This Caterpillar-initiated action signals that Caterpillar's high-level management regards the dealers as valuable. Dealers are concerned about the future of their businesses once they retire, particularly since many of their businesses are family owned. To address this concern, Caterpillar organizes conferences and networking events that introduce dealers' children to Caterpillar and get them excited about the business. Each action is likely to touch dealers emotionally and foster a close personal bond with Caterpillar. As a result, dealer relationships with Caterpillar are deeper, more intimate, and more personal, fostering strong brand love.

Finally, and in terms of enriching benefits, Caterpillar's mission is to make, sell, and tend to machines that make the world work. Dealers feel proud of their position as company representatives because they believe in and identify values embedded in the Caterpillar's mission as their own. In addition, Caterpillar dealers around the world exhibit strong camaraderie. Such camaraderie is fostered, in part, by Caterpillar's annual event that brings all dealers together. By being part of the Caterpillar organization, dealers feel recognized, accepted, and cared for. They feel a sense of pride in being an accepted member of the dealer community. Moreover, as members of the community, they believe that they are doing good things for the world. This belief gives dealers a sense of pride, and it provides a powerful signal to others about who they are and what they do. Pride and identity signaling behind it reinforce Caterpillar's identity *as a partner that dealers want to work with*.

These self-esteem enhancing actions are highly *consistent* with the brand identity (*Caterpillar as a partner that dealers want to work with*). It is unlikely that dealers who lack pride in their association with Caterpillar would be passionate members of Caterpillar's business system. Moreover, camaraderie among dealers around the world and their shared beliefs in doing good things for the world complement each other, fostering strong brand respect.

POSITIONING STATEMENT AND FINANCIAL GOALS

We don't include financial goals like sales or market share as part of the brand's positioning. They are outcomes that emanate from all areas of the company, not just the marketing area. They should be based on coordinated support and relationships among functional areas such as marketing, sales, production, R&D, and distribution/logistics. The positioning statement should only include elements directly under the control of marketing: target market identification, brand-identity development, and implementing marketing actions that communicate and deliver on the brand's identity. That said, estimating financial goals such as market share and total revenue is always difficult, particularly for a new brand. However, estimates are likely to be better justified and more accurate when they are based on the brand's *ability* and *opportunity* to communicate and deliver on the brand's identity. Moreover, considering marketing actions that will communicate and deliver on the brand's identity also allows managers to develop the rational and well-considered budget that is required to perform these actions.

KEY TAKEAWAYS

1. Building a brand that customers admire starts by identifying a market opportunity in which desired benefits have yet to be met. The opportunity may involve providing new benefits (what) that enable, entice, and/or enrich customers, and/or providing benefits for when, where, and how customers would like to receive them.

2. The attractiveness of a potential target market is greater when it is regarded as (1) highly responsive, (2) large, (3) accessible, and (4) no cannibalization, and when the company can credibly provide these benefits better than competitors can.

3. Marketers can best understand what specific benefits to incorporate in their company's brand identity when they develop a need profile, and clarify who customers are and what they want when, why, and how they want it.

4. Brand identity is the face of a brand. It represents the key promise that the brand makes to its customers.

5. Marketers create brand trust, love, and respect most efficiently when their marketing actions are synergistic; that is, their actions are consistent with the brand's identity and they complement one another in communicating and delivering the brand identity.

6. Considering what marketing actions will be used to communicate and execute on a brand's identity (and the 3 Es) places marketers in a better position to develop a budget that supports these activities.

WHAT ABOUT YOUR BRAND?

1. How did you choose your target customers? To what extent have you considered the factors in Table 5.1 in identifying a new market opportunity? How have these factors impacted your choice of a target market?

2. How do you describe your current target customers? Does your description contain information regarding their need profile (e.g., what they need and want, and why, when, where, and how they want it)?

3. What is your brand's identity? How did you choose this identity?

4. How did you choose various marketing actions? Can you classify them into three different Es? Are they supportive of your brand identity in their own unique manner, following the 3 Es?

5. How similar is the implementation (mix of marketing actions) of your brand's identity to those of SIA and Caterpillar?

6. Was your budget based on a consideration of consistent and complementary marketing actions, or were your marketing actions based on a predetermined budget?

NOTES

1. The information in this paragraph was largely based upon the following source: Francis J. Kelley and Barry Silverstein, *The Breakaway Brand* (New York: McGraw-Hill, 2005).
2. Martin Roll, *Asian Brand Strategy: Building and Sustaining Strong Global Brands in Asia* (New York: Palgrave, 2015).
3. Woojung Chang and Steven A. Taylor, "The Effectiveness of Customer Participation in New Product Development: A Meta-Analysis," *Journal of Marketing* 80, no. 1 (2016): 47–64.

Chapter 6

Building Top-of-Mind Brand Recall

Brand names and visual design elements must embody the brand.

Introduction

Since salt is an ingredient in many products, customers typically care more about the taste of the final product (such as soup) than whether it's made with Morton or another salt brand. Yet the Morton Salt brand has had high top-of-mind (TOM) brand recall for over a century. A brand has strong TOM brand recall when it comes to mind on its own (without any hints or prompts) when customers think about the product category. Note that TOM brand recall is not the same as brand recognition. Recall is a stronger form of memory. One not only recognizes the brand, but one can think about it without any external cues bringing it to mind. How did Morton achieve such a strong TOM brand recall? Some might argue that TOM brand recall comes from superior product quality. Morton Salt certainly passes the test on this criterion; however, it is difficult to argue that quality is the primary reason for its superior TOM brand recall; consumers may not be able to differentiate Morton Salt from competing alternatives. Some might argue that Morton Salt has strong TOM recall because it's been around for so long that we're simply familiar with it. But other brands—such as Red Bull, Google, iPhone, and Victoria's Secret—haven't been on the market for all that long, yet we can recall them easily. We argue that the brand's package, logo, and brand name offer important clues as to why the brand's TOM recall is so strong.

Figure 6.1   Morton Salt Package, Logo, and Brand Name
Source: Morton Salt Inc., A K+S Group Company

Morton Salt's package is functional; it allows salt to pour even in damp weather. It is also symmetrical and beautiful. The brand name (Morton Salt) and its logo (Umbrella Girl) are part of the package (Figure 6.1). The cute little girl with an umbrella logo is clearly eye catching. The *cutely beautiful* package design, logo, and the easy-to-pronounce brand name work together to capture attention and encourage memory of the brand name. Indeed, we believe that the brand's name, its logo, and its package (or product) design are critical brand-recall tools. We explain how and why in this chapter.

OVERVIEW

In Chapter 3 we indicated that when brand admiration is high, customers have developed strong connections with the brand (brand-self connections) and they can easily recall it (TOM brand recall). In Chapter 5 we examined how marketers can cultivate brand admiration by ensuring that marketing actions associated with the 3Es are consistent with the brand's identity and complementary to one another. Many (*consistent and complementary*) marketing actions are critical to communicating and implementing the brand's identity, thereby building brand-self connections and TOM brand recall (Chapter 5). But we believe that certain marketing actions are particularly important in fostering strong TOM brand recall: (1) the brand name, (2) the logo, and (3) the product/package design.

Indeed, these three elements are *the most powerful* facilitators of TOM brand recall. The reason why is that often customers are exposed to and experience these elements most frequently. They are *visual elements* that *embody or represent* the brand. As brand symbols they serve as the *umbrella* under which customers categorize all other marketing actions. Moreover, they are *inherent elements* of a product. Brand names, logos, and product/package designs *also serve as brand identifiers and differentiators*. We argue that these three elements can be *used strategically* to maximize TOM recall. First, though, let's address two key issues associated with TOM brand recall.

KEY ISSUES IN TOM BRAND RECALL

Consider the following two issues associated with TOM brand recall: (1) the importance of TOM recall for brand admiration, and (2) what drives TOM recall in the first place.

Importance of TOM Brand Recall

As we've said before, two things are true when customers admire a brand. They've developed a strong connection with the brand and they can recall it easily and without difficulty. Both are true of highly admired brands. Consider a photo album that has family photos spanning four generations. It's clearly representative of the album holder's family and her/his connections with it. But how truly meaningful is it to the holder if it is hidden deep in a closet and rarely thought about? Through the 3Es, an admired brand has built strong brand-self connections *and* it's easily recalled. Being recalled easily is particularly important, not only because it is one of the two key characteristics of brand admiration, but also because it is directly tied to a brand's financial performance.

Highly recalled brands are more likely to be considered when customers think about what brand they should buy. For this reason, it's not a surprise that previous research consistently shows a strong positive relationship between TOM recall and brand market share. But the financial benefits of TOM recall are not limited to market share. Brand recall should also affect need share, too. *Need share* is defined as the brand's share relative to all the products that are designed to satisfy the same need during a fixed period of time. To illustrate, the need share for Coke for customer A is based on how much that person spent on Coke during a particular period relative to expenditures on all other products that serve the same need (e.g., water, tea, sports drinks, etc.). If this customer buys only Coke for all his or her beverage needs, Coke's need share for this person is 100 percent. As TOM brand recall increases, need share should increase too.

What Enhances TOM Recall?

The ease with which customers can recall a brand is determined by a variety of things, but most important among them are (1) how much attention people pay to brand information when they perceive (or encode) it, (2) how deeply they think about (or elaborate on) it, and (3) how the information is presented (e.g., visually, verbally, aurally, etc.).[1]

Attention and Encoding

Memory begins when information (pictures, words, sounds, smells, touch, and tastes) is *encoded* or processed through one or more of the perceptual senses so that it can be transferred to memory. Encoding binds together the various verbal and sensory features of the things we're exposed to (e.g., a brand name, logo, product, or package) into an integrated memory representation. For example, when you see a brand logo, you encode its shape, its color, any associated sound or voice, and its name. These pieces of information create an overall memory representation through a process called *consolidation*. Consolidation makes the memory representation stable in long-term memory.

Encoding is critical to TOM recall. If we haven't encoded a brand name, logo, or package, we obviously can't remember it. Encoding begins when customers pay attention to the entity to be encoded. When attention is divided or impaired, encoding is weaker and later attempts to remember it are likely to fail. Thus, attention is the first critical driver of TOM recall. To have any hope of having our brand name recalled in today's crowded marketplace, we need to consider how we can make it *attention getting* so that it will be encoded.

Elaboration

Our ability to remember something is also impacted by how much we think about, or elaborate, on it. *Elaboration* is the process of thinking about information; that is, spending time and attention on what we are being exposed to and relating it to what we already know. For example, when meeting people for the first time, you might forget their names immediately. But if you pay attention and deeply encode information about someone (e.g., name, facial characteristics, political views), you'll likely remember a lot about that person. The more deeply we think about something that we're exposed to, the more integrated and enduring our memory for that entity is, which makes it easier to recall.

How Information Is Presented

The number of modalities in which the brand information is presented and encoded (e.g., visual, acoustical, verbal, etc.) also affects memory. Visual information is encoded through imagery processing.[2] Auditory information is encoded by what's called the phonological loop, where encoded sounds are subvocally rehearsed. To illustrate: If someone calls your name, you can still "hear" what that person said in your mind a few seconds after he or she said it. Touch, taste, and scent are also encoded as distinct modalities. Verbal information refers to written descriptions or words that have meaning. Individuals encode verbal information semantically; that is, as meaningful words. For example, customers may infer that Apple stands for innovation and creativity because its tagline says, "Think different."

Information is remembered better when it's encoded in multiple modalities because there are more pieces of information consolidated together to represent that item in memory. Information presented in multiple modalities activates more areas of the brain, making it easier to recall something from memory.[3] For example, a visual logo (say the AFLAC duck) that has an auditory cue (say the AFLAC duck's quack) should be remembered better than a visual logo without an auditory cue. In addition, a brand logo that has a tagline (e.g., Nike's swoosh logo with its tagline "Just Do It") is better remembered than either logo or tagline alone. When information is encoded in multiple modalities, thinking about any one modality (say Nike's swoosh) helps to retrieve the others (the Nike name).

Creating TOM Brand Recall Efficiently

In the rest of the chapter, we discuss how marketers can *use brand logos, names, and product/package designs* to facilitate TOM brand recall, and how they can do so by ensuring that these elements are *encoded in multiple modalities*. Figure 6.2 represents the elements *that can be used strategically to maximize TOM brand recall*. Note that the three elements

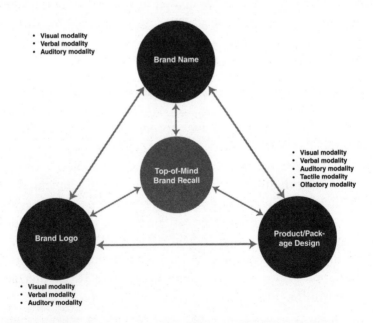

Figure 6.2   Marketing Actions That Enhance Brand Recall

are marketing action variables, and like any other marketing actions, must also honor the brand identity consistency and complementarity principles, regardless of which E each belongs to. As emphasized in Chapter 5, each of these three marketing actions should reflect brand identity and complement other marketing actions for any E they belong to. They should contribute to the process of building trust, love, and respect toward a brand like other marketing actions do by following the consistency and complementarity principles.

Enhancing TOM Brand Recall Using Logos

Logos can be classified by type. One type depicts only the brand name. Examples include Coca-Cola, Google, and IBM. The other type uses separate visual symbols that may or may not include the brand name. Examples include Ferrari's prancing horse logo, Rolex's pointed crown, and the three-pointed star of Mercedes-Benz. Logos that feature only the brand name can use visual elements, such as color and typeface, to foster attention and elaboration. Yet, our research shows that logos that have pictorial elements (either just the pictorial symbol or a combination of pictorial symbol with a verbal element) are more easily recalled because they are more attention getting and elaboration inducing.[4] Brand logos are also important for brand identification. For luxury brands, logos are particularly powerful symbols that convey one's social status or image, though customers vary in whether they want the logo to be quiet and subtle (e.g., less conspicuous and smaller in size) or large and conspicuous.[5]

Visual Modality

Figure 6.3 shows examples of attention-getting and elaboration-inducing logos that use the visual modality together with the brand name. Baskin Robbins' logo brings out the inner child in each of us; one who acts with sheer delight at the prospect of eating ice cream. The logo looks as if a kid might have drafted it. A pink 31 in the center of the logo cleverly represents the brand's 31 flavors. The blue and pink cones in the center of the logo convey that the brand is for everyone, males and females alike. Target's logo creates an attention-getting

Figure 6.3   Examples of Well-Known Logos
Source: Dunkin' Brands Group Inc.; Land Rover UK

contrast with its eye-catching red color and bull's-eye design set against a white background. And it visually communicates Target's fundamental promise of literally hitting the mainstream shopper's mark for finding good-quality products at value prices. The Jaguar logo attracts attention because it is visually stunning and pleasing to the senses (enticing benefits), with its classic styling and the dark background. The animal's fierce look and controlled movements, its ability to leap at the right moment, communicates and fosters elaboration of the car's ability to protect customers and give them the power and control they need for a fulfilling driving experience (enablement benefits). Moreover, the rareness of the animal (wild jaguars in nature) communicates the prestige value of the brand and its enrichment benefits. The logo communicates that the experience of driving, let alone owning a Jaguar, is restricted to the wealthy few (enrichment benefits).

Verbal Modality

Brand logos that include verbal elements such as taglines can be attention getting and elaboration inducing (Figure 6.4). As verbal

Figure 6.4   Brand Logos with Taglines
Source: Nike Inc.; McDonald's; Apple Inc.

elements, taglines can help people to process the logo information at a deeper level. The examples shown in Figure 6.4 not only draw people's attention visually, but also help people to process the logo in a more elaborate way because the logos themselves also contain meaning (e.g., Just do it!).

Auditory Modality

Auditory (sonic elements) refer to the sound associated with a given entity; here, the brand logo. Sonic elements enhance TOM brand recall for several reasons. First, they are engaging in their own right as they create interest in and draw attention to the logo. Second, by associating a logo with an auditory cue, customers will encode the logo more deeply and in yet another modality. They will elaborate more on its meaning, provide more connections to the logo, and relate it to their personal knowledge and experiences. As such, adding the sonic modality to visual and verbal elements of a logo can make it more recallable. Some sonic cues also enhance TOM recall because we anticipate and mentally rehearse them in our minds before and after we hear or see them.[6] One can recall the AFLAC duck's quack just by looking at the duck symbol. The same is true with the Pillsbury Doughboy's cute giggling sound and Tony the Tiger's "They're Gr-r-reat!" Because customers anticipate, pay attention, and mentally rehearse the sonic element, memory for the sonic element and all that's connected to it should be enhanced.

In sum, recall of the brand logo (and hence the brand itself) is enhanced when the logo is verbally, visually, and acoustically attention getting and elaboration inducing.

ENHANCING TOM BRAND RECALL USING BRAND NAMES

Beyond the logo, and holding promotion costs constant, brand-name recall is greater when the *brand name* arouses more interest and attention and it is more deeply encoded and elaborated. For these reasons, it is important to consider how the name can be represented in visual, verbal, and acoustic modalities when brand names are first developed.

Visual Modality

Brand names are depicted in different typefaces, fonts, and colors. Fonts are critical because they can say something profound about the brand's identity.[7] A sans serif font communicates a cleaner and more modern impression than a slab serif or a more block-like font does. A hand-drawn font conveys a more personal touch. The font Disney chose clearly communicates the brand's whimsical and magical character. Brand names can also evoke mental pictures, particularly when the name is concrete and can be imagined. The brand name *Tide*, for example, evokes the image of the sea and powerful churning water—an image that complements the brand name and its benefits.

Verbal Modality

Brand names can also be more recallable when the name is attention getting and elaboration inducing, for instance by including descriptions of brand benefits. Some names are quite difficult to remember, either because they're not very distinctive, too abstract to visualize (e.g., Pledge), or not associated with any inherent meaning (e.g., Mondelez). Others are highly recallable because they're unique or perfectly descriptive of the brand's benefits. A recent interesting trend in branding has been to use a phrase as a brand name. For example, I Can't Believe It's Not Butter is distinctive among brand names because most are quite short. Moreover, the name embodies the brand's benefits. It facilitates elaboration by evoking the customer's imagination about and delight from tasting a product that seems like butter when it's not. Other examples include Bath & Body Works, Food Should Taste Good, and The Walking Company. Although there is limited research on the recall efficacy of phrase-based brand names, they do have attention-getting and elaboration-inducing characteristics that enhance brand-name recall.

Auditory Modality

The sonic mode of brand names also affects our TOM brand recall. For example, brands that have repeated sounds (e.g., Hubba Bubba, Lululemon) can be pleasing and attention getting when spoken aloud, so much so that we mentally rehearse them. V8 vegetable juice's use of the sonic *bop!* in advertising helps brand recall. Beyond attracting attention, sounds can convey meaning.[8] *Phonetic symbolism* means that the mere sound of a word itself conveys meaning. The back vowels in words like *dull*, *blunder*, and *clumsy* convey a negative sense and could easily suggest an item that is heavy or large. In contrast, words such as *pinch* and *slim* have front vowels, which convey a sense of smallness. Another study found that an ice cream named *Frosh* was perceived to be creamier, smoother, and richer than an ice cream named *Frish*.[9] Back vowel sounds like the *u* in *putrid* are often found in words expressing disgust and so may create negative impressions. Sound symbolism makes people connect a brand name with a specific label, concept, or image, facilitating brand-name recall.

In summary, brand-name recall is enhanced when the name is visually, verbally, and acoustically attention getting and elaboration inducing.

ENHANCING TOM BRAND RECALL USING PRODUCT (PACKAGE) DESIGN

The third key element to fostering strong TOM brand recall has to do with the design of the product or its package.

Visual Modality

Research finds that two product/package design features affect brand recall: designs that are cute (e.g., Hello Kitty or Beats Pill speakers) and those that are beautiful (e.g., the Rolex Datejust watch, Chanel's classic flap bag).[10] Both are attention getting and elaboration inducing, but in different ways. People call something that's attractive *cute* when it has certain visual features that connote youthfulness, naiveté, and innocence because those features are reminiscent of babies and children. On the other hand, people call something *beautiful* when its features connote maturity, sophistication, and classiness. Impressions of beauty are typically tied to the symmetry and unity of the product. Cute-looking designs typically have round shapes and a large upper-to-lower portion ratio. Beautiful-(elegant) looking designs are typically slim and have a more balanced upper-to-lower portion ratio.

Our research finds that people show a strong visceral interest in and desire to approach and own cute-looking and beautiful (elegant) designs. However, cute and beautiful designs elicit two very different motivations. A cute product or package design elicits a *nurturing motivation*—a desire to take care of and keep the product, to hold it dear to our hearts and never let it go. The beautiful product or package design elicits a *self-expressive*, or *signaling, motivation*—a desire to express oneself to others through product ownership. But cute and beautiful designs also have downsides. Certain types of cute products can be associated with a lack of sophistication or seriousness, which can undermine performance expectations (lowering perceived enablement benefits). Beautiful-looking designs may not attract attention over time because people become desensitized to them.

It's possible, though, to design products/packages that incorporate both cute and beautiful design elements, avoiding the downsides of one with the upsides of the other. We call such designs *cutely beautiful*. Figure 6.5 shows two interesting examples. These cutely beautiful product designs may be maximally appealing to customers because they contain both elements of aesthetic interest. They don't suffer from problems of perceived quality that might be associated with an exclusively cute design. Nor do they suffer from the sensory fatigue or desensitization associated with an exclusively beautiful design. Moreover, people should *encode them more deeply and think about them more because* they evoke both a motivation to take care of the product and to showcase it to others. For all of these reasons, cutely beautiful product designs should be highly memorable.

Verbal Modality

Beyond the visual modality, any unique information that draws customers' attention to and induces elaborate processing of brand-related information may be highlighted as part of the product's (package) design. For example, PMO (see Chapter 2) uses its product packaging to vividly display and describe the brand's manufacturing principles in

Vespa Scooter Design

The Vespa scooter design is both beautiful and cute. The curves of the scooter are linear and sleek, exhibiting its Italian aesthetic roots. However, what makes the Vespa scooter truly appealing is its cute features. As it does not have a central support spar, the rider can step through the bike and place her feet inside the scooter while riding. In addition, the size of the scooter adds to its cuteness, as it exudes a vibrant and youthful energy.

Braun's Coffeemaker

Braun Coffeemaker is eye catching because of its sleek shape. The design is elegant and minimalist with balanced proportions. In addition, there are cute elements present in the design, such as the soft round shapes and big, graceful handle. The combination of both cute and elegant features makes this coffeemaker endearing and lovable.

Figure 6.5 Examples of Cutely Beautiful Brands
Source: Piaggio Group; Delonghi Group

simple terms to draw customers' attention and to help them understand and appreciate PMO's core principles. Or consider WD-40's
"can with thousands of uses." WD-40 uses verbal product descriptions
on its can to share handy tips for the multiple ways of using the
product, ranging from metal protection against rust and corrosion
to displacing moisture to lubrication of just about anything. It also
describes the unique history behind the WD-40 name on the can,
noting it came from the fact that it took founder Norman Larsen 40
attempts to create the product. The verbal product description helps
draw customers' attention, makes the brand name more salient, and
helps customers elaborate more on the brand.

Auditory Modality

The audio characteristic of a product design can increase TOM
brand recall by attracting attention and inducing elaboration. For
example, consider the fizz of Perrier when it is first opened, and the
volume and pitch of the sound from an aerosol can. Axe deodorant
spray, which targets men, has a forceful sound compared to the more
pleasant sound of Dove's female-targeted deodorant. Product design
elements can include sounds (or the lack thereof!) in some capacity.
Consider Miele washing machines with noise control to afford you
precious silence, the deep full-throttle exhaust sound of a Porsche
911 Turbo you can feel in the pit of your stomach, the "delicious"
snap of Kit Kat bars separating, and Mercedes car doors' distinctive,
reassuring closing sound. One can also use auditory cues in package
design to affect brand recall. For example, Kellogg's Frosted Flakes
has "They're Gr-r-reat!" on its package. Describing the verbal sound
of its tagline on the package connects people to the brand logo while
internally reinforcing the auditory cue of the brand. This can draw
customers' attention to its package and induce further elaboration
about it. In fact, we cannot get "They're Gr-r-reat!" out of our heads.

Tactile Modality

Product (package) design also influences people's attention and elaboration through touch.[11] Touch is the first of the five senses to develop in

life, emerging relatively early in embryonic development. Touch receptors have the widest bodily distribution of any modality. People not only like to touch products, but they also will put effort into seeking out such opportunities, as revealed by *webrooming* (i.e., evaluating products online and visiting retail locations to actually purchase products) and by *showrooming* (i.e., visiting physical stores to interact with and evaluate products, but purchasing them online).

Touching a product or package can stimulate elaboration, conveying sensory, perceptual, and higher-order cognitive information about the brand. Each dimension of touch—weight, texture, and hardness—is mentally represented as a physical sensation, but also in abstract and metaphorical terms.[12] Hardness and heaviness, for example, lead to perceptions of strictness and stability. Have you realized how heavy the doors of a BMW are? The attention-getting and elaboration-inducing power of touching a product or its package in impacting TOM brand recall clearly should be recognized.

Olfactory Modality

Finally, the scent of a product and its package can influence the meaning we infer from a brand and our ability to recall it. Smell is known for its ability to retrieve memories associated with the scent. Memories evoked by smell tend to be deep and intense, and they can create strong emotions. People can recall smells with 65 percent accuracy even after 12 months, compared to people's visual-recall ability, which drops to 50 percent after only 3 months. The Mandarin Oriental and the Ritz Carlton, for instance, each has its own signature fragrances that are used in lobby areas and guest rooms.[13] Singapore Airline's scented towels are also noteworthy. Scent memories are long lasting, and they help facilitate TOM recall in a powerful way.

DESIGNING LOGOS, BRAND NAMES, AND PRODUCT/PACKAGE DESIGNS JOINTLY

Figure 6.2 shows that the three marketing action elements impact TOM recall jointly. Beyond their individual contributions to TOM recall, these three elements interactively influence TOM brand recall. They should thus be designed in such a way that they reinforce one another. Because they often appear together (they are physically proximal), they are intrinsically linked. It is for this reason that each element should be jointly designed so that each can maximize recall of the other.

For example, the meaning of the brand name itself helps customers elaborate on the brand logo and package design, and vice versa (think about Jaguar and Red Bull). Reinforcement among these three elements increases the number and the strength of memory connections that customers form with the brand name. An integrated and stable memory representation of a brand is consequently formed in long-term memory. The stronger, more integrated, and the more stable this memory representation is, the more likely it is to be recalled. Morton Salt (Figure 6.1) illustrates the effective use of these three elements in jointly contributing to TOM brand recall. People associate the name, logo, and package with one another. The *cutely beautiful* package design and the logo as well as the easy-to-pronounce two-syllable brand name work beautifully together to create strong TOM brand recall. Each element reinforces the other in creating attention and elaboration of the brand name.

KEY TAKEAWAYS

1. Three marketing action variables are strong facilitators of TOM brand recall, independent of the level of promotional activity that the company engages in: the brand logo, the brand name itself, and the product/package design. They are relatively stable and inherent product elements that customers encounter in multiple contexts (in ads, in stores, on websites, on social media, etc.).

2. The strength of brand recall is primarily determined by how the brand logo, the brand name, and the product/package are processed. Brand-name recall is enhanced when these elements are attention getting: they foster deeper processing when they are represented in visual, verbal, auditory, tactile, and olfactory (scent) modalities.

3. Brand logos are best recalled when they combine visual, verbal, and auditory elements.

4. Recalling a brand name is also influenced by how the name itself is communicated visually, verbally, and acoustically. Each of these presentation modes can affect the meaning of the brand and what it stands for.

5. Recalling a product/package design is influenced by how it is presented in visual, verbal, auditory, tactile, and olfactory modes.

6. Both cute and beautiful designs arouse strong interest in the product. But they elicit two different motivations regarding product ownership (nurturance and self-signaling). Designs that are most recallable may be those that use a beautiful form with cute elements or a cute form with beautiful elements.

7. Product design, brand logo, and brand-name decisions should be represented in multiple modalities, and they should complement one another in facilitating what people come to understand about the brand and their memory of it.

WHAT ABOUT YOUR BRAND?

1. How readily are the names of your brands recalled? How could you improve their recall potential?

2. To what extent do your brand logo, brand name, and product (package) design work together to foster brand-name recall and brand identity? Do they reflect the identity you want customers to associate with your brand?

3. Does your brand logo attract attention and evoke the meaning that corresponds with your brand's identity? Does it also have an auditory element? A visual component?

4. Does your brand name have visual and auditory appeal, as well as a certain specific meaning that people can associate with your brand name?

5. Does your product and/or package design contain both cute and beautiful (elegant) elements?

6. Do you think that the logo, the name, and the product design of your brand work synergistically to help facilitate TOM recall of your brand?

NOTES

1. Wayne D. Hoyer, Deborah J. MacInnis, and Rik Pieters, *Consumer Behavior* (New York: Cengage Learning, 2013).
2. Deborah J. MacInnis and Linda L. Price, "The Role of Imagery in Information Processing," *Journal of Consumer Research* 13, no. 4 (1987): 473–91.
3. Michael J. Houston, Terry L. Childers, and Susan E. Heckler, "Picture-Word Consistency and the Elaborative Processing of Advertisements," *Journal of Marketing Research* 24, no. 4 (1987): 359–69.
4. C. Whan Park, Andreas B. Eisingerich, Gratiana Pol, and Jason Whan Park, "The Role of Brand Logos in Firm Performance," *Journal of Business Research* 66, no. 2 (2013): 180–187; C. Whan Park, Andreas B. Eisingerich, and Gratiana Pol, "The Power of a Good Logo," *MIT Sloan Management Review* 55, no. 2 (2014): 10–12.
5. Young Jee Han, Joseph C. Nunes, and Xavier Drèze, "Signaling Status with Luxury Goods: The Role of Brand Prominence," *Journal of Marketing* 74, no. 4 (2010): 15–30.
6. Daniel M. Jackson, Richard Jankovich, and Eric Sheinkop, *Hit Brands: How Music Builds Value for the World's Smartest Brands* (New York: Palgrave, 2013).
7. Terry L. Childers and Jeffrey Jass, "All Dressed Up with Something to Say: Effects of Typeface Semantic Associations on Brand Perceptions and Consumer Memory," *Journal of Consumer Psychology* 12, no. 2 (2002): 93–106.
8. Jennifer J. Argo, Monica Popa, and Malcolm C. Smith, "The Sound of Brands," *Journal of Marketing* 74, no. 4 (2010): 97–109.
9. Eric Yorkston and Geeta Menon, "A Sound Idea: Phonetic Effects of Brand Names on Consumer Judgments," *Journal of Consumer Research* 31, no. 1 (2004): 43–51.
10. He Jia, Gratiana Pol, and C. Whan Park, "I'll Keep the Cuddly One: Effects of Visual Cuteness versus Elegance on Product Retention," research in process.

11. Aradhna Krishna, *Customer Sense: How the 5 Senses Influence Buying Behavior* (New York: Palgrave, 2013).
12. Rajeev Batra and Colleen Seifert, *The Psychology of Design: Creating Consumer Appeal* (London: Routledge, 2015).
13. Colleen Clark, "Why Do Fancy Hotels Pipe in Such Powerful Fragrances?," *Bloomberg*, September 18, 2015, www.bloomberg.com/news/articles/2015-09-18/scent-branding-101-why-do-fancy-hotels-use-such-powerful-fragances-.

SECTION 3

STRENGTHENING AND LEVERAGING ADMIRED BRANDS

CHAPTER 7

Strengthening Brand Admiration

T he world does not stop turning and brands should not stop striving to strengthen brand admiration over time.

INTRODUCTION

Since the iPhone's introduction on June 29, 2007, Apple has done anything but sit around and bask in the brand's success. Instead, it has consistently and proactively sought new ways to improve on its brand.[1] In essence, it has been on a continual quest to strengthen brand admiration. Let's consider how.

When it was first introduced, the iPhone reframed the idea of what a cell phone could be. It wasn't just a phone: it was a mobile computer/phone/entertainment system. Though its price was higher than those of other cell phones, the ability to integrate phone, computer, and music—and hence offer so many diverse benefits in a single product—was unprecedented. Importantly, Apple didn't stop there. It continued to offer innovative enabling and enticing benefits that made customers' lives easier and more enjoyable. It added GPS, voice control (Siri's precursor), precision control (important for gaming), a front camera (allowing for selfies and FaceTime calls), a find-my-iPhone feature, and Apple Pay (a mobile payment service). Apple made the phone thinner and reduced its price. With these and many other changes, the iPhone wasn't just a cell phone. Its benefits were sufficiently strong and broad so as to compete with cameras, music devices, computers, and even video entertainment (TV/movies).

These iPhone improvements might look random. But they had a purpose: systematically enhancing the value of the iPhone. Specifically, Apple *manipulated benefits* by adding, improving on, or deleting benefits or features that no longer served the brand well. It *adjusted the importance weight of various benefits*. For example, it made the perceived price difference between the iPhone and competitors' products negligible. It increased the importance of thinness as a desirable product attribute, and it even got customers thinking about the importance of taking selfies, staying connected (with FaceTime calls), and finding their phones if they were lost (with Apple's find-my-iPhone app). Apple also *changed the referent alternative* to which the iPhone was compared from just other cell phones to cameras and other modes of entertainment.

OVERVIEW

The Apple example illustrates two important ideas detailed in this chapter. First, beyond creating an admired brand, companies need to also *strengthen brand admiration* over time. Figure 1.1 explicitly addresses the issue of strengthening brand admiration. Stronger brand admiration means that the brand *becomes even more valuable* than when it was first introduced. Customer needs and the competitive marketplace are constantly evolving. Admired brands can't just sit on their laurels. Marketers must continually invest in the brand to ensure that brand love, trust, and respect—and hence brand admiration—endure over time. Unfortunately, far too many brands have experienced drastic declines or outright failure because they didn't focus on enhancing brand admiration.

Second, there are various value-enhancement strategies that companies can consider to continually strengthen brand admiration through marketing actions. These strategies are noted in Table 7.1 and will be described in detail shortly. Here, marketers focus on besting their own brands while also continuing to differentiate them from competitors' brands. Apple used several such strategies. Very briefly, these strategies involve (1) manipulating brand benefits (e.g., adding and/or improving on and/or deleting brand benefits), (2) changing the importance (or valence) of benefits, and (3) framing the referent alternative to which its brand is compared.

Table 7.1 A Customer's Value Judgments

Benefits Cirque du Soleil: Ringling Brothers	Worse Than Referent			Same As Referent		Better Than Referent		Benefit Importance (Weight)	Subtotal
	-3	-2	-1	0	1	2	3		
Excitement (Enticement)						✓		0.1	$0.1 \times 2 = 0.2$
Comfort (Enablement)						✓		0.2	$0.4 \times 2 = 0.4$
Fun (Enticement)					✓			0.3	$0.3 \times 1 = 0.3$
Ticket Price (Enablement)		✓						0.2	$0.2 \times -2 = -0.4$
Sophistication (Enrichment)							✓	0.2	$0.2 \times 3 = 0.6$
Total									1.1

VALUE-ENHANCEMENT STRATEGIES THAT STRENGTHEN BRAND ADMIRATION

In Chapter 1 we defined a *brand* as a value-generating entity (name) relevant to both customers and the brand owner. If no one wants to buy the brand, it fails to provide value to either customers or the company. This chapter returns to the concept of value and links value to the value-enhancement strategies shown in Table 7.1.

Brand Value Judgments

Hundreds of academic studies in marketing, and presumably in an equal number of consulting models, suggest that buying decisions are based on three basic factors:

1. The first is *whether and to what extent the brand provides customers with relevant benefits*: in our model, benefits that enable, enrich, and entice the customer. These are the benefits customers care about and want to see in a brand.

2. The second is *how important the benefits are*. For any given product, certain benefits may be more important than others. Brand choice reflects how well the important benefits that consumers want line up with what the brand provides.

3. The third is that customers don't make choices in a vacuum. Decisions are often based on what the brand can provide *relative to something else* (e.g., to another brand, to a brand in a different category, or to not buying).

In short, a brand is more likely to be chosen when it provides more value; that is, it provides (1) more important benefits (2) that customers want (3) than an alternative option provides.

Table 7.1 illustrates a particular customer's perceptions of the benefits associated with Cirque du Soleil relative to a referent brand (here Ringling Brothers). The check mark indicates that relative to the referent (Ringling Brothers), this customer perceives Cirque as better than Ringling on all benefits except ticket price. It might be tempting to conclude that this customer will definitely decide to see a show by Cirque du Soleil because it offers more benefits than Ringling Brothers does. However, we also need to consider that customers don't regard all benefits as equally important. Most critical to this particular customer is fun, with a relative importance weight of 0.3, followed by comfort, price, and sophistication (each with an importance weight of 0.2). Excitement is least important (a weight of 0.1). Note that we regard lowered costs to customers (costs related to time and effort, as well as emotional, psychological, and financial costs) as benefits. Less time, money, and effort expended means that the brand saves customers time, money, and effort. These are benefits. Thus, all else equal, a higher-priced brand offers less value than a lower-priced one.

This customer's decision about whether to see a Cirque du Soleil or Ringling Brothers show depends on how well each brand fulfills the enticement, enablement, and enrichment benefits, *weighted by how important those benefits are to him or her*. For example, this customer gives Cirque du Soleil a 3 on sophistication relative to Ringling Brothers, and its importance weight is 0.2, giving it a weighted score of 0.6 ($3 \times 0.2 = 0.6$). This customer is likely to choose Cirque du Soleil over Ringling Brothers, since the sum of the brand's benefits ratings multiplied by their importance weights is positive relative to Ringling Brothers (see the right-hand column and the total score of 1.1 in Table 7.1). Another way of saying this is that Cirque du Soleil offers this particular customer more value than does Ringling Bros because *it fulfills important enticement, enablement, and enrichment needs better than the alternative*. Other customers who have the same need profile as this customer does are in the same segment (see Chapter 5).

Value-Enhancement Strategies

Knowing how customers make buying decisions (and how they judge the relative value of one brand over another) is important because it provides insights into the different value-enhancement strategies *marketers can use to enhance the brand's value and strengthen brand admiration.*

- First, a company can *manipulate brand benefits* by improving on or adding to one or more important benefits that enable, entice, or enrich customers. Alternatively, a company could delete a benefit that customers don't regard as important and is irrelevant to what makes the brand strong.

- Second, the company can *change the importance weight* of one or more benefits. It can increase the importance weight of a benefit on which the brand is strong and/or reduce the importance weight of benefits on which other brands are better.

- Third, the company can *create a referent or change an existing referent* so that the brand compares favorably to the referent. The referent could be a brand in the same product category, one in a different category, *the company's current brand*, or not buying at all.

In all, companies have 15 potential *value-enhancement strategies* from which they can choose to strengthen brand admiration; specifically, five strategic options applied to the three types of benefits (enablement, enticement, and enrichment). Table 7.2 identifies these 15 strategies. These value-enhancement strategies require a company to implement a set of marketing actions as discussed below.

STRATEGIES THAT MANIPULATE BRAND BENEFITS

Let's first consider strategies that manipulate brand benefits; specifically, improving on, adding to, or deleting brand benefits (see the first three columns in Table 7.2).

Improving Benefits That Enable Customers

In 2001, Hyundai initiated new quality improvements in manufacturing, and it made design and engineering improvements to its models. It also gave customers a 10-year, 100,000-mile warranty. The warranty far exceeded the industry's standard 3-year warranty, and it nearly guaranteed that customers would not be responsible for high-priced repairs for their cars' expected working life. These improved benefits transformed Hyundai's reputation for quality.

Table 7.2 Brand Value–Enhancement Strategies

Methods 3Es	Manipulating Brand Benefit			Enhancing/Reducing Benefit Importance	Creating (Changing) the Referent
	Improve	Add	Delete		
Enabling Benefits	Hyundai's extended warranty Amazon's Prime membership	Samsonite Best Buy shops in Macy's stores	Miele	Listerine Enjoy	National Pork Board Gatorade in Korea
Enticing Benefits	Cleveland Clinic Zappos	Age 20's	Burger King Swatch	Volkswagen	Avis
Enriching Benefits	CAPiTA	Starbucks' education benefit Gravity Payments	New Balance Lush, The Body Shop	Hermès Birkenstock	Tower of Love Thermometer

Amazon improved its Prime membership. Beyond offering free shipping, Prime members can stream music and videos. Moreover, on Prime Day members can take advantage of exclusive sales and promotional prices throughout the site. With these benefits, Amazon Prime membership now covers about 25 percent of American households and it is expected to cover 50 percent by 2020.[2]

Improving Benefits That Entice Customers

The Cleveland Clinic offered improved *enticement* benefits. Antiseptic aromas were replaced with scents akin to the signature fragrances favored by four-star hotel chains. Hospital gowns were designed by Diane von Furstenberg to combine ease of access to patients' bodies while maintaining their dignity. Staff members were asked to adopt the 10-4 rule: "when 10 feet away from a patient, smile and make eye contact; when 4 feet away, address the patient by name." Hospitals can be terrifying environments. So empathy, friendliness, and pleasant, dignity-preserving experiences go a long way toward patient well-being and comfort.

Zappos realized that the lifetime value of a customer who calls (for any reason) is five to six times as much as the value of a customer who never calls. So Zappos improved customers' opportunities to connect with the company, offering friendly service and warming their hearts. Zappos lists its phone number on every page of its website and encourages customers to call if they have questions or concerns. Allowing customers to contact Zappos easily enables customers, but warming their hearts through friendly and pleasant service entices customers. In contrast, often customers can't find a customer service phone number for many e-commerce sites unless they Google it.[3]

Improving Benefits That Enrich Customers

In a world dominated by mass-marketed goods sold at chain stores, some consumers want authentic products whose heritage involves a commitment to quality and time-honored principles. CAPiTA Snowboards improved on its ability to enrich customers by emphasizing the brand's authenticity. Improved web content tells about the brand's heritage and humble origins as one of snowboarding's "weirdo companies," highlighting the founding members' commitment to overcome "sleepless nights" and "flirtations with bankruptcy" to realize their dream.[4] It also shares CAPiTA's commitment to responsible manufacturing and information about its new snowboard factory, called The Mothership, which has zero CO_2 emissions and is 100 percent hydropowered.[5] Emphasizing the brand's unique and rich history and focusing on responsible manufacturing help CAPiTA more strongly position itself as authentic "Purveyors of the Wildlife" and resonate with customers who share the same beliefs.

Adding Benefits That Enable Customers

Beyond improving on benefits, companies can enhance the value of their brands by adding new benefits. Samsonite has introduced a new line of GeoTrakR suitcases that contain a cellular-enabled baggage-tracking system. This added benefit solves one of travelers' (and airlines) most vexing problems—finding lost luggage. Macy's recently announced that it will add 10 Best Buy shops to Macy's stores to offer electronic gadgets that Macy's did not carry.[6] The benefit? Macy's customers now have access to a new range of products.

Adding Benefits That Entice Customers

Age 20's, a Korean make-up brand of AeKyung Corporation, used a home shopping channel to visually demonstrate the brand's power in moisturizing skin, keeping it soft. The clip showed water dripping from its Essence Cover Pact foundation when placed on a woman's skin. This visual was astoundingly powerful in demonstrating the brand's superb moisturizing abilities. Age 20's sold 1,199,066 units in 2015, up significantly from its initial 2013 sales of 54,867 units.[7]

Adding Benefits That Enrich Customers

Starbucks adds benefits to employees by investing in their college education. Any Starbucks employee who works at least 20 hours a week in the United States and has the grades and test scores to gain admission to Arizona State University can take advantage of the college program. Enrollees can study whatever they like, and they can leave Starbucks without paying back the tuition that Starbucks has paid on their behalf. Starbucks also is leading a new initiative to provide more opportunities to 16- to 24-year-olds living mostly in low-income neighborhoods.[8] People appreciate Starbucks' principles and its social cause–related movements, identifying themselves with its socially conscious conduct. In addition, Starbucks has consistently added unusual benefits such as stock options and health insurance, even for part-timers. The 31-year-old CEO of Gravity Payments (a credit-card processing company) recently set a new minimum salary of $70,000 for his 120 employees. He slashed his own million-dollar pay package to make it happen. This move made a huge difference for those employees who were struggling to live and pay bills on much lower salaries. The move drew enthusiastic attention and support from people worldwide who applauded the CEO's effort to fight income inequality.

Deleting Benefits That Fail to Enable Customers

Marketers can also eliminate benefits that fail to enable customers. Sometimes less is truly more. This type of value-enhancement strategy can also cut company costs. The increasing number of functions on consumer electronic products often confuses end users, so eliminating features can be enabling. Miele enhanced the value of its washing machines by eliminating certain functions while promising top product performance and noise control. Fewer functions mean greater simplicity and ease of use, and fewer things that might require product repair. Interestingly, Walter Isaacson's biography of Steve Jobs indicated that the consumer-electronics good Jobs was most excited about was a Miele washing machine, given the simplicity of the brand's elegant design.[9]

Deleting Benefits That Fail to Entice Customers

Marketers can also delete benefits that do not entice customers. Burger King dropped fountain drinks from its kids' menus. Soft drinks are still an option, but they are not listed on the King Jr menu. Instead, the kids' menu offers fat-free milk, 100 percent apple juice, and low-fat chocolate milk. This parent-approved move increased parents' willingness to take their kids to Burger King. Swatch, the Swiss-made watch brand, deleted expensive stainless steel wristbands, opting instead for cheerful, colorful, and cheaper plastic wristbands. The move saved costs and allowed Swatch to offer wristbands in a wide range of styles and colors, making the brand a loved fashion item.

Deleting Benefits That Fail to Enrich Customers

New Balance eliminated leather from some of its running shoes because wearing leather goes against some consumers' beliefs about using products that cause harm to animals. Likewise, Lush and The Body Shop do not offer products that use animal testing. In fact, Lush goes so far as to say that it only buys ingredients from companies that do not conduct or commission tests on animals. Instead, it tests its products on humans. Deleting benefits (the testing of products on animals) that fail to enrich customers helps Lush stand out in the marketplace and build a strong following among consumers who share the brand's values.

STRATEGIES THAT ADJUST A BENEFIT'S IMPORTANCE WEIGHT

The second set of strategies shown in Table 7.2 aims to alter how important customers perceive certain benefits to be. With this strategy, marketers can enhance the perceived importance of competitively strong benefits that enable, entice, or enrich customers. Alternatively, they can reduce the perceived importance of benefits on which competing brands are presumed to be superior. Sometimes, changing a benefit's importance weight can turn a negative benefit into a positive one (see the forthcoming Hermès example).

Change the Perceived Importance of Benefits That Enable Customers

In its early days, Warner-Lambert positioned Listerine's strong and relatively unpalatable taste as evidence of the brand's effectiveness in killing germs and eliminating bad breath. In so doing, the brand deemphasized the importance of taste and instead increased the importance consumers placed on killing germs. In fact, Listerine used bad taste as proof that Listerine was strong and effective at eliminating germs and bad breath. On-demand companies such as Enjoy are challenging Amazon by also offering same-day delivery, but with an added twist.[10] Enjoy sends experts who hand deliver tech products and help customers set up their new devices. Enjoy's reps also help customers transfer data from their old smartphones to their new ones, train them to shoot and edit videos on a GoPro, and explain how to add music to their Sonos audio systems, all at no additional cost. It's increasing the importance consumers place on after-sales service.

Change the Perceived Importance of Benefits That Entice Customers

Volkswagen's classic "Think Small" advertising campaign for the Beetle went against the bigger-is-better mantra of the day. It made small cool. In an era in which other manufacturers were competing on speed, size, and muscle benefits, VW linked the car's small size to advanced engineering, gas conservation, reliability, and friendliness. In fact, VW was shockingly honest in its "Think Small" print ads, openly stating that "a VW won't go over 72 mph." However, VW also let customers know that even a Beetle can "easily break almost any speed law in the country." VW thus deemphasized the importance of excessive power and speed and changed people's perceptions, such that smallness became friendly, cool, and fun.

Change the Perceived Importance of Benefits That Enrich Customers

Most customers consider wait time for product delivery to be a negative. This could be difficult for companies like Hermès, whose customers have to wait six months or more to get its Kelly or its Birkin handbag. Hermès could turn this potentially negative problem to its advantage by linking wait time to the search for the highest quality raw materials, and the precision tooling required by skilled craftsmen who make the bag by hand. Customers would feel pride in owning a bag that is so rare and that involves painstaking craftsmanship to produce. In the same vein, the German-manufactured sandal brand Birkenstock has attracted attention from American consumers since the 1960s for its aesthetically unappealing but incredibly comfortable foot bed. To some, the shoe is associated with hippies and making one's feet look big. However, the brand is now being positioned as one that helps consumers express to others who they are, reducing the importance customers place on how they look.[11]

STRATEGIES THAT CREATE (CHANGE) THE REFERENT

As Table 7.1 suggests, customers' choices and their assessment of the 3Es are *relative*, or context-specific. What we mean is that when making choices, customers look at the benefits a brand provides *relative to something else* (called the *referent alternative*). Imagine that you have to travel from New York to Philadelphia. You're considering flying business class on Virgin Air in a Boeing 747. But your final choice could easily be impacted by the alternatives that you compare this flight option with. For example, you might consider (1) a *competing brand* in the same category (e.g., flying on Virgin versus American), (2) a different brand in a different category (e.g., flying on Virgin versus taking Amtrak or renting a car from Hertz), (3) a different alternative of the same brand (e.g., a Virgin Boeing 777 versus a Virgin 747 aircraft), or (4) not buying any product. Marketers can sometimes influence the referent that customers consider when they make their choices. Specifically, marketers can choose the referent that best supports their brands as offering the greatest value. The examples below show how.

Create (Change) the Referent Such That One's Own Brand Strongly Enables Customers

In 1987 the National Pork Board positioned pork as "the other white meat." This campaign came at a time when concerns about the fat in beef appeared frequently in the popular press, and chicken was the most popular lean meat protein source. Framing pork as a white meat made it distinctive from beef and more similar to chicken while promoting its enabling benefit. The campaign increased sales of pork by 20 percent between 1987 and 1991. The National Pork Board claims that today pork is the world's most consumed protein. In the early 1990s, Gatorade was promoted in Korea by comparing it with water instead of other thirst-quenching brands. The claim: Gatorade hydrates the body faster than water. Although Gatorade initially struggled when brought to Korea, today Korea is one of the countries with the highest per capita consumption of Gatorade.

Create (Change) the Referent Such That One's Own Brand Strongly Entices Customers

In its early days Avis used the famous slogan, "We're #2. We try harder" for its car rental service. By positioning itself as #2 (behind Hertz), it led consumers to believe that Avis was right after Hertz and was trying very hard to be as good as, if not better than, Hertz. Avis struck a chord with consumers who identified Avis as an underdog who was true to itself and its customers. This heartwarming advertising campaign also advanced Avis's competitive standing. At that time many rental car companies were competing with one another and Hertz was clearly an industry leader. Avis was able to successfully position itself as the #2 brand, not #3 or #4 brand, on the market, ensuring that customers did not even think about renting other competing brands.

Create (Change) the Referent Such That One's Own Brand Strongly Enriches Customers

Since 2000, 17 major cities in Korea have held a yearly winter ceremony that erects a tower named the Tower of Love Thermometer. The love thermometer's temperature rises one degree for each percent of funds raised for that year. Koreans can track their city's donation progress each day. When the campaign goals are fulfilled, the love thermometer reaches a temperature of 100 degrees. Fundraising success using this love thermometer has been impressive. Since 2000, use of the thermometer as a referent has allowed the campaign to beat its yearly fundraising goal. The Tower of Love Thermometer as a referent in this example serves a different purpose from other referents used in Table 7.2. It is portrayed as a symbol of care for those in need and donors feel pride in participating.

Thinking Broadly about Value-Enhancement Strategies

Although we've discussed five value enhancement strategies in various contexts, these contexts may be better understood in terms of a transaction cycle (pre-purchase, during purchase, usage, and disposition). Brand benefits can not only be appreciated at the usage stage but also at the other stages of the transaction cycle. In addition, although we just discussed benefits that aligned with a particular E, a given benefit can be associated with more than one E. In fact, it's highly powerful and cost efficient to have a single brand benefit that enables, entices, and enriches customers at the same time. We discuss these points next.

Benefits at Each Stage of the Transaction Cycle

First, whether they are establishing a new brand or strengthening an existing one, managers should consider benefits at each stage of the transaction cycle—from *prepurchase* to *during purchase* to *usage* to *disposition*. Consider that ShopAdvisor incorporates data analytics that filter a shopper's preferences and let retailers send personalized alerts to customers who have downloaded the brand's app. ShopAdvisor enables retailers by pinpointing the customer's whereabouts so that retailers can offer discount and product information at the customers' prepurchase stage. Benefits may occur during purchase to facilitate the purchase transaction. Benefits also occur during usage (consumption), as customers appreciate the product benefits in use. For example, Create-A-Book offers benefits to parents and children at the purchase and usage stages of consumption. When the book is bought, the children and their pet are featured as the main characters of the story, an exciting experience at the purchase stage. The children who are the stories' heroes are thrilled when their parents buy the books and read the stories. And benefits may also occur at the disposition stage, as customers try to rid themselves of products that they've outgrown. In the earlier days, BMW offered Japanese customers a free pick-up service for their old cars, facilitating product disposition. *Benefits need not be limited to the product usage stage.*

Benefits That Cut Across Multiple Es

Second, a particular benefit may apply to multiple Es. Caterpillar's dealer advisory group (discussed in Chapters 2 and 5) not only offers enabling benefits (e.g., those that signify an equal partnership with Caterpillar) but also enticing benefits (e.g., those that warm their hearts). Earlier we mentioned Starbucks' free college education program. The program certainly enables its employees by providing them with an educational experience that supports a more secure life. But it also entices employees by offering cognitive stimulation. Moreover, it enriches employees by offering a benefit that is consistent with employees' values, offering opportunities to connect with others, and feel good about their own accomplishments. The more Es a benefit covers, the more powerful and cost efficient it becomes in creating or enhancing the value of the brand.

Template for Value-Enhancement Strategies

Table 7.3 integrates the two points we've just made. In each of the 12 cells in Table 7.3, brand managers can consider any one or a combination of the five value-enhancement strategies (see Table 7.2) and marketing actions appropriate to them. Also, as noted earlier, the more Es a benefit covers, the more powerful and cost efficient it becomes in creating or enhancing the value of a brand and supporting brand admiration. It becomes even more valuable to a company *if the benefit decreases, or at least does not exceed, the brand's unit cost.* For example, Cirque du Soleil eliminated animal acts because this benefit was failing to entice customers. Not having animal acts actually resonated with many customers, warming their hearts (enticing benefit) and also making them believe that Cirque du Soleil shares their own beliefs (enriching benefits). The move also reduced unit costs, among which are the cost of animal tamers, animal feed, medical care, animal housing, and insurance. Progressive Insurance used a similar value-enhancement strategy. Fraudulent claims cost over $80 billion

Table 7.3 Integrated Value-Enhancing Strategies

		From Where		
		Enabling Benefits	Enticing Benefits	Enriching Benefits
Transaction Cycle	Pre-purchase			
	During Purchase			
	Usage			
	Disposition (Post-purchase)			

a year, and companies have to charge higher premiums to recover these costs.[12] Progressive changed how its claims process worked by dispatching a claim agent to the accident site within two hours of the accident. This improved benefit appealed to customers who want fast, seamless service when they need insurance help (enabling benefit). The agent's presence at the accident site significantly lowered fraudulent claims, helping Progressive cut costs and allowing it to charge a lower premium than other leading competitors (enabling benefit). Finally, the agent's professional service at the accident site warmed the hearts of customers who had suffered emotional stress (enticing and enabling benefits).

Managers can therefore use Table 7.3 as a template when considering the value-enhancement strategies that will most effectively build or strengthen their brand's admiration.

KEY TAKEAWAYS

1. Brand admiration and the value a brand offers to customers and companies will likely wane over time unless marketers use value-enhancement strategies to continuously strengthen brand admiration.

2. Customers' choices are based on how much value the brand offers vis-à-vis referent alternatives. Inputs to brand value include the benefits offered, their importance weight, and

the referent with which the brand is compared. This choice (value) equation provides significant insight into how brands can build and strengthen brand admiration over time.

3. Brands can use a number of value-enhancement strategies. They can:

   a) Manipulate benefits that enable, entice, and enrich customers, (add, improve on, or delete benefits).

   b) Change the importance weights of such benefits (enhancing or reducing the importance of benefits that enable, entice, or enrich customers).

   c) Create (change) the referent alternative against which the brand is compared (to a competing brand in the same category, a brand in a different category, a different product from the same company, or not buying).

4. Brand holders can search for value-enhancing strategies that are specific to a particular stage in the transaction cycle.

5. Brand holders can search for value-enhancing strategies specific to a given type of benefit (one that enables, entices, or enriches customers) or specific to multiple benefits.

WHAT ABOUT YOUR BRAND?

1. How have you enhanced the value of your brand so as to strengthen brand admiration over time?

2. How many of the benefits that you have addressed belong to each of the 3Es?

3. To what extent have you considered manipulating the benefits of your brand, enhancing/reducing the importance of benefits, and creating (changing) the referent for your brand?

4. How many of the benefits that you have addressed enhance more than one E?

5. Do the benefits your brand is offering apply to each of the four transaction cycle stages (from pre-purchase to brand disposition)?

NOTES

1. There are also warning signs that Apple may have lost some of its strong focus on brand admiration building and strengthening, as it has been distracted by competitors and litigations. Any brand must continually focus on building and strengthening on its brand admiration.

2. Hiroko Tabuchi, "It's Amazon and Also-Rans in Retailer's Race for Online Sales," *New York Times*, December 31, 2015, www.nytimes.com/2015/12/31/technology/in-online-race-its-amazon-and-also-rans.html?_r=0.

3. Christopher Mims, "The Customer-Service Quandary: Touchy Feely or Do It Yourself," *Wall Street Journal*, November 2, 2015, accessed April 20, 2016, www.wsj.com/articles/the-customer-service-quandary-touchy-feely-or-do-it-yourself-1446440460.

4. "The History of CAPiTA Snowboards," *Whitelines*, accessed April 20, 2016, http://whitelines.com/videos/history-capita-snowboards.html.

5. "The Mothership," CAPiTA, accessed April 20, 2016, https://www.capitasnowboarding.com/mothership

6. Phil Wahba, "Macy's, Best Buy to Test Consumer Electronics Shops," *Fortune*, September 8, 2015, http://fortune.com/2015/09/08/macys-best-buy-electronics.

7. The sales information was obtained from the brand managers of Age 20's of AeKyung Corporation, Mr. G. S. Ryu and Mr. J. H. Lee.

8. Julie Jargon, "Starbucks Leads Multi-Company Initiative to Hire 100,000 Young, Minority Workers," *Wall Street Journal*, July 13, 2015, www.wsj.com/articles/starbucks-leads-multi-company-initiative-to-hire-100-000-young-minority-workers-1436770801.

9. Walter Isaacson, *Steve Jobs* (New York: Simon & Schuster, 2011).

10. Manjoo, Farhad, "Two Retail Veterans Take Aim at Amazon's E-Commerce Reign," *New York Times*, May 6, 2015, www.nytimes.com/2015/05/07/technology/personaltech/two-retail-veterans-take-aim-at-amazons-e-commerce-reign.html?_r=0.

11. Rebecca Mead, "Sole Cycle," *New Yorker*, March 23, 2015, www.newyorker.com/magazine/2015/03/23/sole-cycle-rebecca-mead.

12. John Standish, "Speed to Detection: A Progressive and Strategic Concept Using Advanced Anti-Fraud Analytics," *Insurance Though Leadership*, August 13, 2013, http://insurancethoughtleadership.com/speed-to-detection-a-progressive-and-strategic-concept-using-advanced-anti/#sthash.GjaMlOvT.dpbs.

CHAPTER 8

Leveraging Brand Admiration: Extension and Feedback Effects

L everaging an admired brand fuels opportunities for synergistic brand growth.

INTRODUCTION

What began as a movie about characters in a galaxy far, far away has captivated the hearts and imagination of people around the globe, and in a way that few brands have managed to emulate. Since its 1977 debut, *Star Wars* has spawned a series of films. But the brand's success is not limited to the movie business. *Star Wars* has also given birth to myriad media entertainment–related offerings in other product categories. Among them are *Star Wars* comic books, *Star Wars* video games, *Star Wars* trading cards, and *Star Wars* role-playing games. Cobranding opportunities with Lego, Microsoft, and Sony include Lego's hugely popular *Star Wars* product line and *Star Wars* video games for the PlayStation. For admirers of the *Star Wars* brand, there are few areas of life in which they are unable to connect with the *Star Wars* brand.

OVERVIEW

Companies have the potential to enhance the value of their brands to customers and the company when they leverage an admired brand. That is, using an existing brand's name (*Star Wars*) on a new market offering (e.g., subsequent *Star Wars* films, comics, games, cereal, clothing, and toasters) allows the brand to expand its market base and unlock *new revenue streams*. Extending the *Star Wars* name to new products also allows *Star Wars* to strengthen and broaden the brand's identity (what the brand does and what it stands for) to customers by creating something we call feedback effects. This strengthened and broadened brand identity allows customers to connect with the brand more frequently and use it more often in their lives, resulting in additional brand-self connections and stronger top-of-mind (TOM) recall, boosting brand admiration further. Although leveraging a brand can heighten brand admiration and achieve financial benefits for the company, sometimes using an existing brand name on a new marketplace offering can hurt the parent brand *and* its new offering. The new offering might be a flop, or it might create confusion (versus clarification) about what the brand stands for. In this case, feedback effects are negative, not positive. Rather than strengthening and broadening the brand's meaning, the brand's meaning is diluted. This chapter and the next discuss why, when, and how companies can benefit (versus being hurt) when they leverage an admired brand.

Why Leverage an Admired Brand?

What does *leveraging* an admired brand mean? If the brand decides to use its name on a new product or service, it is leveraging its name. In essence, a brand uses its name (e.g., Alibaba) as a springboard for introducing a new market offering (e.g., Alibaba Cloud Computing). The more the brand is admired, the more power this springboard has in helping the rapid success of a new market offering. Let's explore two distinct advantages to leveraging an admired brand: *extension effects* and *feedback effects*.

Extension Effects

Developing a new market offering provides new opportunities for added revenue and growth. When companies pursue these opportunities and the new offering includes the parent name, the new offering can add revenue and growth efficiently, with less time and cost to the company than would be true had the new offering not used the parent brand's name. For example, if customers have seen Alibaba's web portals and they know that these portals are easy to use, safe, and reliable, they will probably automatically transfer these same (or similar) associations to Alibaba Cloud Computing without even realizing that they are doing so. Knowing what Alibaba does makes it easier for customers to understand what Alibaba Cloud Computing might be. This means that Alibaba can establish the new offering's identity quickly and with a more limited marketing budget than would be true if the new offering didn't have the Alibaba name.[1] Distribution and retailing costs may also be lower because value-chain partners already know and trust the Alibaba name. We call these opportunities for efficient revenue generation and growth *extension effects* (Table 8.1).

Feedback Effects

Leveraging an admired brand not only has the potential to enhance the success of the new product/service (creating positive extension effects), but the new offering can also feed back into customers' understanding

Table 8.1   Why Leverage an Admired Brand?

Extension Effects: Effects of the Parent Brand on the Extension	
Enhanced Company Value	Opportunities for efficient revenue growth.
Enhanced Customer Understanding	Opportunities to enhance the understanding of the extension benefits quickly.

Feedback Effects: Effects of the Extension on the Parent Brand	
Strengthening Brand Meaning	Deeper understanding of what the brand stands for.
Broadening Brand Meaning	Broader understanding of what the brand stands for.
Additional Brand-Self Connections	Additional opportunities for customers to connect with the brand.
Enhanced TOM Brand Recall	Additional opportunities for customers to remember the brand.

of and admiration for the parent brand.[2] One set of positive *feedback effects* is that the new product can *strengthen* customers' understanding of the brand's identity, while also *broadening* the identity and adding new associations to the brand (Table 8.1). For example, extensions of Caterpillar—to, say, Caterpillar snowplows—would reinforce Caterpillar's identity as a brand that makes powerful machines to move heavy materials. These extensions would also broaden customers' understanding of the contexts in which Caterpillar can be relevant (the brand is useful not just for moving earth, but for moving snow too). Or Alibaba's extensions to cloud computing could reinforce Alibaba's associations to "getting what you want when you want it." They would also broaden the meaning of Alibaba: customers would understand that the company is not just relevant to trade in goods, but also to information access and management.

The strengthening and broadening feedback effects that result from successful extensions, in turn, strengthen customers' admiration of the parent brand. They do so by augmenting the very elements that constitute brand admiration—*brand-self connections* and *TOM brand recall* (see Table 8.1). Going back to the opening example, new *Star Wars*–branded products give customers more opportunities to interact with the *Star Wars* brand, building new brand-self connections. Since the brand name is now linked with more than one product, exposure to one of the brand's products (e.g., *Star Wars* toasters) cues memory for the other products linked to the brand (e.g., *Star Wars* movies). Each can reinforce TOM recall of the other. Stronger brand-self connections and TOM brand recall, in turn, further strengthen brand admiration.

Negative Feedback Effects

While feedback effects can be positive, sometimes using an existing brand name on a new offering can create negative feedback effects, weakening (versus strengthening) customers' understanding of the parent brand's identity and confusing them about what the brand stands for.[3] For example, musical instruments with the Yamaha name (e.g., Yahama pianos) do not appear to be strengthened by using the same name as its motorcycles. It is most likely to cause difficulty in strengthening Yamaha as an admired brand for musical instruments. We call the phenomenon of the failure to either strengthen or maintain the original brand identity *brand dilution*. Admired brands want to avoid brand dilution at all costs. This is why it's so important to think strategically about how to leverage one's brand so that companies realize positive (and not negative) feedback effects.

We continue the discussion about extension and feedback effects in the rest of Chapter 8 and into Chapter 9.

HOW TO LEVERAGE A BRAND: PRODUCT AND BRAND EXTENSION STRATEGIES

How can a brand extend its offering? Companies can leverage their brands by using several broad types of brand naming, one of which we highlight in this chapter (Chapter 10 describes other types): namely, direct extension. Direct extension branding (and other types) can be applied in two different ways: through product extensions and through brand extensions. With *product extensions*, the company uses the parent brand name on a new variant *in the same product category*.[4] With *brand extensions*, the company uses the parent brand name on an offering that's *in a different product category* from the one in which the parent brand currently operates. We explain these strategies next.

Product-Extension Strategies

Let's explore three product-extension strategies that achieve *positive extension* and *feedback effects* (Table 8.2). From a positive extension perspective, each strategy (1) encourages current customers to use the brand more often, (2) keeps them from switching to competing alternatives, and, importantly, (3) helps attract new customers who didn't previously use the brand. From a positive feedback perspective, each strategy also (4) strengthens the brand's identity and its expertise in the product category, (5) while broadening the associations that customers link to the brand. (6) And they all provide more opportunities for customers to interact with the brand, enhancing brand-self connections and TOM brand recall.

Table 8.2 Leveraging Brand Names Using Product Extensions

Types of Product-Extension Strategies	Definition	Examples	Strengthens	Broadens
New Performance Benefit	A new variation of an existing product that offers *new benefits* to customers.	Gatorade introducing low-calorie Gatorade; Boeing introducing a quieter, more fuel-efficient aircraft.	The brand's association with the product category.	Benefits provided by the brand (*why* the brand is used; e.g., no sugar, fewer calories, less noise, etc.).
New Usage Application	A new variation of an existing product that offers *new usage applications* to customers.	John Deere introducing tractors for special terrains; SAP software solutions for health care, insurance, chemicals, industrial machinery, and so on.		Benefits provided by the brand (*where* or *when* the brand is used; e.g., using a John Deere tractor in vineyards).
New Usage Mode	A new variation of an existing product that offers *new modes or ways of using* a product to customers.	Car companies (Tesla, BMW, etc.) introducing driverless cars.		Benefits provided by the brand (*how* the brand is used; e.g., relaxing and resting while being chauffeured to one's destination).

New Performance-Benefit Extension

This strategy strengthens and broadens a brand by giving customers a new reason as to *why* they should buy the brand's offering (and buy more of it). This strategy could appeal to current customers. More significantly, it has a potential to appeal to customers who *don't* currently use the product. Low-calorie Gatorade illustrates this strategy. Here the new benefit is very clear: lower calorie intake. Current customers who want to reduce calorie intake might drink it. But it will most likely also attract new customers who previously didn't buy the original Gatorade drink, given its calorie count. Positive feedback effects are also likely. For example, because Gatorade is expanding its range of sports-drinks offerings, this strategy strengthens the brand's sports-drinks identity, as opposed to emphasizing its calorie content. Customers also add the information about low calories and low carbs to their memory associations with Gatorade, thus broadening their memory associations with the brand. Furthermore, being aware of both versions of the product and making a choice between the two (i.e., drinking low-calorie Gatorade on some occasions and regular Gatorade on others) provides more opportunities for customers to connect with the brand and enhances TOM brand recall, thus strengthening brand admiration for Gatorade.

Let's explore an example in the B2B setting: Boeing might introduce a more fuel-efficient aircraft that helps airlines save costs. Boeing might also introduce a quieter and more spacious aircraft, which enhances customers' in-flight experience. These Boeing airplane variants may motivate companies who buy planes to buy the new Boeing offering. Making a choice between the two types of airplanes and/or using them on different occasions also provide more opportunities for airlines to strengthen brand admiration for Boeing through enhanced brand connection and TOM brand recall. These extensions can also attract airlines that have not previously bought from Boeing, but who want to upgrade customers' in-flight experiences.

New Usage-Application Extension

Here the company introduces a product extension that offers new usage applications, that is, the extension affects *where* or *when* customers are able to use the brand. When the Nintendo Entertainment System (NES) was launched in North America in 1989, people were only able to play Nintendo games at home (the gaming console needed to be linked to a TV). The Nintendo Game Boy, introduced to North America in July 1989, became an instant hit because it made gaming portable. One did not need a TV to enjoy Nintendo. Customers could enjoy playing video games anywhere. This product-extension strategy had a huge impact on *when* people could enjoy gaming and *where* they could use Nintendo products. Moreover, Nintendo's Game Boy attracted an entirely new customer group who wanted entertainment on the go. This strategy clearly reinforced Nintendo's gaming identity. But it also broadened customers' memory associations with Nintendo, because they now also added *portable, on-the-go entertainment* to their memory associations with the brand. And since the extension allowed customers to engage with the brand *when*ever (when waiting for a bus, when on a holiday) and *where*ver (on their cozy sofas at home, on an airplane), it gave customers a greater chance to connect with the brand and recall it more frequently, boosting the two defining properties of brand admiration.

John Deere's four-wheel drive tractors for special and rough terrain lets users maneuver in tight spaces (expanding *where* customers can use the brand) and in adverse contexts (e.g., in bitter cold, ice, or mud). As such, it expanded *when* and *where* customers could rely on the brand. John Deere has also attracted new customers who have specialized tractor needs; for example, customers who own vineyards. Alternatively, consider the myriad of industries in which (*where*) customers can use SAP's specialized software solutions: aerospace and defense, automotive, banking, chemicals, consumer products, health care, and so on. New usage-application extensions help brands expand their market boundaries, and they help companies capture new markets. They also induce positive feedback effects, as was with John Deere's extension.

New Usage-Mode Extension

This product-extension strategy allows customers to use the brand in a new way, by changing *how* customers use the brand. Giving customers new ways of using a brand is potentially a game changer, making this strategy highly effective at attracting new customers and encouraging current customers to use the brand more often. For instance, in the not-too-distant future, we are likely to see groundbreaking new usage-mode extensions in the car industry: driverless cars and trucks for transporting passengers and freight, respectively. While driverless cars will strengthen car brands' transportation identity, they are likely to significantly broaden customers' memory associations in terms of what the brand can do for them (e.g., a transportation mode that provides so much more than merely bringing one from point A to point B). Such transformation of how people use cars in their daily lives is likely to create new touchpoints to connect and recall a particular car brand more frequently, significantly impacting which car brands remain the same, decline, or gain in brand admiration.

Combined Strategies

Using one product-extension strategy does not preclude using another. Using them jointly can increase the chances that the company's offerings cover the entire product market. That is, the company can own the product category by catering to different customer needs for a product. These strategies also allow a company to increase revenue while spreading fixed costs, such as R&D, production, and promotion. And they can help a company preempt market entry by competitors.

Think about Caterpillar's product extensions. Customers may use Caterpillar because its product extensions offer a new *performance benefit*, such as particularly lightweight, fuel-efficient loaders or dozers (e.g., saving costs on fuel, meeting environmental targets set by governments, etc.). Or they may use Caterpillar because its extensions offer a new *usage application* that affects *when* (e.g., summer, winter, etc.) and *where* (e.g., underground, steep mountains, etc.) Caterpillar can be used. Finally, new *usage-mode* product extensions, such as loaders and dozers with remote-control capability, give customers a chance to use the brand in new ways. In addition to strengthening customers' association with the product category, these extensions broaden the set of benefits (*why*, *when*, *where*, and *how*) that customers associate with Caterpillar, thus adding new memory associations to the brand. These extensions impact brand admiration by reinforcing its central subcomponents: brand-self connections and TOM brand recall.

Brand-Extension Strategies

With brand-extension strategies, the company introduces a new offering in a *different* product category from the one it currently competes in. We define five such strategies (Table 8.3). Each helps *efficient growth* and also (1) *strengthens the core benefits* customers associate with the brand's identity, and (2) *broadens* the meaning of the brand by linking it to a more diverse array of product categories.

Note that brand extensions strengthen and broaden the parent brand in ways opposite from the ways product extensions do. *Product extensions strengthen the brand's association with the product category and broaden the benefits associated with it. Brand extensions strengthen the brand's benefits and broaden the product categories (and benefits) to which it is associated.* We discuss each strategy below.

Joint Consumption–Based Extension

Here the new offering is designed to be used *with* the parent brand; each enhances the usage experience of the other, creating positive extension and feedback effects. For instance, Doritos dips may be perceived to taste better when used with Doritos chips. Intel processors may be perceived to function faster, more reliably, and in a more energy-efficient manner when used together with Intel's chipsets. If the brand is highly admired, its jointly consumer brand extension is readily accepted by customers and may also be able to command a premium price. This strategy also reduces promotion costs, since the jointly consumed products can be promoted together for the same customers.

Perceived positive benefits from using the extension strengthen the parent brand's appeal on a particular benefit or set of benefits, creating positive feedback effects. Google's e-mail (Gmail) and Google Calendar, for instance, work well together (each enhancing the usefulness of the other), strengthening customers' *enabling benefits* associated with Google. In B2B and B2C markets, joint extensions are often seen as augmented service and product solutions, allowing a brand to provide an entire ecosystem of product/service solutions relevant to customer needs. Brand extensions based on joint consumption can also enhance customers' memory associations to a brand's *enticing benefits*.

Table 8.3 Leveraging Brand Names Using Brand Extensions

Types of Brand-Extension Strategies	Definition	Examples	Strengthens	Broadens
Joint Consumption–Based	An extension that is used jointly with the parent brand to enhance the brand's 3Es benefits.	Google's e-mail (Gmail) and Google Calendar; Hello Kitty toy and Hello Kitty blanket.		Product category to which the brand is relevant (*how* brand is used; with which other products).
Consumption Alternation–Based	An extension that provides the same benefits as the parent brand but in different contexts.	Kellogg's cereals and breakfast bars; Samsung Galaxy smartphone and Samsung laptop; Red Bull energy drink and chocolate.	Brand's enabling, enticing, or enriching benefits.	Product category to which the brand is relevant (*when* or *where* brand can be used).
Substitution-Based	An extension that substitutes for the original one and serves as a fallback option to hedge against technological obsolescence.	IBM computers and IBM outsourcing services.		Product category to which the brand is relevant (*why* brand is used).

(*continued*)

Table 8.3 (*continued*)

Types of Brand-Extension Strategies	Definition	Examples	Strengthens	Broadens
Feature-Based	An extension that shares a highly regarded product feature.	Rolls-Royce car (engines) extending to Rolls-Royce aircraft engine.	Key product features	Product category to which a parent brand's key feature(s) is relevant.
Concept-Based	An extension that makes the brand stand for something broader than what was true before the extension.	Ghostly (music) extending to coffee beans, notebooks, and art prints; Amazon (books) extending to videos, music, and the like.	Brand concept or image	Product category which is relevant to the concept or image of the parent brand.

For example, customers may feel good or feel right when using a Hello Kitty plush cuddle toy while sleeping with their very own Hello Kitty bedsheets and blankets.[5] Stiegl beer may taste better when enjoyed in Stiegl's signature curved pilsner glass. People may think that Starbucks coffee is more delicious in a Starbuck collector's cup with the famous mermaid logo on it. Or Harley Davidson motorcycles, helmets, and other branded products may feel right because their joint usage augments the brand's *enrichment benefits* (e.g., symbolizing one's status as a member of the Harley Owners Group). Wearing a Kawasaki helmet wouldn't have the same effect. In addition, memory associations with the parent brand are broadened through the joint consumption-based brand extensions because the parent brand becomes relevant to the new extension product category and the new extension through joint usage.

The feedback effects of the joint consumption-based brand extensions increase each time the two products are used together. Joint usage occasions deepen personal connections with the brand through its enhancing effects on the 3Es, as noted earlier. The number and strength of memory associations with the brand should also be augmented, enhancing TOM brand recall. By enhancing brand-self connections and TOM brand recall, brand extensions based on joint consumption can make the brand even more highly admired than before.

Once customers are accustomed to using two products from a brand together, and once they believe that usage of one enhances the usage experience of another, it's more difficult for them to consider replacements. This creates psychological inertia, which demotivates brand switching. Just think about Apple's Mac, iPod, iPad, and iPhone ecosystem, and how easy it is to save, share, and do other things with data across these devices. Or consider that customers want to use Hello Kitty toys and blankets, or Harley Davidson helmets and jackets, together. Switching to another brand that doesn't provide this ecosystem might seem daunting to customers. Brand extensions based on joint consumption can therefore create very *powerful brand lock-in*.

Consumption Alternation–Based Extension

Here the new offering serves the same general need as the parent, but its use can be alternated with that of the parent. Why alternate?

Typically, it's because alternation provides variety or convenience, or it just seems to make more sense to use one product in one context and the other in a different context. For example, eating cereal for breakfast all the time can be boring. People may get sick and tired of it. Alternating Kellogg's cereals with Kellogg's breakfast sandwiches or breakfast bars creates more variety in usage, avoiding brand fatigue and burnout. Moreover, customers might find it more convenient to use Kellogg's breakfast bars at certain times since they can eat them anywhere (at home, on the go, at the office). But Kellogg's breakfast sandwiches or cereals may be preferred at home.

Critically, this strategy helps keep current customers from switching to competing alternatives by preempting competitors who might otherwise offer variety or convenience that the current brand doesn't offer. It also attracts new customers. The parent brand (Kellogg's) and the brand extension (Kellogg's breakfast bars) aren't likely to be used together, as with joint consumption–based extensions. But because they both have the parent's name in common, in addition to strong extension effects, the extension creates opportunities for strong feedback effects. Extension to the breakfast bar and sandwich categories *strengthens* Kellogg's core association with breakfast. Kellogg's identity is also substantially *expanded* from cereals to breakfast bars and breakfast sandwiches. Over time, customers recall Kellogg's not just in response to breakfast bars and breakfast cereals, but also with respect to the general category of breakfast foods. To the extent that this type of brand extension enhances opportunities for variety, it is more likely to generate greater brand-self connections and TOM brand recall.

Consider Samsung's big screen Galaxy smartphone that can be used alternately with Samsung's super lightweight laptop. While customers might buy both products, using one might make more sense in one situation (say, using the laptop when one needs to prepare fancy presentation materials) while the other product might make more sense in another (say, using the smartphone to listen to music while walking). Red Bull's Fliegerschokolade (or pilot's chocolate) is another example. Its natural caffeine boost does what a Red Bull drink does, but uses a different method to provide the caffeine. Since both brands fulfill the same general benefit, customers are likely to use one or the other, not both at the same time.[6]

Substitution-Based Brand Extensions

Here the brand extension serves as *a fallback option* in the event that customers no longer favor the brand's original product. This is often the case in technology-based markets, in which new solutions hedge against the original product's obsolescence.[7] Many brands have failed because the brand owners haven't considered or taken advantage of this option. For example, Kodak's unwillingness to move forward with digital photography left it vulnerable when digital cameras changed the playing field. Sony was unwilling to cannibalize the sales of its compact discs (CDs) and so failed to introduce MP3 technology. That failure left Sony exposed to Apple's hugely successful iPod. Xerox failed to commercialize inventions such as its personal computer, word processor, and Ethernet for fear of cannibalizing the sales of its printer and photocopier divisions.

Like the other brand-extension types just described, substitution-based brand extensions can grow efficiently by attracting a sizable number of *existing customers* and by attracting a sizable number of *new customers* who did not use the initial product. Substitution-based brand extensions also offer strong feedback effects. The improved substitute strengthens the positive memory associations customers have with a brand. When successful, this strategy can also broaden memory associations and *rejuvenate a parent brand, ensuring that it remains relevant to customers over time*. Together the substitute enhances brand-self connections and TOM brand recall, augmenting the parent brand and enhancing brand admiration. Not all substitutable extensions *completely* replace the brand's original product. For example, instead of investing in IBM computers, customers can purchase IBM's IT outsourcing service. The option of using the IBM outsourcing service provides an additional purchase opportunity for customers whose needs may not require its in-house IT systems. IBM secures additional revenue from these customers.

Feature-Based Brand Extension

Here a feature of the parent brand that is well known and highly regarded is leveraged to a new product category in which the feature is also relevant and valued.[8] Product features are concrete attributes of a product. When Rolls-Royce extended its name to aircraft engines, airline companies readily transferred Rolls-Royce's reliable, high-performance car engine features to reliable, high-performance aircraft engines. Put differently, airline companies viewed the feature of Rolls-Royce's engines positively because the brand's expertise in producing a feature (reliable, quality automobile engines) was extremely important in the extension category. Whereas product extensions allow companies to own (dominate) the product category, feature extensions allow companies to own the feature for which the parent brand is known (e.g., engine reliability and quality, etc.).[9] Arm & Hammer's brand extensions to toothpaste, laundry detergent, saline wound wash, and other products (see Chapter 9) all use Arm & Hammer's deodorizing and cleaning features, yet in entirely new product categories.

A strong association between the brand name and the feature makes it *efficient* for companies to grow and extend the brand name to other product categories, significantly expanding the brand's customer base into areas in which the feature is also important—even if the feature is in an entirely different product category. It also helps strengthen customers' memory associations with the brand's feature (Rolls-Royce reliable, quality engines) and broadens them (Rolls-Royce engines can also be used in airplanes). Rolls-Royce's feature extension unlocked a completely new customer base, namely aircraft manufacturers and airlines around the world. Rolls-Royce has been so successful in the aircraft engine market that its aircraft business dwarfs the revenue generated from its luxury car business. In fact, Rolls-Royce is now the second-largest aircraft engine manufacturer in the world. Imagine how much growth and profit Rolls-Royce would have lost had it only manufactured automobiles. By tying the brand name to the feature and to different product categories, the brand creates greater opportunities for customers to connect with the brand, and the brand becomes known as the *exemplar* (or best example) of that core feature. When they think about the feature (e.g., cleaning and deodorizing), the brand (e.g., Arm & Hammer) is the first one to be retrieved from memory.

Concept-Based Brand Extensions

Here companies leverage a well known and highly regarded concept tied to a brand's identity and extend it to a different product category for which the concept is likely to be highly valued by customers. Brand concepts are abstract meanings associated with the brand's identity (e.g., think about Hermès and luxury, or Hello Kitty and kawaii—cuteness). A concept emerges from a collection of features that share the central characteristics of the concept. For example, customers might regard a particular brand as upscale because it is associated with a high price, expensive-looking design, prestigious stores, and professional service employees. Abstract associations give the parent brand room to maneuver when it wants to extend to other product categories. This is so because customers see the extensions as fitting naturally under the more inclusive parent brand name. For example, Hermès, which began as a saddle company and extended to other leather products (bags, purses, and wallets) and more (scarves, watches, perfume, and jewelry), has retained its associations of fine, handcrafted, quality goods. These goods also convey high fashion, sophistication, and an upper-class lifestyle. In contrast to joint consumption-based brand extensions, concept-based brand extensions do not have to be used together during consumption.

Notably, concept-based brand extensions need not have any one particular feature-based relationship with the parent brand. For example, one can accept Armani's sunglasses and Armani's suits although sunglasses and suits don't have the same features. Prestige or fashion brands that signify a certain lifestyle (such as Tiffany, Rolex, Chanel, etc.) and brands that symbolize group membership can all grow efficiently and generate strong feedback effects through concept-based brand extensions.

Ghostly International is an example of a brand that has leveraged its name through concept-based extensions. Ghostly has grown from a boutique music record label to a globally successful platform that showcases musicians and music genres from around the world. Beyond music, Ghostly International also sells notebooks, coffee beans, gallery-quality art prints, messenger bags, and more. Why? Because Ghostly wants to first build and then solidify its identity as a hipster lifestyle brand—"an arbiter of fine goods" for the "taste-conscious cultural consumer." The unique, artisan back story of each product, whether it is a leather wallet or a messenger bag, is shared with the brand's customers in vivid detail. The brand presents itself more as a community of like-minded consumers than a shop selling music. By carefully sourcing these diverse products, Ghostly can build relationships with its customers who care about provenance. The offering strengthens Ghostly's hipster identity, and it gives consumers more opportunities to connect with the Ghostly brand and relate it to who they are. Moreover, each product sold by Ghostly can serve as a retrieval cue for other Ghostly-branded goods.

The examples we've just mentioned reflect abstract symbolic brand concepts that leverage the enrichment benefits (e.g., a lifestyle, a badge of group membership) of one product (Ghostly music) to others (other categories that convey the hipster identity). However, these abstract brand concepts can also be based on enablement benefits. For example, Amazon has extended its business from solely books to all manner of product categories, making the concept of "shopping convenience and selection" salient. This concept is activated not only by the diverse array of products Amazon offers (creating the shopping convenience identity) but also by the identity-consistent search functions (by brand, by attribute, by price, by reviews), easy payment, and seamless product returns that Amazon enables.

Abstract concepts can also be based on enticement benefits. IMAX, known for its immersive theatre experience technology, could extend the IMAX name to other areas related to immersive sound experiences, such as the development of sound systems, sound insulation, and TVs and headphones, that allow an immersive experience from the comfort of one's home or on the go.

KEY TAKEAWAYS

1. Leveraging an existing admired brand name by using product or brand extensions provides new and efficient

revenue-generating opportunities (i.e., using minimal time and resources), resulting in strong *extension effects*.

2. Successful extensions augment brand admiration through positive *feedback effects*. They strengthen and broaden the meaning of the parent brand, which, in turn, strengthen brand-self connections and TOM brand recall (i.e., the core properties of brand admiration).

3. The three product-extension strategies shown in Table 8.2 strengthen customers' associations of the brand with the product category in which the brand competes. They also broaden the benefits customers associate with the brand.

4. The five types of brand extensions described in Table 8.3 strengthen customers' understanding of the brand's identity. They also broaden customers' brand associations with the parent brand to include other product categories that are either product need-related, feature-related, or concept-related.

WHAT ABOUT YOUR BRAND?

1. Which of the product extensions and brand extensions does your brand use?

2. Do the product and brand extensions that you currently use create both strong extension *and* positive feedback effects?

3. What types of product and brand extensions might you use to leverage the impact of your (highly admired) brand?

NOTES

1. David A. Aaker, *Brand Portfolio Strategy* (New York: The Free Press, 2004).
2. Others have called these effects *spillover effects*. Subramanian Balachander and Sanjoy Ghose, "Reciprocal Spillover Effects: A Strategic Benefit of Brand Extensions," *Journal of Marketing* 67, no. 1 (2003): 4–13.
3. Chris Pullig, Carolyn J. Simmons, and Richard G. Netemeyer, "Brand Dilution: When Do New Brands Hurt Existing Brands?" *Journal of Marketing* 70, no. 2 (2006): 52–66; Deborah Roedder John, Barbara Loken,

and Christopher Joiner, "The Negative Impact of Extensions: Can Flagship Products Be Diluted?," *Journal of Marketing* 62, no. 1 (1998): 19–32; Sandra J. Milberg, C. Whan Park, and Michael S. McCarthy, "Managing Negative Feedback Effects Associated with Brand Extensions: The Impact of Alternative Branding Strategies," *Journal of Consumer Psychology* 6, no. 2 (1997): 119–140; Sanjay Sood and Kevin Lane Keller, "The Effects of Brand Name Structure on Brand Extension Evaluations and Parent Brand Dilution," *Journal of Marketing Research* 49, no. 3 (2012): 373–382.

4. We use the term *product extension* rather than *line extension*. The latter is frequently used to refer to an extension in terms of price (e.g., a high-end versus a low-end line). Product extensions go beyond this narrow definition, as we discuss in this chapter.

5. Ryan Rahinel and Joseph P. Redden, "Brands as Product Coordinators: Matching Brands Make Joint Consumption Experiences More Enjoyable," *Journal of Consumer Research* 39, no. 6 (2013): 1290–1299.

6. Intended brand extension strategies may not be perceived by customers in the manner intended. For example, managers may intend to have Red Bull chocolate and Red Bull drinks used on alternative usage occasions; however, customers may end up substituting one for the other instead.

7. Larry Downes and Paul F. Nunes, "Big-Bang Disruption," *Harvard Business Review* 91, no. 3 (2013): 44–56. Note that brands can create substitution-based products without using brand extensions but instead with a standalone, new brand. In this case, however, they will not benefit from positive feedback and extensions effects.

8. C. Whan Park, Sandra Milberg, and Robert Lawson, "Evaluation of Brand Extensions: The Role of Product Feature Similarity and Brand Concept Consistency," *Journal of Consumer Research* 18, no. 2 (1991): 185–193.

9. Paul M. Herr, Peter H. Farquhar, and Russell H. Fazio, "Impact of Dominance and Relatedness on Brand Extensions," *Journal of Consumer Psychology* 5, no. 2 (1996): 135–159.

CHAPTER 9

Leveraging Brand Admiration: Implementation Issues

W hat might your brand stand for tomorrow?

INTRODUCTION

Leveraging a brand so that customers connect with it in a more frequent, more deep, and more engaging way creates positive feedback effects that strengthen brand admiration (Chapter 8). Not expanding on these connection opportunities limits the brand's efficient growth and reinforcement of customers' brand admiration. But will these positive feedback and extension effects always be realized? What should companies consider before deciding about whether to use product and brand extensions and which ones to use? Think about the following example: Hello Kitty, the beloved kitten adored by customers around the world, recently launched a health clinic in Hong Kong. Everything from Band-Aids to scales carries images of the charming kitten with the bow. This move might seem quite strange at first. How do cute toys fit with health? They seem quite removed from the cold, sterile environment and medical expertise typically associated with doctors and clinics. Customers may wonder whether Hello Kitty has the gravitas and the expertise to extend to this divergent service category. Will Hello Kitty fall victim to the brand dilution observed with other (low-fit) extension failures, such as Bic underwear, Jell-O cola, and Zippo golf balls?

But after one thinks about it, an association with health clinics might actually be appropriate for the Hello Kitty brand. Hello Kitty delights with its sense-pleasing and heartwarming design. Wouldn't one want compassion, empathy, and heartwarming benefits in a clinic? People who visit health clinics are sick and anxious. Associating the clinic with the warm feelings of the Hello Kitty brand may calm patients and make them feel at ease. Moreover, Hello Kitty's heartwarming benefits are atypical of most sterile health clinics. Using the Hello Kitty name in a health-related context could induce strong WOM because it's so unexpected. Additionally, if Hello Kitty is successful in the area of health clinics, the brand may be in a better position to extend the Hello Kitty name to other categories associated with health (e.g., Hello Kitty antistress blankets) and well-being (e.g., Hello Kitty body massagers and spas). Was Hello Kitty's move into health clinics a good one? How can one tell? In this chapter, we address these questions by describing *when* (under what conditions) companies should consider pursuing product and brand extensions.

OVERVIEW

Chapter 8 suggested that admired brands can use product and brand extensions to achieve efficient growth (*extension effects*) and to create stronger and broader memory associations with a brand (*feedback effects*). But not all brand-leveraging strategies are successful. More often than not, extensions don't create the desired effects. Brand managers therefore need to understand *when* these extension strategies should be used. In this chapter, we explore the marketplace and extension characteristics that can impact the success of specific product- and brand-extension strategies. A lot of research suggests that successful extensions must somehow fit the parent brand. But low-fit extensions (such as Hello Kitty and health clinics) can sometimes be even more successful. We explain when and why. Finally, we consider how product and brand extensions should be sequenced over time.

WHEN ARE PRODUCT AND BRAND EXTENSIONS MOST LIKELY TO BE SUCCESSFUL?

To maximize extension and feedback effects, companies should consider the guidelines described below.

Company Considerations

The following company considerations are relevant regardless of which product or brand-extension strategy one follows.

Degree of Brand Admiration

It's less costly and more time efficient for companies to market an extension when the parent brand is already admired (based on strong trust, love, and respect). When the brand isn't admired, customers may be uncertain about the extension's benefits and how much they will like it. When the parent brand's admiration is very weak, it's better not to use an extension. Instead, the new product should be given a name different from the parent brand. It's possible that a less-admired brand could introduce a successful brand extension, but it will not yield the marketing efficiencies that an extension to an admired brand can realize.

Extension Differentiation

Using the 3Es, extensions should be meaningfully distinguished from the parent brand. Customers must understand *why* they should purchase the extension(s) in the first place. Otherwise, there's no reason for customers to buy the extension. Diet Coke is different from Coke because it has no sugar. Maersk's Triple-E shipment service is different from other shipping options because it offers improved shipment capacity and reduces CO_2 emissions. Extension differentiation is particularly important for product extensions. If there is no significant differentiation between a potential extension and the parent brand, it may be better to use the value-enhancement strategies discussed in Chapter 7 to grow the brand (e.g., does a company really need to market 18 different types of shampoos?).

Extension Cannibalization

Target markets should be distinctively different to minimize the extension's cannibalization of the parent brand, as is true with FedEx, whose air and ocean freight shipment services clearly cater to different customer groups. The only exceptions to this general guideline are

(1) when the extension tries to satisfy customers' desires for variety (as with consumption alternation–based extensions), or (2) when the company is developing a substitution-based brand extension so as to rejuvenate the parent brand. For example, different types of breakfast cereals give customers a way of fulfilling variety-seeking needs without switching to a competitor's brand. Or Intel might want its cloud computing services to cannibalize its solid-state data center products because it wants to retire the old product and have the brand stand for something new.

Resources

All extensions require some investment of talent, time, and money on behalf of the company. It's important to realistically assess the financial, temporal, and human resources needed to successfully develop and market the extension. Spreading resources too thin risks undermining the success of the extension, as well as the parent brand. Japanese electronics company Sharp is facing financial difficulty, due in part to its proliferation of product and brand extensions.

Competitor Considerations

Brand managers need to check the following competitor considerations carefully when considering the use of product or brand extensions.

Unique Benefits in the Extension Category

Extension and feedback effects are most significant when the brand offers unique and relevant benefits (the 3Es) that competitor brands in the extension category don't or can't offer. As with any new product, the extension must be differentiated from competing offerings, and it must provide value to customers (see Chapters 5 and 7). Apple's iPhone introduced such significant new benefits that it created a new category of cell phones called *smartphones*. In the best of all worlds, this type of extension changes how customers think about the extension category and what benefits products can (or should) offer. The Apple watch has had only a lukewarm marketplace response, perhaps because it didn't provide a sufficiently unique configuration of the 3Es that would resonate with customers in the smart-watch category.

Market Competitiveness

Companies should consider the number and strength of existing and *potential* competitors in the extension category.[1] For example, FedEx, DHL, UPS, and even Maersk need to be watchful of e-commerce giants, such as Amazon and Alibaba, who plan to offer their own delivery services.

Customer Considerations

Several customer considerations also affect whether or not companies should develop product and brand extensions.

Market Size

Extensions should only be pursued if added revenue from growth exceeds added unit costs in the long-term. Companies need to ask what the current and future potential size of the customer pool and customers' degree of receptivity to the new extension will be. While large markets are potentially attractive from the standpoint of brand extensions, companies should also consider future market size and avoid being *myopic*. Foxconn, the world's largest electronics contract manufacturer, started its computer components business when the outsourcing market was small. Today, as a supplier to brands such as Apple, Sony, Nintendo, Microsoft, and the like it manufactures a stunning 40 percent of *all* consumer electronics products sold globally.

Perceived Fit with the Parent Brand

Finally, there should be something that meaningfully connects the parent brand with the extension. Will a Bic computer-tablet stylus, Bic perfume, or Bic underwear make sense to customers? When customers don't see a meaningful connection between the brand (e.g., Bic) and its extension (e.g., underwear), they often respond poorly to the extension.[2] Therefore, customers should see *some* type of connection, or *fit*, between a parent brand and its extension. We'll say more about fit shortly.

Considerations Relevant to Specific Product- and Brand-Extension Strategies

Consider the following points before adopting a *particular type* of product or brand extension to help grow the brand.

Product Extensions

With product extensions, the goal is *to own (dominate) the product category* in which the parent brand currently competes. To achieve this goal, brand managers should market brands that offer different performance benefits, different usage applications, and/or usage modes that meet the diverse needs of customers in the category. For example, SAP offers industry-specific software for customers in the automotive, banking, health care, and transportation industries. Its product extensions employ configurations of the 3Es that give users the exact solutions and functionality they need—*where, when*, and *how* they need it. When customers think about the business software category, SAP is often the first brand that comes to mind.

Joint Consumption–Based Brand Extensions

Joint consumption–based brand extensions should enhance the consumption experience. They complement the brand's original product to mutually reinforce each other's benefit to customers. Their goal is to *own a certain need category* (breakfast need, efficiency need, etc.). Aunt Jemima pancakes and its syrup go together and can make the brand more salient for customers' breakfast need. Or consider Kuka's industrial robots and intelligent robot software for a safe and efficient human-machine interaction in the B2B market. In this case the extension product (software) made the use of the original product safer, more convenient, more efficient, thereby helping grow the market for industrial robots substantially. Another example is Stahl industrial driers and sound absorbers, making for a less noisy, more pleasant usage of the industrial driers when used together. Unless a brand has a sizable number of customers who believe it's first in class, joint consumption–based brand extensions might not offer significant extension and feedback effects. It's more difficult to convince customers that their consumption experience will be enhanced when the extension is from a mediocre brand.

Consumption Alternation–Based Brand Extensions

Consumption alternation–based brand extensions allow customers to meet their needs by using different versions of the brand interchangeably over time. These work best when the goal is to *own a certain need category* (but in a different way from the joint consumption–based brand extensions). The only way this strategy works is if the brand extension can truly provide the parent brand's benefits in different contexts. Cisco's data center solutions and cloud service solutions are interchangeable, making Cisco a one-stop solution for its business clients' data storage needs. It also gives business customers the flexibility to use different data storage solutions from a single trusted partner (Cisco).

Substitution-Based Brand Extensions

Substitution-based brand extensions work best when the goal is to *own a certain need category* (but in a different way from the above two brand extensions). Porsche Consulting Academy offers advice on how to build effective internal consulting teams that facilitate change and operational excellence. The Academy offers the very service that lets clients do future consulting jobs themselves (without relying on external consulting providers, including Porsche Consulting). These strategies are also appropriate in converging and/or rapidly changing markets. Internet, satellite, electronics, and car companies are competing in ways previously thought unimaginable. When considering substitution-based extensions, companies need to take a broad view of their markets and avoid marketing myopia.

Feature-Based Extensions

With feature-based extensions, the brand aims to *own a specific feature*. Feature-based extensions are advantageous when the company has a patented technology for which it is known and in which it has made a significant investment. By using the feature in other categories, the company can amortize its investment over several distinct products. Feature-based extensions can also make the company less dependent on the market conditions (e.g., the growth rate, the competition) of the parent product category.

Dupont's Kevlar brand, for example, provides a strong, lightweight, protective fiber that is used in ballistic protection products (e.g., bulletproof vests), cut protection products (industrial gloves and other body armor), foot protection products (shoes and socks), theft protection products (cable locks), and leak protection products, among others. Expanding to new and distinct markets has allowed the company to significantly expand its customer base.

Concept-Based Extensions

The primary goal of concept-based brand extensions is to *own a particular concept or idea*. They are most relevant when the identity (or meaning) of an admired brand can be abstracted to stand for something more general. Admired lifestyle brands (such as Ralph Lauren, Nike, and Red Bull), prestige brands (such as Tiffany and Rolex), fashion brands (such as Versace and Michael Kors), brands symbolic of group membership (such as Harley Davidson and *Star Wars*), and décor brands (such as Martha Stewart) can all benefit from concept-based brand extensions, because these brands want to reflect a certain style or sensibility. The impact of concept-based extensions is greater when the categories to which the general concept extends are growing.

Fit Considerations

Earlier, we suggested that brand extensions are often more successful if they somehow fit the identity or meaning of the parent brand. High (low) fit means that customers can (can't) find something (anything) that connects the parent brand and its extension. Bic might extend more readily from pens to a tablet stylus than to underwear because a pen and a stylus have similar forms (shapes) and functionalities. The connection to underwear is less clear. High fit seems to facilitate the transfer of positive feelings and memory associations about the parent brand to the extension. The fact that these memory associations and feelings transfer readily to the extension is what creates positive extension effects.[3]

Low fit does not mean that the extensions are *inconsistent with* or *contradict* the parent brand.[4] One would never want high-end, luxury brands such as Bentley and Prada to enter a low-end market of the same product category, or to make cheap sunglasses, perfume, or travel bags with the same brand name. Instead, low fit means that there is no immediate basis on which customers can see a connection between the parent and its extension. The product and brand-extension strategies we described in Chapter 8 are based on a high fit with the parent brand in different ways, as we'll describe next.

Product Category Fit

With product extensions, high fit means that the new offering *fits the product category*. Product extensions that involve new performance benefits, new usage applications, and new usage modes in the same category all have a high category fit because they are in the same product category as the parent brand. Intel processors for laptops and Intel processors for smartphones are both types of processors. The product category is the same (processors), even if the specific benefits (3 Es) that each extension provides are different and geared toward different market segments.

Usage Fit

Joint consumption–based brand extensions are based on high *usage fit*. The jointly consumed products may be in completely different product categories and have completely different features. An Airbus aircraft is a physical product (an aircraft). The Airbus flight operations service is an operations solutions service. They each require different expertise and know-how (building an aircraft is very different from offering a service that makes aircraft fleet usage more efficient). But since aircraft and flight operations services are often used together, they have high usage fit.

Benefit Fit

Consumption alternation–based or substitution-based brand extensions have strong *benefit fit*, meaning that the parent brand and brand extension meet the same cluster of customer needs. For example, Red Bull's energy drink and Red Bull's chocolate both boost energy. Moreover, usage fit is not high, since one would (should) probably not consume Red Bull chocolate together with Red Bull energy drinks.

Feature Fit

Feature-based extensions are based on high *feature fit*. The feature is important to all categories in which it is used. Kevlar body armor, gloves, cables, and footwear make sense because they all share the fabric protection and impenetrability offered by Kevlar fabrics.

Concept Fit

With high concept fit the parent brand and the brand extension share a common identity. Chanel, with its upscale and sophisticated identity, fits well with handbags, shoes, and suits, but not with running shoes, backpacks, and sweatpants. Nike, with its athletics identity, fits well with running shoes, backpacks, and sweatpants, but not with handbags, high-heeled shoes, and suits. Goldman Sachs, with its professional investment-management identity, fits well with investment advisory and trading, but not with cinema movies, dating websites, and music.

IS HIGH FIT ALWAYS NECESSARY?

Are there any situations in which low-fit brand extensions can benefit companies? Consider Virgin, which uses its name on apparently unrelated businesses, such as Virgin Trains and Virgin Active Gyms. Will Hello Kitty's introduction of a Hello Kitty health care clinic dilute or augment the parent brand? Are there any situations in which low-fit brands can have strong and positive extension and feedback effects? Some recent research suggests that the answer is yes.

We find that low-fit brand extensions can yield positive extension effects and *even more positive feedback effects* than high-fit extensions, but

Table 9.1   Strategic Use of Low-Fit Brand Extensions

When to Use a Low-Fit Extension	How It Works	With What Effects	
		Extension Effects	Feedback Effects
• Brand is admired. • Extension offers innovative benefits.	• Customers are surprised. • Customers are curious about the relationship between the parent and extension. • Customers are motivated to think deeply about the extension (and its innovative benefits).	• Customers like the low-fit extension as much as the high-fit extension.	• Stronger parent brand identity. • Broader parent brand identity. • Enhanced brand admiration (brand-self connection and TOM recall). • Openness to other low-fit extensions (future growth opportunities).

this effect only holds under the conditions shown in Table 9.1. Specifically, the parent brand must be admired and the benefits that are offered in the extension category must be innovative.

Strong Brand Admiration

Admired brands have the reputation and credibility to pull off the use of a low-fit extension. When brands are not strongly admired, customers are not even sure that they like the brand's current benefits (3Es), let alone its extension's.

It might cost more to promote a low-fit (versus a high-fit) extension because a company needs to explain itself to customers (who may ask themselves why on earth a company would introduce a low-fit extension). But these promotion costs can be offset by the information-processing benefits that low-fit extensions enjoy.

Specifically, when an admired brand uses a low-fit extension, customers are surprised. Surprise motivates customers to think more deeply about what connects the parent brand (e.g., Hello Kitty) and its extension (e.g., Hello Kitty health clinics). That deeper processing should increase the impact of the company's communication efforts and help customers identify a meaningful basis on which the parent brand and its extension are related (e.g., care, tenderness, compassion). Low fit has another benefit. The connection between an admired parent brand and a low-fit extension is memorable and distinctive because it is surprising. Because customers are surprised by the brand extension, they might tell others about it and talk about why the extension makes sense.

Innovative Benefits in the Extension Category

Our research shows that feedback effects to the parent brand from low-fit extensions are positive *only if* the brand extension offers *innovative benefits* in the extension category. A Hello Kitty clinic that is just like any other health clinic doesn't offer anything distinctive. But a Hello Kitty clinic that has comfy plush Hello Kitty chairs, cuddly Hello Kitty blankets, and pillows and smiling staff dressed in Hello Kitty uniforms creates a unique and distinctive experience. Interestingly, we find that low fit does not dilute the highly admired parent brand's identity when the brand offers innovative benefits in the extension category. Instead, the brand's core associations (Hello Kitty as heartwarming) are reinforced.

Even more significant is that when benefits in the extension category are innovative, a low-fit extension can *broaden the identity* of the admired brand. Because the low-fit extension is surprising, and since customers can eventually figure out what connects the low-fit extension with the parent, customers' understanding of what the parent brand stands for is expanded to include the new extension and its benefits.[5] For example, by extending the Hello Kitty brand to health clinics, customers may associate Hello Kitty with more than just cute toys and accessorizing. Instead, they may associate it with a broader benefit—*comfort and care*—whether one is sick or well.

This broadened understanding of the brand provides opportunities to build additional brand self-connections and strengthen TOM brand memory, resulting in stronger brand admiration. It also makes customers more open to other extensions that fit with this broadened identity. For example, Hello Kitty's extension to health clinics opens the brand up to a potentially wide array of extension categories related to comfort or care. Each new extension gives the company more maneuverability in terms of the product categories to which it might extend next. Customers would no longer limit their understanding of Hello Kitty to a narrowly defined context or category. Instead, they would accommodate any product relevant to the broadened identity of the brand.

Our research shows that customers like low-fit extensions of admired brands as much as they do high-fit extensions, but for different reasons. The connection between the high-fit extension and the parent brand is obvious and easily accepted. However, an extension to a high-fit category creates no psychological curiosity or surprise that motivates customers to think about the brand more deeply. In contrast, the low-fit extension creates surprise, and it motivates customers to find a connection between the parent brand and the brand extension. Finding a connection is pleasurable because it resolves what initially seemed to be a puzzle. The connection also provides new meaning to the brand and gives customers more reasons to like the parent brand.

Companies can't frequently utilize low-fit brand extensions, because the conditions under which they are effective are limited to (1) admired brands that (2) have innovative benefits in the extension category. Brands that are not admired should not use a low-fit extension, even if the benefits it offers in the extension category are innovative. Instead, they are better off extending to high-fit extension categories.

ACHIEVING OPTIMAL EXTENSION AND FEEDBACK EFFECTS OVER TIME

Many companies offer not just one type of product or brand extension, but several. How should companies decide what types of extensions to offer first, and which might be offered later in the brand's evolution? The issue here is how various product- and brand-extension strategies should be *sequenced over time*.[6] Both product and brand extensions aim to keep current customers and to attract new ones in the most efficient way possible (creating extension effects). Equally important is the effect of extensions on what customers know and think about the parent brand (feedback effects).

Sequencing Considerations

Is it better for companies to use certain types of extensions before they use others? Let's consider these issues next.

Value Enhancement before Product or Brand Extensions

Product and brand extensions create the strongest extension and feedback effects when the parent brand is admired. Hence, before opting for any product or brand extension, brand managers should do as much as they can to build trust, love, and respect for their brands, following the ideas in Chapters 3 through 6. They should also continue to enhance the brand's value to customers following the value-enhancement strategies described in Chapter 7. Before using product or brand extensions, brand managers should invest the time and effort to ensure that their existing brands offer value to customers, particularly as the competitive marketplace evolves.

> Recommendation 1: Invest in building brand admiration before developing product or brand extensions.

Product Extension before Brand Extension

Product extensions solidify the parent brand's relevance and competence in the category at hand. They provide additional reasons as to why customers should trust, love, and respect the brand in the parent category. With product extensions companies can take advantage of operating resources like manufacturing, R&D, distribution, and so on, which makes growth efficient. Solid product market share in the original product category puts the company in a strong position to leverage its brand as an asset in different product categories later on. This can be accomplished by product extensions that (1) encourage initial customers to consume the product more often or in larger quantities, (2) attract competing brand users, and importantly (3) convert nonusers to brand users by developing product variants that meet the needs of different segments who have previously not considered the product.

> Recommendation 2: Use product extensions to make the admired brand highly relevant to customers in the initial product category before using brand extensions. Strong credibility in the original product category paves the way for brand extensions in new product categories.

Brand Extensions Follow Product Extensions

When an admired brand is known and credible in the parent category, it's in a solid position to extend to new product categories. But which of the five brand-extension strategies should be pursued at this point? We recommend using either joint consumption–based, consumption alternation–based, or substitution-based brand extensions. These strategies allow the company to own a specific need category related to the parent brand product. They also capitalize on the brand's current customer base and operating resources (e.g., manufacturing, R&D, distribution, etc.), which facilitates efficient growth. Moreover, they strengthen the core memory associations of the brand and broaden them through their linkage to other product categories. This latter outcome helps the brand to earn a reputation not only for a single product category, but for fulfilling a specific consumption need that is relevant to customers across product categories.

> Recommendation 3: After developing a highly admired brand using product extensions, focus on brand extensions that allow the brand to address user needs related to the consumption of the original product.

Feature-Based or Concept-Based Brand Extensions as the Ultimate Goal

Finally, when an admired brand is known for addressing a generalized need, the company is in a stronger position to pursue either feature-based or concept-based extensions. The goal here is to secure efficient growth while broadening (and not diluting) the memory associations linked to the brand. This can be accomplished by extending the brand to new markets for which a dominant feature associated with the parent brand is relevant. Swarovski, known for luxury cut lead glass in figurines and jewelry, has also extended its name to high-end optical equipment, such as binoculars, rifle scopes, and telescopes. Through these feature-based extensions Swarovski can achieve efficient growth (extension effects). Moreover, Swarovski's core memory associations (i.e., precision cut glass) are strengthened, not diluted. New memory associations are also added to Swarovski, which broadens the brand's identity. Similarly, companies may also follow concept-based brand extensions. Brands such as Chanel, Virgin, and Nike have achieved similar extension and feedback effects using concept-based extensions.

> Recommendation 4: The ultimate goal is to extend the brand to diverse categories using feature- or concept-based extensions. These strategies allow the brand to grow efficiently, while also strengthening and broadening memory associations.

Of course, these recommended sequencing considerations shouldn't be followed blindly. As noted earlier, considerations about the company, the competition, and customers also affect which extension strategy is used. For example, no matter how great the extension opportunities are (e.g., no competition and strong customer demand), they may not be capitalized on by a company if it doesn't have necessary resources to pursue such opportunities.

Illustrative Brand Evolution (Strategic Growth Path) Maps

The preceding four recommendations generally square with the brand evolution process used by a number of successful companies. For example, Nike first developed a set of value-enhancement strategies that improved its shoes and enhanced the brand's relevance to diverse segments (see Figure 9.1). Product improvements included

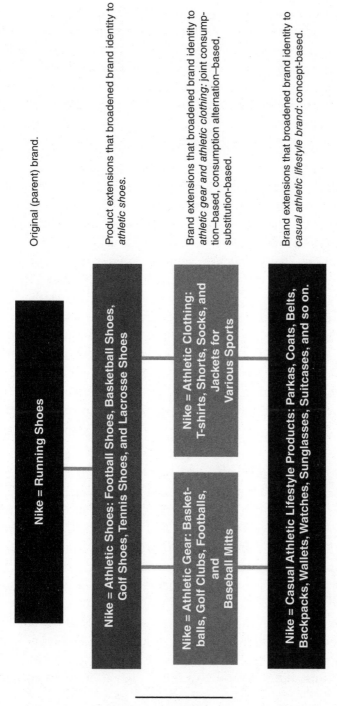

Figure 9.1 Nike Brand Evolution Map

air cushioning, enhanced ankle protection, and customized patterns. Next, Nike extended the Nike name from running shoes to other athletic shoes. Football shoes, basketball shoes, golf shoes, and others broadened the associations linked to Nike. This move strengthened Nike's core running shoes identity ("Just Do It" = "do that marathon," "start running," etc.), and broadened its identity from a running shoe brand to an athletic shoe brand ("Just Do It" = "practice your football game," "go ahead and exercise," etc.).

Nike's extensions to athletic shoes opened up opportunities for Nike to subsequently extend its brand to other categories associated with athletics. Athletic gear and athletic clothing used in a variety of different sports reinforce the Nike athletic identity, but also broadened its relevance beyond shoes to other categories associated with the *needs* of athletes. Subsequent extensions to casual clothes, travel bags, and accessories (belts, watches, sunglasses, etc.) further broadened memory associations linked to Nike, transforming it from a company completely focused on athletic paraphernalia (gear and clothes) to an athletic lifestyle brand that exudes a casual clothing and casual active lifestyle identity. Here, Nike's concept-based brand extensions broadened the general concept of Nike as a casual, athletic lifestyle brand. Today, Nike is no longer dependent on the growth of the running shoe market. Its extensions give Nike opportunity to balance its risk by making the brand relevant to and grow in a set of diverse categories.

Let's illustrate this evolution and brand growth path process again using a different brand. Arm & Hammer's value-enhancement strategies gave customers another strong reason as to *why* they should use Arm & Hammer baking soda (e.g., for deodorizing one's refrigerator). This move gave Arm & Hammer the ability to develop extensions to other contexts where deodorizing was needed; for example, Fridge-n-Freezer for refrigerators and freezers and Fresh-n-Natural for bathrooms. These product extensions broadened the brand's identity and moved the brand from being merely a baking ingredient to a brand that had powerful deodorizing associations. Interestingly, unlike Nike, Arm & Hammer did not offer joint consumption–based, consumption alternation–based, or substitution-based brand extensions that are related to the needs of baking and deodorizing. Instead, it directly introduced a variety of feature-based brand extensions in such areas as pet care (puppy pads, pet wipes, etc.), personal care (nasal wands, toothpaste, antiperspirants, etc.), and fabric care (fabric softener, detergent boosters, etc.), further broadening the brand's identity from deodorizing to *cleaning*.[7]

Through its extensions, Arm & Hammer showed that the brand is appropriate for every living (customers, their pets) and nonliving (the refrigerator, clothes) entity in customers' houses. People have warm and positive feelings about their homes. The affection and love associated with its extensions,[8] in turn, helps Arm & Hammer further leverage its brand. Today, Arm & Hammer has become much more than just a company that markets a relatively undifferentiated baking ingredient. Arm & Hammer's identity is evolving to an even more general concept of "home care." The case of Arm & Hammer shows that a series of feature-based extensions can also transform a brand's identity to a more abstract, concept-based identity.

We invite brand managers to consider the specific growth path and the memory associations that they want to develop, and then identify and implement a set of product and brand extensions that steer a brand toward these associations. This last point brings us to an additional recommendation regarding mapping the brand's evolutionary trajectory over time:

> Recommendation 5: When developing product and brand extensions, companies may wish to begin with the *end game* they have in mind, addressing what identity the brand has now, and what identity it could efficiently and effectively achieve over time.

A brand should be leveraged proactively so as to first enhance its competitive marketplace value while also aiming to own the product market by the use of product extensions. It can then extend to offerings in different product categories that are jointly consumed with, alternate with, or substitute for the original brand. Finally, it can extend to offerings in different categories using feature-based or concept-based brand extensions. Brand admiration can continue to grow and strengthen when companies consider the strategic and evolutionary paths by which they use product and brand extensions.

KEY TAKEAWAYS

1. In order to benefit from efficient growth and strong feedback effects, first build brand admiration (Chapters 3-6), and then enhance it using value-enhancement strategies (Chapter 7).

2. Product extensions can then strengthen the parent brand's core memory association, broadening the brand's identity and enhancing TOM brand recall.

3. Joint consumption–, consumption alternation–, and substitution-based extensions boost a brand's relevance to a specific need.

4. Feature extensions heighten the brand's relevance in the delivery of a product/service feature across diverse markets and categories.

5. Concept-based extensions enhance the brand's relevance to a diverse set of markets and categories in which the concept itself is also relevant.

6. Product and brand extensions typically create stronger extension and feedback effects when they extend to categories that have high fit (e.g., category fit, feature fit, usage fit, benefit fit, and concept fit). However, the strongest feedback effects occur when an admired brand offers innovative benefits in low-fit extension categories.

7. Keep the end game or destination in mind when developing product or brand extensions. Consider not only the brand's current identity, but also the ultimate identity that it could have in the future.

WHAT ABOUT YOUR BRAND?

1. How are you using product and brand extensions in your organization?

2. To what extent have you considered employing low-fit extensions?

3. To what extent have you considered following the strategic brand evolution map (growth paths) for the long-term health and success of your brand?

NOTES

1. Lan Luo, "Product Line Design for Consumer Durables: An Integrated Marketing and Engineering Approach," *Journal of Marketing Research* 48, no. 1 (2011): 128–139.
2. See David A. Aaker and Kevin L. Keller, "Consumer Evaluations of Brand Extensions," *Journal of Marketing* 54, no. 1 (1990): 27–41; C. Whan Park, Sandra Milberg, and Robert Lawson, "Evaluation of Brand Extensions: The Role of Product Feature Similarity and Brand Concept Consistency," *Journal of Consumer Research* 18, no. 2 (1991): 185–193.
3. C. Whan Park, Bernard J. Jaworski, and Deborah J. MacInnis, "Strategic Brand Concept-Image Management," *Journal of Marketing* 50, no. 4 (1986): 135–145.
4. Susan Spiggle, Hang T. Nguyen, and Mary Caravella, "More Than Fit: Brand Extension Authenticity," *Journal of Marketing Research* 49, no. 6 (2012): 967–983.
5. Michael J. Barone and Robert D. Jewell, "The Innovator's License: A Latitude to Deviate from Category Norms," *Journal of Marketing* 77, no. 1 (2013): 120–134; Mita Sujan and James R. Bettman, "The Effects of Brand Positioning Strategies on Consumers' Brand and Category Perceptions: Some Insights From Schema Research," *Journal of Marketing Research* 26, no. 4 (1989): 454–467; HaeEun H. Chun, C. Whan Park, Andreas B. Eisingerich, and Deborah J. MacInnis, "Strategic Benefits of Low Fit Brand Extensions: When and Why?" *Journal of Consumer Psychology* 25, no. 4 (2015): 577–595.
6. See Kevin L. Keller and David A. Aaker, "The Effects of Sequential Introduction of Brand Extensions," *Journal of Marketing Research* 29, no. 1 (1992): 35–50.
7. We call Arm & Hammer's move to these extensions feature-based because deodorizing and cleaning are closely related features.
8. Catherine Yeung and Robert S. Wyer Jr., "Does Loving a Brand Mean Loving Its Products? The Role of Brand-Elicited Affect in Brand Extension Evaluations," *Journal of Marketing Research* 42, no. 4 (2005): 495–506.

CHAPTER 10

Brand Architecture Design

The brands that make up your company are part of an ensemble ... each piece should fit the whole.

INTRODUCTION

High-end grocery chain Whole Foods Market has been quite successful globally. Despite the popularity of organic food, however, the brand is facing slowing growth. In order to attract people who don't currently shop at Whole Foods, the company launched a sister chain of lower-priced grocery stores called 365 by Whole Foods Market (365 is a Whole Foods private label brand). This new chain aims to attract younger customers who want affordable natural foods. To fulfill this promise, Whole Foods hopes that 365 costs less to run. It also hopes to give 365 a hip, cool, tech-oriented identity. Was Whole Foods' decision to name its new brand *365* a good idea?

Google offers a variety of Google-branded services, among which are Google Scholar, Google Finance, Google Maps, and Google Images. Furthermore, Google offers Google-branded services to other businesses (Google AdWords), consumers (Google Chrome), and even start-ups (Google Ventures). Yet it also has brands that don't use the Google name (e.g., biotech company Calico and Next smart-home products). Google recently reorganized. The Google brand now falls under an overarching holding company called Alphabet. The market reacted positively to this announcement: Google's share price rose 5 percent.[1] Was this a good long-term decision for Google? How can one tell?

OVERVIEW

The opening examples relate to a concept called brand architecture design, which we define as the hierarchical representation of a firm's portfolio of brands to secure optimal financial, asset-building, and organizational benefits.

We discuss this definition and the benefits of brand architecture design in this chapter. Just as architects must design buildings such that their collective components make for strong structures of enduring value, so too must managers design companies such that their collective brands work together to build a strong company of enduring value. Brand architecture design decisions influence how stakeholders, including customers and investors, perceive the company. They also affect employees' understanding of the company and its goals, and their own roles in delivering brand value.

The concept of brand architecture design suggests that companies should have an overarching strategic focus that guides the individual and collective identities of their brands. Such a focus helps customers understand the company and what it does and stands for. Adopting an overall strategic focus on the set of brands that the company offers also helps the company secure optimal financial, asset-building, and organizational benefits. Unfortunately, brand-naming decisions are often ad hoc. Criteria like a new product's market opportunity and growth potential typically loom large. Considerations of what the new brand brings to the set of brands that comprise the company are rarely thought through. One reason why, is that the brand architecture design concept is somewhat nebulous. We hope to clarify its meaning in this chapter. Specifically, we aim to:

- Identify key brand naming options that companies can consider when designing their brand architectures.

- Describe how brand managers can design their company's brand architecture so as to effectively accommodate various branding decisions of a company.

- Articulate key financial, asset-building, and organizational criteria that companies should consider when developing their brand architecture designs.

BRAND NAMING OPTIONS
IN BRAND ARCHITECTURE DESIGN

We noted in Chapter 1 that a *brand name* helps customers identify what the brand is and how it is different from other brands. When thinking about what to name a new brand, it's helpful to have a typology or a way of evaluating potential brand naming options. Ideally, the branding options in this typology should represent the set of brand naming options from which the company can choose. It should also clarify how this new brand relates to other brands marketed by the company. Table 10.1 shows such a typology.

The typology includes three broad types of brand naming options: (1) extension branding, (2) association branding, and (3) individual branding (see Table 10.1). These three types vary in how close or distant they are to the parent brand name. With extension branding, the name of a new offering is strongly related to (close to) the parent brand. With individual branding, the name of the new brand is unrelated to (farthest from) the parent brand. Association branding is a middle-ground option.[2] A second thing to note is that there are different options for each broad brand naming type (again, see Table 10.1). Extension branding includes direct and linked branding options. Association branding has four branding options: subbranding, endorsement branding, indirect branding, and cobranding. Individual branding has two options: word-based and phrase-based.

The final thing to note is that each option can include or not include a modifier. A modifier is a descriptor that adds information to the selected branding option. It is nested in the eight branding options. Table 10.1 thus shows a typology of eight brand-naming options, which can use or not use a modifier. We explain the meaning and significance of these branding options next.

Extension Branding

There are two types of extension branding options that companies can consider: (1) direct-extension branding and (2) linked-extension branding.

Table 10.1 Types of Brand Naming Options

Branding Options	Extension Branding				Association Branding								Individual Branding			
	Direct		Linked		Sub-branding		Endorsement Branding		Indirect Branding		Co-branding		Word-Based		Phrase-Based	
	Modifier	No Modifier	Modifier	No Modifier	Modifier	No Modifier	Modifier	No Modifier	Modifier	No Modifier	Modifier	No Modifier	Modifier	No Modifier	Modifier	No Modifier
Modifier																

Direct-Extension Branding

With *direct-extension branding*, the company uses an existing (parent brand) name for a new business or product. For example, Google used direct-extension branding when it moved from general Internet search to maps (Google Maps), scholarly articles (Google Scholar), and shopping (Google Shopping). With extension branding, the parent brand (Google) is the single dominant driver of the new brand's identity (e.g., Google Maps). Chapter 8 focused extensively on this direct-extension branding option.

Linked-Extension Branding

With *linked-extension branding*, a *key element* of the parent brand name is used to name the new product. For example, McPotato and McCafe include *Mc*, which is a key part of the McDonalds brand name. China's Xiaomi, the world's most valuable technology start-up and electronics company, has used *Mi* to name new products such as Mi headphones, MIUI 7 (a software platform), Mi 4i (a smartphone), and so on. Alibaba uses this branding option for its online payment system (Alipay) and online retail services (AliExpress).

As noted in Chapters 8 and 9, it takes time and resources to build brand awareness (let alone brand admiration) for a new brand. Using an existing (parent) brand name for a new business or product lets customers transfer what they know and have experienced with the parent brand to the new business or product. Customers make these associations naturally. So companies should spend less to create associations for the new product when they follow the extension branding option, as opposed to an entirely new brand name. This is particularly true when positive extension and feedback effects can be realized.

But extension branding is not without risks, since the parent brand is vulnerable to potential dilution. If there's no meaningful connection between the parent brand and the extension, customers may become confused about what the brand stands for, which can hurt the brand's identity. Extensions that fail to deliver on their brand promise in the marketplace can also backfire and tarnish the parent brand's reputation. Moreover, with extension branding, customers might generalize a mishap associated with the extension to include the parent brand.

Table 10.2   Meaning and Examples of Different Branding Options

Extension Branding

- Definition: Uses the same brand name (of the holding company, corporation, or product) to introduce a new offering (e.g., company, strategic business unit [SBU], or product).

- Examples: Virgin Atlantic, Virgin Money, Virgin Books, Virgin Holidays, Virgin Wine; Oracle Cloud, Oracle Mobile, Oracle Database; Maersk Line, Maersk Oil, Maersk Drilling; Mi headphones, Mi 4i; Alipay, AliExpress; CAT Financial, CAT Rental Store; McPotato, McCafe.

Subbranding

- Definition: Adds a new brand name to an existing brand, such that the new brand is a special version of the parent brand.

- Examples: Toyota Prius, Toyota Corolla, Toyota Camry; Microsoft Xbox, Microsoft Lumia, Microsoft HoloLens; Intel Xeon, Intel Atom, Intel Quark.

Endorsement Branding

- Definition: Supports a new brand through the endorsement of the parent brand.

- Examples: Courtyard by Marriott; Disney Presents … *Frozen, Big Hero 6*, and other entertainment; Polo by Ralph Lauren; Solar Turbines—A Caterpillar Company, Turbomach—A Caterpillar Company.

Indirect Branding

- Definition: Indirectly associates a known parent brand with a new brand (e.g., parent name appears, but is not prominent, on packaging, in advertising, or in other marketing formats).

- Examples: General Mills: Wheaties, Cheerios, and other products; BASF: Novasil, Lucarotin, Lutrell, Lupro-Grain, Amasil NA.

Cobranding

- Definition: Two known brands join to produce a new brand that leverages the strengths of each brand.

- Examples: Adidas Porsche Design athletic shoes; SlimFast Godiva cake mix (hypothetical example); Disney · Pixar.

Individual Branding

- Definition: A new brand is introduced whose name is independent of and distinct from the parent.

- Examples: Lexus and Toyota; Innocent Drinks and Coca-Cola; Boeing and Apache helicopters; ESPN and Walt Disney; Alibaba and Taobao; I Can't Believe It's Not Butter; Bed Bath & Beyond.

However, when extension decisions are thought through in the ways suggested in Chapter 9, positive extension and feedback effects generally far outweigh the risks of brand dilution.

Association Branding

With association branding, the new product is less strongly connected to the parent brand than is true for extension branding. As such, the company trades off potentially strong extension and feedback effects for lower risk of damage to the parent brand should the new brand perform poorly. Let's take a closer look at the four association branding options shown in Table 10.1.

Subbranding

Subbranding adds a new brand name to the parent brand name. The parent could be a holding company, corporation, strategic business unit (SBU), or a specific product. Here the company takes advantage of the equity (e.g., trust, reliability, luxury image, etc.) of the parent brand while also developing a unique name and identity for the subbrand. The subbrand is distinct from, but still a member of the parent brand family. Think about Microsoft and Microsoft Xbox (Table 10.2). Xbox (the subbrand) has a younger, cooler image than the Microsoft brand does, and it appeals more strongly to a younger audience of gamers. The Toyota Prius leverages the qualities normally associated with Toyota (e.g., reliability and user friendliness) while developing new associations, such as fuel efficiency and environmental friendliness, in the subbrand Prius. Because a subbrand has its own identity, the extension and feedback effects are somewhat weaker than what can be realized with extension branding.

Subbranding is a viable branding option when the parent brand's characteristics or associations do not readily transfer to the new product, and when the new brand needs to be somewhat differentiated from the parent brand. Take Porsche Boxster, Porsche Cayenne, and Porsche Macan as examples. On the one hand, the Porsche parent brand wants to establish a new business (e.g., in the SUV market and lower-price range segments, etc.) efficiently by supporting it with the trust, love, and respect that customers have for the parent brand. But the company does not want the new business too closely linked with the parent because the parent brand is known for high-performance sports car racing. Subbranding indicates that the new brand is a special version of the parent brand. Subbrands have additional benefits. First, companies can gain cost efficiencies in advertising, promotions, and distribution. The subbrand also allows the company to target new, specialized customer groups whose needs may differ from those associated with the parent brand.

With subbranding, the parent name always comes first so that the new product is still strongly tied to the parent brand and its identity. But the subbrand is subservient to the parent brand. This can make it difficult for the subbrand to establish its own independent identity and equity unless the company promotes the new identity. For example, Ford's Taurus (one of Ford's many subbrands) was the number-one brand in the midsize car market several decades ago. Today its identity and distinctiveness from other Ford brands are less clear. Having too many subbrands aggravates this phenomenon. Other brand naming options (described later) may be better if differentiation from the parent is a key objective. However, when properly managed the parent brand and the subbrand can both drive demand for the new product (e.g., Toyota Camry, Honda Accord, etc.).

Endorsement Branding

With *endorsement branding*, an established parent brand introduces a new market offering. Examples include Courtyard by Marriott, Disney Presents … , Polo by Ralph Lauren, and Solar Turbines—A Caterpillar Company (Table 10.2). Here, the parent brand plays a supportive role by endorsing the new product. Endorsement branding assures customers that a strong, high-quality brand stands behind the new product offering. The parent (endorser) brand thus provides credibility and legitimacy to a new offering while allowing the endorsed brand to operate independently from the parent brand. Movies such as *Frozen* or *Big Hero 6* might have been less successful had they not included the Disney name as an endorsement.

Endorsement branding and subbranding differ in two important ways. First, with endorsement branding, the *emphasis is on strong extension effects* because the new brand is supported by the parent brand. But with endorsement branding, the *feedback effects on the parent are weaker* than is true with subbranding. Second, with endorsement branding, what gets transferred to the new brand are the *legitimacy* and *credibility* of the parent (endorser) brand. With subbranding, what gets transferred to the new brand are the memory associations and identity linked to the parent. Endorsement branding is preferred to subbranding when the new offering needs a unique identity that distinguishes it from parent brand but when it can also benefit from parent brand's credibility.

Sometimes companies use what might appear to be an endorsement branding option by endorsing a new *product category*. For example, the German brand Tchibo calls its line of yoga tops and leggings Active by Tchibo or its children clothing line "Kids by Tchibo." These are not endorsement brands because the new brand is really just a different product category pursued by the company. We would only regard them as examples of endorsement branding if customers considered *Active* or *Kids* to be unique *brand* names. Otherwise, these names are simply variations of extension branding.

Indirect Branding

With *indirect branding*, the new offering is linked only indirectly to the parent brand. Indirect branding and endorsement branding both use a brand name that's separated from the parent's name. But with indirect branding, the parent is less visible, and support of the parent brand is less direct.

For example, Wheaties and Cheerios benefit from their ties to General Mills, given General Mills' history in making cereals. But the General Mills name is not part of the Wheaties and Cheerios name. The General Mills name is inconspicuous, shown only on the top left-hand side of these brands' packages. BASF, one of the world's leading and most innovative chemical companies, uses indirect branding for its Novasil, Lucarotin, Lutrell, and Amasil brands. All aim to provide nutrition to cows and other ruminants, but the parent brand name BASF is only used indirectly.

In light of the relatively wide distance between the parent brand and a new brand name, the extension and feedback effects are weaker for indirect branding than for endorsement branding. This option is appropriate when the company wants to develop a unique identity for the new business. The parent brand provides some credibility and support (as with endorsement branding), but it's the new brand name that's prominent.

This is not to say that the parent brand in the indirect branding cannot play a powerful role in offering credibility and legitimacy or quality assurance to the new brand. In Korea, for example, PMO (see Chapter 2) uses indirect branding with great success. Or consider the extent to which customers trust and value the "Bayer" parent brand name for a variety of consumer health care products. Depending on how a firm promotes its parent brand name (e.g., through corporate advertising), customers may consider the parent brand name as a strong and reassuring seal of quality even if the parent name is not displayed prominently with the new brand.

Cobranding

The fourth type of association branding is *cobranding*. Here, two brands (either from the same company or from different ones) come together to form a new market offering, product, or company (Table 10.2). Examples include Adidas Porsche Design athletic shoes, Tide 2× Ultra with Febreze Freshness laundry detergent, or Disney · Pixar. With this branding option the goal is to convey that a new business (or product) has the strengths of each brand and/or that one compensates for the weaknesses of the other. Think about the hypothetical example of the Godiva SlimFast cake mix.[3] Godiva is known for rich, sumptuous chocolate, but few would associate the brand with low calories. SlimFast has the opposite association—it is well known for low-calorie (though not necessarily good-tasting) food. When combined, Godiva and SlimFast may compensate for each other's weakness (e.g., Godiva SlimFast cake mix).

Cobranding is somewhat similar to endorsement branding, since there are two brands. But with endorsement branding, it is clear which is the endorsing brand and which is the endorsed brand. With cobranding, each brand endorses the other. Also, with endorsement branding, the endorsed brand takes a new name. With cobranding, established brand names are used for both products. Godiva SlimFast cake mix takes the form of endorsement branding, but it's actually an example of cobranding, since Godiva and SlimFast are already well-known and established brands in their own right.

One downside to cobranding is that it may be harder for customers to understand the identity of the cobrand, since it is blending associations linked to each individual brand. When two brands do not have strong built-in reinforcing or compensating identities, customers may not understand how or why they are related, or what this new product or company stands for.

Cobranding creates an extension effect, which helps the cobranded product.[4] Cobranding also has feedback effects. However, it's often unclear as to which brand benefits more from the positive feedback effect. For instance, does Godiva benefit more from its cobranding with SlimFast (i.e., being perceived as a delicious chocolate brand with lower calories) or vice versa (i.e., SlimFast as a low-calorie cake mix with a sumptuous, mouthwatering taste)? When one brand is substantially weaker than the other, it is the weaker brand that benefits from stronger feedback effects.[5] As with all branding options, it's important for the cobranded product to *deliver* on perceptions. If it doesn't, extension effects will be limited, and feedback effects on the parent brand will likely be negative.

Individual Branding

The final branding option is *individual branding*. Here, the new brand has absolutely no relationship with the parent brand. The goal of individual branding is to create a new business (or product) that has its own unique and exclusive name and identity, separate from the parent name (see Table 10.2). For example, no visible marketing action identifies Lexus as a product of the Toyota parent. Nor do a lot of consumers know that civilian aircraft maker Boeing makes the Apache combat helicopter.

This branding option doesn't create any extension effects on the new product, so it is useful when marketing resources are not constrained. This option doesn't create any feedback effects, either.

As such, it's a good option when the company wants to avoid any potential dilution of the parent brand from its association with the new product. For example, Ben & Jerry's ice cream is owned by Unilever. Associating a brand that conjures up the image of two guys in Vermont making homemade ice cream with that of a multinational corporation would clearly not help Ben & Jerry's. Moreover, the Ben & Jerry's identity doesn't necessarily help Unilever's identity, either. The individual branding option is also less likely to cause negative consequences to the company as a whole when a mishap occurs, since the parent brand and the new brand aren't connected.[6] Restaurant Brands International owns Burger King, though most consumers don't know that. If Burger King experienced a crisis, the crisis may not spill over to negatively affect Restaurant Brands International.

An individual branding option is also appropriate when the company wants to diversify into new areas (product categories) that are unrelated to the parent brand, particularly when this new brand can offer its own range of products and brand extensions.[7] Think about Alibaba's move to call its online shopping platform for business customers Alibaba's B2B Marketplace and offer its online shopping platform for retail customers under a different name, Taobao.

Word-Based and Phrase-Based

With individual branding, companies can use either a specific word or a phrase to name the brand (Table 10.1). Word-based brand names are much more common than phrase-based names, but phrase-based brand names are potentially better from an identity perspective. I Can't Believe It's Not Butter; Bed Bath & Beyond; Food Should Taste Good; and the like are examples of brands that have phrase-based names. Phrase-based names may create brand recognition, recall, and favorable brand attitudes more readily than word-based names because they're more unusual and more descriptive of the brand's benefits. As such, it may cost less to communicate the brand's benefits. Phrase-based names can also lead to future brand extensions. For example, Unilever's I Can't Believe It's Not Butter brand might be easily extended to other product categories by building on the same phrase (e.g., I Can't Believe It's Not Milk, I Can't Believe It's Not Hamburgers, etc.), thereby fully taking advantage of both extension and feedback effects.

Modifiers

While a new brand name can create differentiation, companies might also use modifiers to create differentiation. Modifiers *use a descriptor* that conveys the nature of the new offering (i.e., the business, the product benefits, the usage occasion, advanced or upgraded models, or the intended target market). Boeing's 707, 717, and 747, and Johnny Walker's Blue Label or Red Label scotch whiskey are examples. Godiva has a Gold collection, and Hugo Boss has an Orange line. Although these modifiers may not always be legally protected, they are cost efficient because the descriptive or symbolic label indicates that the brand is distinct from others made by the company. Modifiers may be used for, and are thus nested in, any of the eight branding options described earlier in Table 10.1. For example, modifiers can be used with extension branding (e.g., Porsche *911*), subbranding (e.g., Toyota Corolla *L*, Nintendo Super Mario Bros. *2*), endorsement branding (e.g., Disney Presents *Toy Story* 3), and cobranding (e.g., Caterpillar GORE-TEX *safety* boots).

DESIGNING THE STRUCTURE OF THE COMPANY'S BRAND ARCHITECTURE

Whereas Table 10.1 shows the set of branding options companies can consider when introducing a new offering, an effective brand architecture design should also specify *how the brands that make up the company relate to one another at different levels of the business hierarchy*. As Table 10.3 shows, brand naming decisions happen at all levels of the business hierarchy: at the SBU level, at the category level, and so on, down to the name of a specific subproduct. The brand architecture design space, therefore, is potentially described by the matrix of 8 (branding options) × 2 (presence or absence of modifiers) × 5 (business hierarchy levels) shown in Table 10.3.

The structure shown in Table 10.3 can serve several purposes. First, companies can use it to represent *the company's current brand architecture*.[8] Toyota has an SBU called Toyota Financial Services Corporation. This is an example of direct extension branding with a modifier (see Table 10.4). At the same business hierarchy (SBU) level, Toyota

Table 10.3 Brand Architecture Structure

Branding Options		Extension Branding				Association Branding								Individual Branding			
		Direct		Linked		Sub-branding		Endorsement Branding		Indirect Branding		Co-branding		Word-Based		Phrase-Based	
Business Hierarchy	Modifier	Modifier	No Modifier	Modifier	No Modifier	Modifier	No Modifier	Modifier	No Modifier	Modifier	No Modifier	Modifier	No Modifier	Modifier	No Modifier	Modifier	No Modifier
SBU																	
Product category																	
Product line																	
Product																	
Sub-product																	

202

also adopts an individual branding option with no modifier (Lexus). Mapping a company's activity in the manner shown in Table 10.4 clarifies the scope of the companies' brands and how they relate to one another. For example, the addition of Lexus as an individual brand helped Toyota diversify its brand portfolio and enter a luxury market, while retaining associations of the car's affordability in its nonluxury lines. The addition of Toyota Financial Services aids in the transaction process. It also captures the market of Toyota buyers who are making their purchasing and financing decisions at the dealership. DC Tacoma is a cobranded product that involves the Toyota Tacoma truck and the shoe brand DC. The truck has a plow, gear racks, and a carrier for a snowmobile and tent.

Second, this brand-architecture design model can be used to reevaluate a company's current brand architecture to see if improvements are possible. They often are, since companies need to adapt proactively to constantly changing markets and business opportunities. Third, it also helps brand managers think through what to name new businesses (products) as new opportunities arise since it includes all the possible branding options. In the next section we specifically examine how to reevaluate a company's current brand architecture and how to name a new product.

CRITERIA IN CHOOSING A BRANDING OPTION IN THE COMPANY'S BRAND ARCHITECTURE

When companies introduce a new offering as part of their brand architecture, they need to consider the new offering's relationship with the company's other brands. Three criteria can help companies consider which brand naming options to use (regardless of their level in the business hierarchy).

Brand-Leveraging Benefits

The first concerns how important feedback and extension effects are to the company. All else being equal, extension branding has stronger extension and feedback effects than association branding does, which,

Table 10.4 Brand Architecture Structure of Toyota Motor Corporation

Business Hierarchy \ Modifier	Extension Branding				Association Branding								Individual Branding			
	Direct		Linked		Sub-branding		Endorsement Branding		Indirect Branding		Co-branding		Word-Based		Phrase-Based	
	Modifier	No Modifier	Modifier	No Modifier	Modifier	No Modifier	Modifier	No Modifier	Modifier	No Modifier	Modifier	No Modifier	Modifier	No Modifier	Modifier	No Modifier
SBU	Toyota Financial Services													Lexus		
Product category													Lexus hoverboard			
Product line						Toyota Corolla								Lexus NX		
Product						Toyota Corolla LE							DC Tacoma	Lexus NX Hybrid		
Sub-product						Toyota Corolla LE Eco										

204

in turn, is stronger than the individual branding option. IBM's extension to cloud computing enhanced the extension's efficient growth, and also created a strong feedback effect that made IBM seem more innovative and cutting edge than before. Note that extension and feedback effects need to be assessed separately, because their effects may not be equally strong. For example, endorsement branding (such as Courtyard by Marriott) may have a strong extension effect (to Courtyard) but not a strong feedback effect (to Marriott).

Asset-Building Benefits

A second criterion concerns how well each of the branding options will build assets for the company. With brand extensions the company loses an opportunity to create an entirely new brand, which can itself be nurtured and leveraged in the future. Individual branding and indirect branding options are better if this criterion is important. Alibaba's decision to invest in and build an entirely new consumer brand (Taobao) made sense for this reason.

Organizational Benefits

A third criterion concerns the organizational benefits of the branding decisions. Different branding options can clarify or muddy employees' understanding of who is in charge of what and why. They can affect whether employees understand how different parts of a business contribute to the overall profitability and growth of the company. They can also impact whether brand managers see their roles as complementing or competing with managers of other brands in the company. They can thus impact the sharing of assets and information within the company, affecting a company's culture and its practices.

For instance, employees probably have a better understanding of who is in charge of what and why when companies use individual (versus extension) branding options. With individual branding, the brand manager can create a separate brand with its own unique identity and culture. It's clear who's accountable for the brand's performance. Role clarity and performance accountability are less clear with extension branding or association branding options.

But individual branding can create other organizational problems. Having multiple brands, each with a unique identity, can lead to siloed thinking and a lack of coordination across brands. Individual branding can also lead to competition for resources and customers. For instance, Lexus brand managers may be more than happy to steal customers from Toyota's other high-performance models, such as the Avalon Hybrid XLE Premium. The same may be true for subbranding, though to a lesser extent (e.g., Toyota Avalon versus Toyota Camry). *Thus, individual branding provides more clarity in roles and responsibilities, but it creates greater potential for intraorganizational conflict and competition, greater costs, and reduced efficiencies due to a reduction in willingness to share resources and critical information.*

The three criteria we've just described are trade-offs: pursuing one benefit can make it more difficult to pursue another. To make a decision about branding options, then, the company needs to weigh the importance of each criterion. The weight of each criterion can depend on the level of the business hierarchy and the nature of the new offering. For example, organizational benefits may be weighed more heavily when the branding decision involves a new SBU than when it involves a new subproduct. Asset building may be weighed more heavily when the new offering is very different from the company's current offering(s). Organizational benefits are likely to be more important when the new offering and the current one(s) are similar. Because the importance of these benefits varies, companies often use a mix of branding options in their brand architectures. For example, Google systematically used extension branding with modifiers (e.g., Google Fiber, Google X, etc.). However, its brand architecture also includes the individual branding option (e.g., Android, Calico, Nest, YouTube, etc.), allowing it to build new assets.

These same benefits (criteria) can be considered in merger-and-acquisition decisions, since such decisions often require some brand name changes. For example, in the late 1980s DEC (Digital Equipment Corporation) was the second-largest computer company in the world (IBM was number one). When Compaq acquired DEC in 1998, it stopped using the DEC name. HP (Hewlett-Packard) then acquired Compaq in 2002, and the HP name replaced the Compaq name. While replacing the name of the acquired brand with that of the acquiring brand name may have strong organizational benefits (one company and one culture), this practice leads to a loss of the acquired brand's equity. Instead, cobranding or indirect branding might have been used. The ultimate branding decision depends on the importance of the criteria shown in Table 10.5.

The chapter introduction described the branding options offered by Whole Foods in introducing its 365 stores. The three criteria can be used to assess the potential effectiveness of this decision. Both brands existed previously, making the branding decision an example of cobranding. This cobranding strategy is clearly helped by the strength of Whole Foods' reputation, while also compensating for its weakness (i.e., high price). Extension effects appear to be strong (organizational benefits such as resource sharing and coordination benefits fostered through the cobranding option), although how successful this cobranded store will be depends on the potential cannibalization of Whole Foods main store customers by 365 by Whole Foods Markets. Feedback effects should be strong, because Whole Foods maintains its natural food concept while adding *affordability and value-for-money* memory associations to the parent brand name. Therefore, both extension and feedback effects seem to be strong. Although the ultimate success of this new store depends on many other factors, the branding option it chose appears to be a sound one (there is no asset-building criterion in this case, since 365 is an existing brand).

The chapter's opening vignette also described Google's reorganization under the holding company Alphabet. This reorganization suggests that web search and other Internet-related businesses represent just one operating arm of the company. Other operating arms include biotech (Calico) and smart-home products (Nest). Organizing Google in this way seems to be a viable option for pursing long-term growth. Yet Google must also consider how it can build extension and feedback effects from individual brands such as Calico and Nest through their own product and brand extensions. The company's brand architecture design should be assessed periodically in light of changes in the external environment. For example, if a brand suffers from some type of adverse market reaction, the company may need to consider whether a brand name change is in order. However, changing the name might merely

Table 10.5 Brand Architecture Evaluative Criteria

Branding Types		Extension Branding				Association Branding								Individual Branding				
		Direct		Linked		Sub-branding		Endorsement Branding		Indirect Branding		Co-branding		Word-Based		Phrase-Based		
Modifier		Modifier	No Modifier	Modifier	No Modifier	Modifier	No Modifier	Modifier	No Modifier	Modifier	No Modifier	Modifier	No Modifier	Modifier	No Modifier	Modifier	No Modifier	Importance weight
Benefits																		
Brand-Leveraging	Extension effect																	
	Feedback effect																	
Asset-Building																		
Organizational	Management accountability																	
	Use of shared resources																	

hide these problems while at the same time enormous costs would be incurred promoting the new name. We recommend that companies should change a brand name when (1) the current brand name has an inherent liability problem, and/or (2) when a brand name change offers very clear benefits to the company. Philip Morris Companies' name change to Altria made sense, given the first criterion. The company's strong association with tobacco made it difficult for the brand name to represent the portfolio of nontobacco products that Philip Morris marketed. Andersen Consulting's name change to Accenture helped it avoid getting hurt from its association with Enron during the Enron scandal.

KEY TAKEAWAYS

1. Extension branding can create powerful extension and feedback effects. But companies need to be careful because the possibility of parent brand dilution is also greatest in this case.

2. Subbranding can take advantage of the parent brand's equity while also building a unique brand identity. When managed effectively, the parent and the subbrand both drive demand for the new offering.

3. Endorsement branding offers legitimacy and credibility to a new brand while allowing the endorsed brand to operate independently of the parent brand.

4. Indirect branding is appropriate when a company intends to develop a unique brand for a business or product with support from the credibility of the parent brand that the company wishes to be less visible than the support resulting from endorsement branding.

5. Cobranding can convey that a product possesses the strengths of each brand and/or compensates for the weakness of one brand with the strength of the other.

6. The key advantage of individual branding is that a new business will have its own exclusive identity without being associated with the parent brand name.

7. Modifiers are cost-efficient ways of differentiating a business or a product.

8. A company's brand architecture design is a time-dependent, structural description of its business portfolio.

9. Brand architecture designs should be routinely assessed for the (1) financial, (2) asset-building, and (3) organizational benefits they offer to the company.

10. With a company's growth (or shrinkage) in business portfolio, its brand architecture design will also evolve.

WHAT ABOUT YOUR BRAND?

1. Have you considered your company's entire brand portfolio in a way that is suggested by Table 10.3? What concerns do you have about your company's current brand architecture?

2. What logic drove your current brand architecture? Did that logic have anything to do with optimizing the financial, asset-building, and organizational benefits discussed in this chapter (Table 10.5)?

3. How can you improve your current brand architecture so as to generate greater financial, asset-building, and organizational benefits for the company?

NOTES

1. Richard Waters, "Alphabet Reveals Scale of Google's Ambition," *Financial Times*, August 12, 2015, 17.
2. These types incorporate and extend types identified by other scholars (e.g., Liwu Hsu, Susan Fournier, and Shuba Srinivasan, "Brand Architecture Strategy and Firm Values: How Leveraging, Separating, and Distancing the Corporate Brands Affects Risk and Returns," *Journal of the Academy of Marketing Science* 44, no. 2 (2016): 1–20).
3. C. Whan Park, Sung Y. Jun, and Allan D. Shocker, "Composite Branding Alliances: An Investigation of Extension and Feedback Effects," *Journal of Marketing Research* 33, no. 3 (1996): 453–466.

4. Irwin P. Levin and Aron M. Levin, "Modeling the Role of Brand Alliances in the Assimilation of Product Evaluations," *Journal of Consumer Psychology* 9, no. 1 (2000): 43–52.

5. Bernard L. Simonin and Julie A. Ruth, "Is a Company Known by the Company It Keeps? Assessing the Spillover Effects of Brand Alliances on Consumer Brand Attitudes," *Journal of Marketing Research* 35, no. 1 (1998): 30–42.

6. Liwu, Fournier, and Srinivasan, "Brand Architecture Strategy."

7. David A. Aaker and Erich Joachimsthaler, "The Brand Relationship Spectrum: The Key to the Brand Architecture Challenge," *California Management Review* 42, no. 4 (2000): 8–23.

8. At one extreme, a company might use a single brand name on all brands in its brand portfolio. Some people call this a *branded house* approach. At the other extreme, a company might use independent branding for all of the brands in its product portfolio. This has been frequently called a *house of brands*. We do not use these terms, because most companies use a combination of extension, association, and individual branding.

ASSESSING THE VALUE OF ADMIRED BRANDS TO FIRMS AND CUSTOMERS

CHAPTER 11

Measuring Brand Equity

T he ultimate brand destination: brand equity.

INTRODUCTION

Corporate brands such as Amazon, the Bank of China, Coca-Cola, Disney, Samsung, and IBM are among the world's most valuable. Indeed, their valuations (in the billions of dollars) exceed the annual gross domestic product of many countries. The ability to put a financial value on corporate or product brands is important for companies, particularly those making merger-and-acquisition decisions.[1] Unfortunately, valuing brands is not that easy. Some measures assess the brand equity of the company and not the individual brands that comprise it. Different companies also propose different valuation methods. For example, Young and Rubicam's brand asset valuator measures brand equity by differentiation, brand relevance, brand esteem, and brand knowledge.[2] Some brand-valuation models examine market dynamics and residuals from capital, product, packaging, and other components and use these to forecast future earnings and discounts.[3] Some valuation methods use conjoint analysis.[4] Others measure brand equity by the difference between the brand's profits and what the brand would earn if it were compared with a generic (or unnamed) brand. Metrics also differ in whether they include customer data,[5] and whether the estimate of brand equity is revealed by the stock market.[6]

Each metric has its own advantages and disadvantages. Yet there seems to be consensus among marketers that a good measure of the value of a brand is *based on objective (versus subjective) criteria.*[7] It should be *theoretically grounded, intuitive, and reliable*. It should be based on *readily available data*, and it should *result in a single financial number*. An ideal metric should provide *diagnostic information*[8] and should allow the health of the brand to be *tracked over time* and *compared with other (competing or non-competing) brands*. Ideally, it would let managers track the value of the *corporate brand name* and the *individual brands that comprise it*. It would also *work in situations in which there is no generic brand counterpart* and/or where it is difficult to think of a comparable situation in which the brand name is absent. For example, how would Silicon Valley's economic development alliance compare the value of the Silicon Valley brand to a region that has the same features without the Silicon Valley name?

OVERVIEW

In this chapter we discuss the concept of brand equity and describe a measure we've developed to assess it. As Figure 1.1 (reproduced as Figure 11.1 below) suggests, *brand equity reflects the financial value of the brand to the brand holder (the company) based on the company's efforts to build brand admiration among customers*.

We believe our measure addresses some, if not all, of the aforementioned criteria for a good brand-equity measure. It's theoretically grounded in our brand admiration model. It's intuitive and based on objective data that are readily available to brand managers. It results in a single financial number, and it allows for comparisons with any number of entities (e.g., the brand itself over time, brands in the same category, and brands in other categories). It can be used to measure the equity of individual brands that comprise the company as well as the company as a whole. It does not require a generic or fictitious non-named brand as a basis for comparison. Following Figure 11.1, we assume that companies can measure brand equity at any time during the brand's life cycle. Companies can assess brand equity after the brand is first introduced (Chapters 4 through 6), after efforts to elaborate on its value (Chapter 7), and after product and brand extensions (Chapters 8 and 9) and efforts to build on (or redesign) the company's brand architecture (Chapter 10).

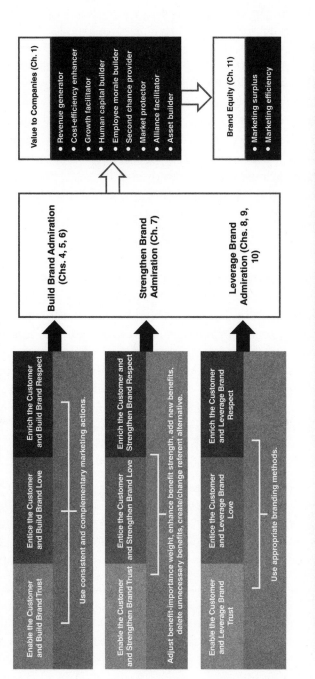

Figure 11.1 The Brand Admiration Management System

PERSPECTIVE ON BRAND EQUITY

Before we get too deeply into our proposed measure, let's link the concept of brand equity to some of the components of Figure 11.1. According to the figure, brands have *equity for the company when they offer value to the company and its customers.* Value to customers is indicated (in part) by how much customers admire the brand and their loyalty toward and advocacy of it. Value to the company is indicated by the outcomes that companies realize from building brand admiration among customers. As Figure 11.1 shows, brands have value to the company when they serve as revenue generators, cost-efficiency enhancers, growth facilitators, market protectors, and so on.

Figure 11.2 represents some of the ideas on the right-hand side of Figure 11.1 but ties them to our proposed measure of brand equity. For example, and as shown in Figure 11.2, the more customers admire a brand, the more likely they are to forgive the brand for mishaps such as product recalls, brand mistakes, or brand crises. Customers' *willingness to forgive* the brand for mishaps provides value to the company because it means that the brand can serve as a *second-chance provider* if mishaps occur. To the extent that the brand provides a second chance, it should cost the company less to recover from mishaps and retain current customers. *Brand advocates* generate revenue from new customers who are persuaded by their persuasive online or offline WOM.[9] The more customers admire a brand, the more willing they are to *pay a price premium* for it.[10] Given these outcomes, companies can more readily *build brand assets* and *attract alliance partners*, and hence generate greater brand revenue. For example, Google can more easily attract partners than can unknown tech companies. Also, the more customers admire the brand, the less willing they are to *buy substitute products* and the more likely they are to *denigrate alternatives.* These outcomes help to *protect the brand* from competitors, minimizing any revenue loss from new market entrants.

Chapter 4 discussed the importance of building brand admiration among employees. It's easier for companies to *attract top talent* and *build employee morale* when employees admire the brand. Cultivating employee brand admiration can also affect how much *customers* admire the brand (see Figure 11.2). Customers admire companies that attract

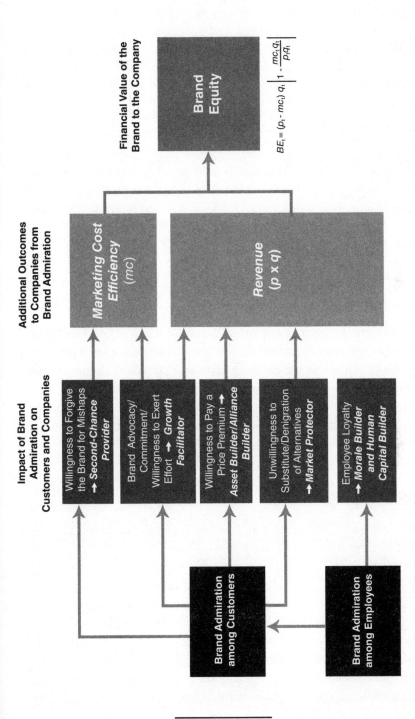

Impact of Brand Admiration on Customers and Companies

- Willingness to Forgive the Brand for Mishaps → *Second-Chance Provider*
- Brand Advocacy/Commitment/Willingness to Exert Effort → *Growth Facilitator*
- Willingness to Pay a Price Premium → *Asset Builder/Alliance Builder*
- Unwillingness to Substitute/Denigration of Alternatives → *Market Protector*
- Employee Loyalty → *Morale Builder and Human Capital Builder*

Brand Admiration among Customers

Brand Admiration among Employees

Additional Outcomes to Companies from Brand Admiration

Marketing Cost Efficiency (mc)

Revenue (p × q)

Financial Value of the Brand to the Company

Brand Equity

$$BE_t = (p_t - mc_t)\, q_t \left[1 - \frac{mc_t q_t}{p_t q_t} \right]$$

Figure 11.2   Brand Admiration: Financial Value

employees who love the brand they work for. They want to support brands that treat their employees well. And they should want to patronize brands whose employees are capable and who respect the brand. Thus, the outcomes of brand admiration shown in Figure 11.2 should increase when employees admire the brand.

Figure 11.2 is important. It provides a theoretical link between our concept of brand equity and the previous chapters. It also suggests that the value to customers and a company noted earlier is in essence reflected in the brand equity measure through the following two critical inputs: (1) the extent to which the brand provides cost efficiencies to the company (shown in Figure 11.2 as mc, or unit marketing costs) and (2) the extent to which it generates revenue (shown in Figure 11.2 as p, or price per unit sold, and q, or quantity sold).

MEASURING BRAND EQUITY

Let's explore our measure of brand equity in more detail. One important point to note right off the bat is that our measure emphasizes customers. Although we've suggested that companies should cultivate brand admiration among employees, the most important reason for doing so is that good employees enhance the customer experience. That's why there's an arrow between employee brand admiration and customer brand admiration in Figure 11.2.

Defining Brand Equity

The notion that unit marketing costs, unit price, and quantity sold are inputs to a financial measure of brand equity squares with our definition of brand equity. That definition states that *brand equity is a financial measure that reflects the financial value to the brand holder (the company) from its efforts to build brand admiration with customers*. Conceptually, and consistent with Figure 11.2, we can think about brand equity as the difference between *customers' endowment to a brand* (e.g., the price they are willing to pay and the number of units they are willing to buy) and the *investment the brand holder* has had to bear to secure this endowment from customers (e.g., the costs incurred to market to these customers).[11]

An important point is that our definition of brand equity focuses on costs the company bears *to market the brand to customers*. This means that when calculating brand equity, emphasis should not be on all costs the company bears (total costs). Instead, the measure focuses on the brand's costs in marketing to customers (*marketing* costs). The third and final important point is that our brand-equity measure is a time-specific measure. It reflects the value of a brand to the brand-holder at time t. It does not include its future value, which always requires an uncertain estimation.

Brand Equity Inputs

Based on the definition of brand equity and Figure 11.2, we suggest that in order to measure brand equity we need to know (1) the unit price (p) customers paid to obtain the brand, (2) the unit marketing cost (mc) marketers have incurred to obtain these customers, and (3) the total quantity sold (q).

Unit Price

Our brand admiration model indicates that when customers admire a brand they are willing to pay a higher price to obtain it. Abundant research supports this proposition. Accordingly, brand equity should increase when a company can increase its unit price (p) from a prior time period (called time $t - 1$) to the current time period (called t) without negatively impacting demand (q) and without additional unit marketing costs (mc) during the same time period. In our metric, *unit price* reflects unit *wholesale* price. It seems reasonable to consider wholesale (versus retail) price in calculating unit price. Wholesale price focuses on the company's efforts alone, as opposed to the combined efforts of the company and its retailers. We calculate wholesale price by total revenue divided by the number of units sold at the wholesale level. Unit marketing costs (aimed at both middlemen and end users) represent the expenditures that the company (not the company and its retailers) has borne to generate this revenue during time t.

Quantity Sold

Research similarly supports the relationship between the value customers place on their relationship with a brand (e.g., how much they admire it) and quantity sold (q). As shown in Figure 11.2, the more customers admire a brand, the more committed they are to it and the more effort they will exert to get it. For example, Microsoft's *Rare Replay* video game was the most preordered video game in 2015. Consumers were willing to wait for it, versus buying a different game before *Rare Replay* was available. Brand commitment and willingness to exert effort should reduce how much it costs the company to market to customers. It also reduces customers' desires to switch to competitors' brands. The more customers admire the brand, the more they speak poorly of competitors' brands, which should dissuade their friends and acquaintances from buying competitors' brands. Because they admire a brand, customers are also more likely to spread positive WOM to others, which secures additional revenue for the company's brand. Based on this logic, brand equity should rise when demand for the brand (q) increases over time (i.e., from $t - 1$ to t, or from the previous period to the current period) without (1) an associated reduction in price per unit (p) and/or (2) an increase in unit marketing cost (mc) during the same time period.

Unit Marketing Costs

Finally, the extent to which customers value (admire) the brand should be related to the marketing costs the company must bear to stimulate brand purchases (called unit marketing costs). As brand admiration increases, customers are willing to spread positive WOM about the brand, which should reduce how much it costs the company to acquire new customers. Furthermore, as brand admiration increases, companies don't need to exert as much effort in marketing the brand to customers. Customers are already committed to the brand and will exert effort on their own to get it (see Figure 11.2). Furthermore, as brand admiration increases, it will cost less to retain customers. Accordingly, brand equity should increase when a company can reduce unit marketing costs from a previous period to the current one (i.e., from time $t - 1$ to time t) without an associated reduction in revenue. Brand equity should also increase when the company realizes a revenue increase without an associated increase in marketing costs per unit (mc). We'll say more about what we mean by *marketing* costs later in the chapter.

Components of the Brand-Equity Measure

The above three variables (unit price, quantity sold, and unit marketing costs) provide the basis for calculating two key components of our brand-equity measure. The components reflect (1) an unadjusted assessment of the *magnitude* of the brand's financial value (what we call *marketing surplus*), and (2) the *efficiency* at which this financial value is achieved (what we call *marketing efficiency*). These two components are shown mathematically in the two formulas shown below. Although they may look complicated, these two components are simple mathematical equations that can easily be calculated.

$$\text{Marketing surplus: } (p_{jt} - mc_{jt})q_{jt}$$

$$\text{Marketing efficiency: } \left(1 - \frac{mc_{jt}q_{jt}}{p_{jt}q_{jt}} \right)$$

In these equations:

- p_{jt} means the unit price of brand j at time t

- mc_{jt} means the unit marketing cost of brand j at time t

- q_{jt} means the quantity sold for brand j at time t

- $mc_{jt}q_{jt}$ means total marketing cost

- $p_{jt}q_{jt}$ means total revenue

Let's describe these two components (marketing surplus and marketing efficiency) in a bit more detail.

Marketing Surplus

One can calculate marketing surplus from price, quantity sold, and marketing costs. As the preceding equation shows, *marketing surplus* reflects the difference between the customer's costs at time t (e.g., the price he or she pays to obtain a unit of the brand) and the brand holder's costs at time t (the unit marketing costs). This equation is consistent with our definition of brand equity, but it doesn't adjust for the cost efficiency with which this surplus is generated. Hence, it represents an *unadjusted* measure of brand equity.

Multiplying the difference between price and unit marketing costs by the number of units sold (q_t) yields marketing surplus. Since willingness to pay represents the customer's side, and the unit marketing costs represent the company's side, both customer and company perspectives are reflected in marketing surplus. A marketing surplus means that companies have created, communicated, and delivered brand benefits at a lower cost than the price customers are willing to pay to acquire the brand. The greater the marketing surplus, the more valuable the brand is to the company in a financial sense. We can think of marketing surplus as an unadjusted measure of the financial *magnitude* of the brand's value.

Marketing Efficiency

Marketing efficiency, the second component of our brand-equity measure, can also be calculated from p, q, and mc. But this component reflects the cost efficiency with which the brand achieves its marketing surplus. Consistent with the preceding formula for marketing efficiency, marketing efficiency is calculated as 1 minus the ratio of total marketing costs to total revenue. The lower marketing costs are in relation to revenues, the greater the company's marketing cost efficiency. Brand equity increases as marketing cost efficiency increases. So the less a company spends on marketing to generate a specific revenue level, the greater its brand's equity is. The marketing efficiency component assumes that the brand's revenue is greater than zero. As with marketing surplus, marketing efficiency involves both customers' input (customers' responses in the form of revenue) and a company's input (marketing costs).

Independence of Marketing Surplus and Marketing Efficiency

Importantly, even though marketing efficiency and marketing surplus include common variables (unit price, quantity, and unit marketing costs), they are independent and unrelated brand-equity components. *Marketing efficiency* serves as a weight for *marketing surplus*. It *adjusts marketing surplus* by the cost required to obtain this surplus. Specifically, even if two brands have the same marketing surplus (($p_t - mc_t$) × q_t), the brand value of each will differ if one brand can achieve this revenue more efficiently than the other.

Table 11.1   Adjusting Marketing Surplus by Marketing Efficiency

	Brand A	Brand B
Price per Unit (p)	$10.00	$20.00
Quantity Sold (q)	10	10
Unit Marketing Costs (mc)	$1.00	$11.00
Marketing Surplus ($p - mc$) $\times q$	$90.00	$90.00
Marketing Efficiency ($1 - mc \times q/p * q$)	$0.90	$0.45
Brand Equity (Marketing Surplus Adjusted by Marketing Efficiency)	$81.00	$40.50

We show this concretely by the simple example in Table 11.1. Brand A has $100 in total revenue (unit price of $10 and 10 units sold) and $10 in total marketing investment (unit marketing costs of $1 and 10 units sold). Brand B has $200 in total revenue (unit price of $20 and 10 units sold) and $110 in total marketing investment (unit marketing costs of $11 and 10 units sold). Both brands have the same marketing surplus ($90). However, each differs greatly in its marketing efficiency. Brand A should be higher in value since it spent less than brand B to achieve the same marketing surplus. Assuming that all other costs for the two brands are equivalent, the difference between the two brands suggests that brand B spent 11 times more in marketing dollars to generate the same unit profit ($p - mc$). This adjustment for marketing efficiency yields a value of $81 for brand A and value of $40.50 for brand B. Simply stated, a brand enjoys the highest (lowest) value when it generates substantial (limited) revenue with limited (extensive) marketing costs.

Brand Equity as Marketing Surplus Adjusted by Marketing Efficiency

Marketing surplus and marketing efficiency form the basis for our brand-equity measure. As shown below and in Figure 11.2, brand equity reflects marketing surplus ($p_{jt} - mc_{jt})q_{jt}$ weighted by marketing efficiency $\left(1 - \frac{mc_{jt}q_{jt}}{p_{jt}q_{jt}}\right)$.

Thus, brand equity can be calculated as: $BE_t = (p_t - mc_t)q_t$ $\left|1 - \frac{mc_t q_t}{p_t q_t}\right|$.

When a brand spends more for marketing than its total revenue ($mc > p$), brand equity becomes negative. Our measure assumes that brand equity cannot be negative and exceed total revenue.

More on Marketing Costs

As we mentioned earlier, we don't focus on all costs: only *marketing costs*. Marketing costs reflect the costs incurred to create, communicate, and deliver brand value to customers over time and across all stages of the transaction process (e.g., prepurchase, during purchase, during use, and disposition). We recommend defining the following costs as marketing costs:

- Raw material costs, costs incurred to develop product functions (a portion of R&D costs), and product design development costs (a portion of R&D). Activities associated with these product-related costs are highly relevant to customers' perception of value, which serves as a key driver of brand choice. For example, raw materials (steel versus plastic, organic versus nonorganic, silk versus synthetic fiber, intellectual capital, etc.) matter a great deal to customers.

- Communication and marketing research. Marketing costs should include value-creating and communicating activities (e.g., advertising, trade shows, publicity, sampling, package design, product design, etc.) and other activities (e.g., marketing research expenses) designed to improve customers' brand experiences.

- Costs from removing transaction barriers. Marketing costs should include the cost of activities designed to remove purchase barriers. Thus, costs associated with getting the brand to the customer at the right time, in the right place (e.g., logistics, distribution costs, flagship store design) should be included in marketing costs.

- Costs from facilitating purchase, ownership, usage, and disposition. Marketing costs should include expenditures that facilitate brand purchase, ownership, usage, and disposition (if borne by the company). These costs would include personal selling, merchandising and brand display, warranties, customer service costs, and the like. Order handling and processing costs (relevant at the during purchase stage), call center operating costs (relevant at the prepurchase stage), and customer service center operating costs and customer support and help (relevant at the postpurchase stage) should also be included.

One might include production method–based costs if these costs contribute to customers' valuation of the brand (e.g., handmade production). Companies could also include other costs. What's most important is that brand managers include the *same* types of marketing costs over time so that the measure makes valid comparisons. Keeping what's included as costs consistent over time means that the measure also provides insight into the brand's relative value (its performance in previous periods and performance relative to other brands, including competitors or generic brands). The larger point is that we gain a more accurate estimate of marketing's contribution to the value of the brand if we include only relevant marketing (versus total) costs.

APPEAL OF THE BRAND-EQUITY MEASURE

In the chapter introduction, we noted an ideal measure of brand equity would:

- Be theoretically grounded.
- Result in a single financial number.
- Be reliable.
- Be intuitive.
- Be based on objective (versus subjective) criteria.
- Be based on readily available data.
- Allow the health of the brand to be tracked over time and compared with competitor brands.

- Enable tracking of both the corporate brand name and the individual brands that comprise it.

- Wouldn't require a generic or no-named brand counterpart in its calculation.

The measure we propose has some real appeal as it relates to these criteria.

Theoretical Grounding

First, our measure is based on our brand admiration system. It is grounded in how the brand provides value to companies and on value from a customer's perspective. By its components of price, marketing costs, and quantity, it incorporates the customer outcomes of creating brand admiration (e.g., willingness to forgive, willingness to exert effort, willingness to pay a price premium, etc.). It's also based on a strong theoretical premise: specifically, brand equity is the difference between *customers' endowment to the brand holder* (e.g., the price they are willing to pay and the number of units they are willing to buy) and the *investment the brand holder* has had to bear to secure this endowment from customers (e.g., the costs incurred to market to customers).

A Single Number That Is Reliable, Intuitive, and Based on Objective and Available Data

The measure we propose is based on available data (on price, marketing costs, and quantity sold). It makes intuitive sense that these financial variables should be included in metrics of brand equity. Multiple people should come up with the same financial estimate of brand equity, since the measure's components are objectively determined. Some brand-equity measures incorporate expected future earnings. Our measure does not. Doing so would make the measure less objective and reliable. Estimates of future earnings potential involve subjective judgment and uncertainty. People might not agree on what these estimates are. One could incorporate future values *after* brand equity has been assessed using our proposed measure. These future values include what brand equity at time *t* may be projected to be in the future. But estimating the potential future values is not part of the measure itself.

Comparability across Brands or for the Same Brand over Time

Our measure allows us to compare the equity of one brand to that of another, or to one's own brand over time. These cross-brand and cross-time comparisons can be very informative. For example, look at Tables 11.2A, 11.2B, and 11.2C, which show the internal financial data for two brands: Cruise and Boom.

Table 11.2A shows financial data for Cruise. Based on this information, it's hard to see if there's a problem (or opportunity) with respect to the brand's operations and value. The fact that the brand's revenue and margins have increased over time is a good sign. The brand's profit, ROI (return on investment), and marketing/sales have been steady over the same five-year period. But the continual decrease in ROS (return on sales) is disconcerting and a potential cause for concern. These analyses become even more complicated when we compare Cruise with another brand, Boom, whose financial information is shown in Table 11.2B. Boom's revenue growth has been substantial and its profits have remained both steady and identical to

Table 11.2A   Assessing Brand Equity and Marketing Performance: Cruise Brand

All $ (thousands)	Cruise				
	Year 1	Year 2	Year 3	Year 4	Year 5
Revenue	$1,320	$1,385	$1,463	$1,557	$1,670
Margin before Marketing	$198	$208	$219	$234	$251
Marketing	$173	$183	$194	$209	$226
Profit	$25	$25	$25	$25	$25
Margin (%)	15%	15%	15%	15%	15%
ROS	1.9%	1.8%	1.7%	1.6%	1.5%
Year-over-Year Revenue Growth	—	5%	6%	6%	7%
Invested Capital	$500	$501	$503	$505	$507
ROI	5.0%	5.0%	5.0%	5.0%	4.9%

Table 11.2B   Assessing Brand Equity and Marketing Performance: Boom Brand

All $ (thousands)	Boom				
	Year 1	Year 2	Year 3	Year 4	Year 5
Revenue	$833	$1,167	$1,700	$2,553	$3,919
Margin before Marketing	$125	$175	$255	$383	$588
Marketing	$100	$150	$230	$358	$563
Profit	$25	$25	$25	$25	$25
Margin (%)	15%	15%	15%	15%	15%
ROS	3.0%	2.1%	1.5%	1.0%	0.6%
Year-over-Year Revenue Growth	—	40%	46%	50%	53%
Invested Capital	$500	$520	$552	$603	$685
ROI	5.0%	4.8%	4.8%	4.1%	3.6%

Note: The above information about Cruise and Boom was taken from Farris et al. (2008), p. 324.[12]

those of Cruise. However, its ROS and ROI have declined over time. It's difficult to assess which brand is better in its equity management and marketing performance.

It's much easier to see which brand is doing better by looking at their marketing surplus, marketing efficiency, and brand-equity indicators, as shown in Table 11.2C. There the verdict is clear. The two brands have similar marketing efficiency. But Boom is much stronger in marketing surplus, and thus brand equity (more than twice the brand equity of Cruise at the end of year 5). Moreover, the Boom brand manager is doing a much better job than her counterpart at Cruise, as revealed by changes in brand equity over time. The increase in brand equity over the five-year period shows far greater potential for Boom than for Cruise.

The fact that one can track brand equity using the same objective inputs over time has some additional advantages.

Reducing Manipulation Potential

No measure, including the one we propose, is immune to misuse or undesirable manipulation. For example, brand managers might be

Table 11.2C Assessing Brand Equity and Marketing Performance: Cruise Brand versus Boom Brand

| | Cruise | | | | | | Boom | | | | |
	Year 1	Year 2	Year 3	Year 4	Year 5	Year 1	Year 2	Year 3	Year 4	Year 5
Total Revenue	$1,320	$1,385	$1,463	$1,557	$1,670	$183	$1,167	$1,700	$2,553	$3,919
Total Marketing Costs	$173	$183	$194	$209	$226	$100	$150	$230	$358	$563
Marketing Surplus	$1,147	$1,202	$1,269	$1,348	$1,444	$83	$1,017	$1,470	$2,195	$3,356
Marketing Efficiency	86.9%	86.8%	86.7%	86.6%	86.5%	46.0%	87.1%	86.5%	86.0%	85.6%
Brand Equity	$997	$1,043	$1,101	$1,167	$1,249	$38.18	$886	$1,271	$1,887	$2,874

tempted to reduce marketing costs as a way to increase brand equity in the short term. Alternatively, they might use aggressive short-term sales promotions, creating short-term revenue spikes. But these tactics come at the expense of long-term brand equity. These temptations are minimized if brand equity is assessed on a longer-term basis, when short-term effects may have settled out. Comparisons across years should also minimize temptations to game the measure. To discourage a short-term orientation, one might assess brand equity yearly, but assess the brand manager's performance over a longer period (e.g., over three years).

Lag Effects

Second, our measure doesn't incorporate a time lag between marketing investments (costs) and their revenue return. This is so for several reasons. First, the appropriate time lag would depend on the type of investments (e.g., advertising, package design, sales promotions, etc.). Since different types of marketing investments have different return horizons, a different time lag must be specified for each type of marketing investment. Estimating the magnitude of the lag effect over time is equally challenging, since it's affected by which marketing investments are made and how effective those investments have been. Lag effects may also depend on market and competitive factors that may change over time. Using one-year and three-year time horizons to measure brand equity allows for time periods that are sufficiently long to let short- and moderate-term lag effects settle out.

Other Adjustments

Whereas our measure meets a number of important criteria, there may be situations in which companies wish to adjust the measure based on certain marketplace changes. For example, when there is an industry-wide demand increase, managers could adjust brand equity by considering that industry demand increase.

Aggregation Potential across Brands within the Company

Another benefit of our measure is that managers can assess brand equity at various levels of the company: at the level of a product line, a product, a branded product that includes brand extensions, a business unit, or the company as a whole. For example, the equity of BMW motorcycles and BMW M models could be estimated separately, since they differ in ways that affect brand equity (differences in markets and the company's relative emphasis on resource investment, etc.). However, by aggregating across the set of brands with the BMW label, one can also calculate the equity of the BMW brand itself.

One can estimate brand equity at a higher level of aggregation in two ways. One way is to assess the brand equity of a corporate brand (e.g., Goldman Sachs) based on its total revenue and total marketing costs. Here, brand equity is not the sum of the equity of its individual product brands but rather the equity of the overall company. This method might be appropriate, because while the marketing-surplus component of our brand-equity measure can be aggregated up from a single brand to a complete line of products (i.e., the marketing surplus of a product line is the sum of the marketing surpluses of each product), the marketing efficiency multiplier cannot be aggregated so readily.

A different way is to multiply the marketing surplus of each product brand of a corporation by a weighted average of the marketing efficiency of that product. The marketing efficiency of a corporate brand is a weighted average of all the individual product-level marketing efficiencies, where the weight associated with each product is its dollar share of the whole corporation.

Measuring brand equity at the company level may help a conglomerate assess royalty fees to its subsidiaries for the use of its brand name. For example, many conglomerates (such as GE, Sony, Unilever, Nestlé, Hitachi, etc.) have subsidiary companies that use their names. Since each subsidiary's equity directly and indirectly influences the conglomerate's brand equity, the conglomerate should ensure that each subsidiary strives to improve its own brand equity. Conglomerates can develop compensation systems (e.g., royalty fee assessments) that reward the CEOs of individual subsidiary companies who augment the brand's equity.

No Need for a Referent Brand

Some people define brand equity as the value of the brand name compared to a referent brand (such as an unnamed or generic brand).

For example, conjoint studies might ask about customers' preferences for a brand in light of all of its characteristics except for the brand name and their preferences for the brand in light of all its characteristics plus the brand name. The fact that our measure doesn't include a referent brand has some important advantages.

First, for some brands it is very difficult if not impossible to identify a credible referent with a fictitious or generic brand name. This problem is particularly serious for services, places, countries, organizations, and sports brands (e.g., New York City, Silicon Valley, World Health Organization, United Nations, or Japan). They don't have referents that can be separated from their names. Second, collecting data on a referent brand is an onerous task, particularly if brand equity is measured and compared to the referent brand across multiple time periods. Third, comparing a brand with a fictitious brand that is identical with the brand with the exception of the brand name assumes that the value of the brand lies only in its name. But the value of the brand to customers entails more than its name. For example, Angelina Jolie's brand equity lies not just in her name, but in her physical beauty, too (Angelina Jolie's physical beauty should be considered as part of her brand equity). Fourth and finally, there is a problem of reliability with referent brand-based measures because depending on the sample of respondents (e.g., teenagers vs. 20+ year olds, rural vs. urban, etc.) who answer the referent brand-based measures, the noted equity is likely to vary.

Our measure does not require a generic or unnamed referent in measuring brand equity. The measure is easy to gather, objectively based, and results in a single financial number. With this measure, companies can assess the value of its corporate brand and product brands at a point in time, over time, or relative to competitors.

KEY TAKEAWAYS

1. The financial measure of a brand's equity should take into account how the brand has built value for the company and its customers.

2. Brand equity is the difference between *customers' endowment to a brand* (i.e., the price they are willing to pay) and the

investment the brand holder has had to bear to secure this endowment from customers (i.e., the costs incurred to market to these customers).

3. Three variables—unit price, unit market costs, and quantity sold—are therefore important inputs to calculating brand equity.

4. These three variables produce the two critical components of brand equity—marketing surplus and marketing efficiency.

5. Marketing surplus reflects an unadjusted measure of the financial *magnitude* of the brand's value and is given by the equation $(p_{jt} - mc_{jt})q_{jt}$. This value is positive when the price customers pay is higher than the costs to market the brand. The more units sold, the higher is this value.

6. Marketing efficiency reflects how efficiently the company earns this surplus. It is given by the equation $\left(1 - \frac{mc_{jt}q_{jt}}{p_{jt}q_{jt}}\right)$.

7. Brand equity is assessed by marketing surplus weighted by marketing efficiency.

8. The measure presented in this chapter has some distinct advantages. It uses information available to marketers, doesn't require the use of a referent brand, and can be compared with other brands or with one's own brand over time.

9. One can also create measures of brand equity at various levels of analysis of the company (at a brand level and at the level of the company as a whole).

10. Our measure can also be used to reward managers based on their performance in managing brand equity.

11. One can include additional information (such as industry-wide demand, lag effects, and expected future earnings) if desirable, but this added information is considered to be an adjustment to the brand-equity measure, not inherent to its assessment.

WHAT ABOUT YOUR BRAND?

1. What is the equity of your brand as based on components of marketing surplus and marketing efficiency? How has your brand equity changed over time?

2. What's the equity of your brand compared to that of competitors? What accounts for discrepancies between the performance of your brand and that of your competitor's over time?

3. Looking at all the brands in your company's brand portfolio, which brands are most successful from a brand-equity perspective? What changes would you make to your brand architecture based on this analysis?

NOTES

1. S. Cem Bahadir, Sundar G. Bharadwaj, and Rajendra K. Srivastava, "Financial Value of Brands in Mergers and Acquisitions: Is Value in the Eye of the Beholder?" *Journal of Marketing* 72, no. 6 (2008): 49–64.

2. Florian Stahl, Mark Heitmann, Donald R. Lehmann, and Scott A. Neslin, "The Impact of Brand Equity on Customer Acquisition, Retention, and Profit Margin," *Journal of Marketing* 76, no. 4 (2012): 44–63.

3. Interbrand, accessed April 22, 2016, http://interbrand.com.

4. Madiha Ferjani, Kamel Jedidi, and Sharan Jagpal, "A Conjoint Approach for Consumer- and Firm-Level Brand Valuation," *Journal of Marketing Research* 46, no. 6 (2009): 846–862.

5. Kevin L. Keller, "Conceptualizing, Measuring, and Managing Customer-Based Brand Equity," *Journal of Marketing* 5, no. 1 (1993): 1–22; Chan Su Park and Veena Srinivasan, "A Survey-Based Method for Measuring and Understanding Brand Equity and Its Extendibility," *Journal of Marketing Research* 31, *no.* 2 (1994): 271–288.

6. Natalie Mizik and Robert Jacobson, "The Financial Value Impact of Perceptual Brand Attributes," *Journal of Marketing Research* 45, no. 1 (2008): 15–32; Natalie Mizik, "Assessing the Total Financial Performance Impact of Brand Equity with Limited Time-Series Data," *Journal of Marketing Research* 51, no. 6 (2014): 691–706; Roland T. Rust, Tim Ambler, Gregory S. Carpenter, V. Kumar, and Rajendra K. Srivastava, "Measuring Marketing Productivity: Current Knowledge and Future Directions," *Journal of Marketing* 68, no. 4 (2004): 76–89.

7. See Kusum L. Ailawadi, Donald R. Lehmann, and Scott A. Neslin, "Revenue Premium as an Outcome Measure of Brand Equity," *Journal of Marketing* 67, no. 4 (2003): 1–17.
8. Stahl et al., "The Impact of Brand Equity."
9. Andreas B. Eisingerich, Hae Eun Chun, Yeyi Liu, Michael Jia, and Simon J. Bell, "Why Recommend a Brand Face-to-Face but Not on Facebook? How Word-of-Mouth on Online Social Sites Differs from Traditional Word-of-Mouth," *Journal of Consumer Psychology* 25, no. 1 (2015): 120–128.
10. Jan-Benedict E. M. Steenkamp, Harald J. Van Heerde, and Inge Geyskens, "What Makes Consumers Willing to Pay a Price Premium for National Brands over Private Labels?" *Journal of Marketing Research* 47, no. 6 (2010): 1011–1024.
11. The material in this chapter was adapted from C. Whan Park, Deborah J. MacInnis, Xavier Dreze, and Jonathan Lee, "Measuring Brand Equity: The Marketing Surplus & Efficiency (MARKSURE) Based Brand Equity Measure," in *Brands and Brand Management: Contemporary Research Perspectives*, eds. Barbara Loken, Rohini Ahluwalia, and Michael J. Houston (New York: Taylor and Francis, 2010), 159–188.
12. See Paul W. Farris, Neil T. Bendle, Phillip E. Pfeifer, and David J. Reibstein, *Marketing Metrics: Fifty + Metrics Every Executive Should Master* (Philadelphia: Wharton School Publishing, 2008).

CHAPTER 12

Brand Dashboards

A brand's health is similar to human's health. We must not take it for granted. It's perhaps the most precious thing we have.

INTRODUCTION

Today Apple is one of the most celebrated and highly valued global brands. Yet it's possible that it has already passed its zenith. Worse still, the brand's health may be at risk and brand managers may not even be noticing. If Apple has passed its peak, the situation is not likely due to lack of data. Apple brand managers are well aware of the precise figures for sales volume, revenue, costs, and profits for Apple products. They probably examine these figures weekly, if not daily. But do they have a solid understanding of what's driving these figures and what to do next? Do they collect diagnostic input on *why* Apple's financial performance might slide, and if it does, *how* to stem it? Will efforts at stemming a decline be sufficient, or will customers regard those efforts as too little, too late?

The field of marketing doesn't lack for marketing metrics. Hundreds exist. In fact, it's quite easy for managers to get to a state of analysis paralysis: having tons of data but not knowing quite what to do with it all. Complicating matters further, many measures are disconnected from the broader overarching framework of what drives brand success. Looking at a particular metric (say a net promoter score or social media "likes") in isolation doesn't provide much insight into how a brand got where it is and what should be done next to improve it. The problem is not the lack of measures, but rather the lack of insight into (1) *which* measures to use, (2) *how* to use them collectively to arrive at a solid picture of a brand's health over time, and (3) *what* to do next when signs of decline emerge. We tackle these issues in this chapter.

OVERVIEW

In the prologue, we stated that our book is distinct in providing an integrative perspective on building, strengthening, and leveraging brand admiration so as to provide value to customers and companies. According to our framework, the ultimate destination point for brands is brand equity (see Chapter 11). This financial measure of brand health is critical to CMOs, CEOs, and CFOs. Indeed, it provides C-suite insight into the financial value of brands to the organization. But brand equity is an *outcome* measure of all previously executed branding decisions. Brand equity describes *how well* (in monetary terms) the brand is doing. But it doesn't provide insight into *why* brand equity might be higher or lower than expected and *what managers should do* given the brand's current equity level.

To get to that level of understanding, we need to assess the *drivers* of brand equity; specifically, the nonfinancial factors shown in Figure 12.1. These metrics include measures of the 3Es; brand trust, love, and respect (and mind, heart, and spirit share); brand admiration; and brand loyalty and advocacy behaviors. These measures reflect how *customers* think about their relationships with the brand. Brand managers can clearly add other metrics. However, we believe that these metrics are essential components of a brand admiration dashboard. They help brand managers and others in the organization (1) assess the brand's current performance, (2) assess what's driving its performance, and (3) assess what actions should be taken next.

We call the set of measures shown in Figure 12.1 the *brand admiration dashboard*. We suggest that it's not just brand managers who benefit from the brand admiration dashboard. Its use can cascade down through the organization and up to the C-suite in light of its metrics' potential to affect how the brand moves forward. Notably, these dashboards can be used at any level in the organization—at the product level, business unit level, and corporate level—indeed, at any of the business hierarchy levels discussed in Chapter 10.

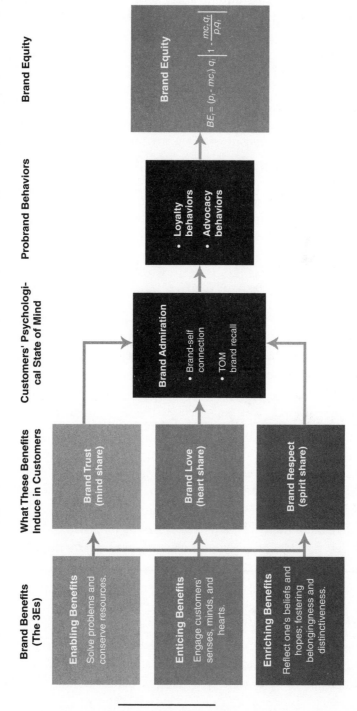

Figure 12.1 Metrics That Comprise the Brand Admiration Dashboard

241

To best explain the brand admiration dashboard and its diagnostic and prescriptive power, we base our illustration on data we've collected from customers of a major supermarket. This illustration shows how managers use brand admiration dashboards to gain insight into how the brand is currently doing and to diagnose what the brand needs to do to sustain its success or to improve. But first, let's clarify the benefits of using dashboards.

What a Brand Admiration Dashboard Can Do for You?

Put simply, a brand admiration dashboard offers five key benefits (see Table 12.1).

Help Assess Current Status

First, like the dashboard of a car, a brand admiration dashboard indicates the brand's status at a specific point in time. It indicates *where the brand currently is*. It gives managers an idea about what is going on with the brand *right now*.

Facilitate Action Plans to Reach Goals

A brand admiration dashboard also provides insight into *what needs to be done next* to strengthen brand admiration. How often have you been given brand-related data that provide no clue as to what steps you should take next? Without a plan or some simple guidance, the brand's health cannot improve—and clearly having no plan won't help it. Metrics that provide guidance on how you can improve the value of your brand are worth their weight in gold.

Track Progress toward Goals

A brand admiration dashboard lets brand managers track real-time progress toward a goal. Imagine that you want to increase customers' perceptions of how well your brand enables customers. You make product improvements, train your sales force to discuss these new enabling benefits, and put hundreds of thousands of dollars into marketing communications to get these ideas across. After a year, you find that your customers aren't really seeing the ways in which the brand is better than before. Wouldn't you rather have known that your marketing efforts were ineffective earlier? By collecting real-time data on a consistent basis, we can be assured that we are moving toward our goal and that our marketing investments are paying off.

Enhance Action/Performance Accountability

Accountability of actions is an important element that affects marketing's influence within the company.[1] A useful brand admiration dashboard emphasizes accountability for contributing to and achieving strategic goals. Performance goals for those who are responsible for building, strengthening, and leveraging brand admiration can be tied to brand dashboards. Doing so clarifies what employees are working toward. It motivates them to work toward a goal because they see that they have some personal responsibility for making it happen. This information also provides a common goal that all employees involved in branding can work toward. It enhances the likelihood that everyone is on the same page, and that all oars of the organization are rowing in the same direction. A brand admiration dashboard can also provide accountability at the divisional level. For instance, comparing brand admiration dashboard results across geographical divisions can provide insight into where investments are paying off and where future investments are needed.

Enhance Knowledge Sharing

To be maximally useful, brand admiration dashboard findings need to be shared across the organization. It's vital to keep employees in the loop and empower them to act toward the brand's strategic goals, particularly since these individuals represent the brand to customers and often deliver the brand's promise to the outside world (see Chapter 4). Involving employees and equipping them with brand dashboard information also gives employees a sense of ownership over brand success and a sense of urgency about acting on behalf of the brand.

Table 12.1   Do's and Don'ts of a Good Brand Admiration Dashboard

Brand Admiration Dashboard Benefits	Good Brand Admiration Dashboards...	Brand Managers Should...	Brand Managers Should Not...
Assess Current Status	Assess where the brand currently is.	Develop a brand admiration dashboard that is aligned with strategic objectives of the brand.	Have measures that are disconnected from the brand's strategy and from strengthening brand admiration.
Facilitate Action Plans	Help brand managers decide what to do next.	Examine dashboard results to plan future actions.	Ignore the brand's goals, not analyze data pertinent to them, or fail to use dashboards to plan future actions.
Track Progress toward Goals	Check progress made toward a specific goal.	Ensure that data are as real time in nature as possible.	Collect dashboard data irregularly or inconsistently.
Enhance Action/ Performance Accountability	Hold employees accountable for progress toward goals.	Analyze data such that accountability for and contribution toward strategic goals can be tracked.	Rely solely on financial metrics of accountability. Nonfinancial metrics can provide more diagnostic information.
Enhance Knowledge Sharing	Facilitate knowledge sharing and communication within the organization.	Create involvement with the brand's financial and nonfinancial performance.	Make data inaccessible to employees who are responsible for the brand.

A brand admiration dashboard that achieves the effects described in Table 12.1 increases the likelihood of the brand's success in the marketplace, the credibility of marketing within the company, and the brand's stock market performance.[2] It gives *brand managers* a glimpse of the brand's progress, providing valuable time to lead the brand in the right direction or turn things around before financial damage is done. It gives *employees* useful information about where their actions are best directed. Finally, it helps members at the C-suite level evaluate where investments in the brand should be made, and whether these investments in branding are paying off from a financial and a nonfinancial perspective. Many of the nonfinancial measures of the brand admiration dashboard reflect the intangible value of a brand—metrics that are not considered in accounting assessments of brand value.

THE BRAND ADMIRATION DASHBOARD: AN ILLUSTRATIVE EXAMPLE

To make the discussion of brand dashboards concrete, we provide an illustrative example using data from customers of a major supermarket brand in the United Kingdom. Our goal is to show that even a small-scale survey can provide relevant diagnoses that can inform a brand's future steps. Small-scale data collection efforts can always be augmented by larger-scale ones (online, offline, panel, for customers and employees, etc.).

Sample and Measures

We first identified a panel of consumers who had purchased items from the supermarket on at least one occasion. Panel members were representative of the general population of customers who shopped at the store. We asked panel members a set of questions related to each component in the brand admiration framework shown in Figure 12.1. (We refer readers to Chapter 3 for definitions and examples of these components.) Table 12.5 in the appendix of this chapter shows the questions we asked. Some of our measures used 9-point scales, while others used percentages. To make the measures comparable, we converted the 9-point Likert-scaled items (1 = not at all, 9 = very much) to 100-point scales. For example, a score of 9 on the 9-point Likert scale was converted to a score of 100. In this way, all of metrics are on the same (100-point) scale. We used two types of measures for brand trust, love, and respect. One assesses the absolute level of these concepts. The other measures how much customers trust, love, and respect the brand relative to competing brands. We call these *share* measures, since they're assessed relative to competitors (see the appendix).

The measures that comprise the brand admiration dashboard were all reliable, and they had good face validity, meaning that they seemed to directly tap into the components of the brand admiration model (as we discuss next). Brand managers can always add additional (specific) items. Or they might change the wording of certain items based on the brand in question. Hence, the measures we used should be regarded as illustrative versus definitive. That said, our past research has used these metrics to empirically test our brand admiration model, and these metrics have been used across brands, across industries, across nations, and with different customers.[3] Here, we show that even a small-scale survey can shed important light on the relevant issues a brand is faced with.

Analyzing Dashboard Findings

We used structural equation modeling (SEM) on the data we collected. SEM is a statistical procedure that allows us to see the strength of the relationship among measures, such as those shown in Figure 12.1. The procedure is like regression analysis, but all variables in the model are considered in the analysis simultaneously. Before brand managers interpret the brand admiration dashboard metrics, they first need to check the overall *goodness of fit* of the model that contains the dashboard metrics.[4] The better the model's fit with the data, the more confidence we can have in the results.[5] The model for the brand dashboard data (Figure 12.1) had a good fit[6] and it properly represents the underlying process of how the 3Es lead to brand loyalty and advocacy behaviors.[7] We therefore proceed with our analyses and diagnose the results of the grocery supermarket brand with confidence that the model depicted in Figure 12.1 is satisfactory in fit.

Assessing the Brand's Current Status: Where Is the Brand Right Now?

Let's first focus on how the brand dashboard data can help the company assess the brand's current status, the first objective of the brand admiration dashboard shown in Table 12.1.

Brand Loyalty and Advocacy Behavior

The first column of Table 12.2 shows that the tested supermarket brand scored 41.44 (out of 100) on customers' willingness to engage in brand loyalty behaviors. Since the scores have a theoretical range of 0 to 100, these scores say that the brand has considerable room for improvement in building brand loyalty. It scores 29.33 (again, out of 100) on brand advocacy behaviors. The brand really has its work cut out for it in boosting customers' willingness to engage in brand advocacy behaviors. Table 12.2 also shows that the brand is doing only modestly well on the other dashboard metrics. What's behind these scores? What can the brand do to improve these scores?

Brand Admiration: Brand-Self Connection and TOM Brand Recall

The second column of Table 12.2 shows how brand admiration and its two components (brand self-connection and TOM brand recall) *predict* loyalty and advocacy behaviors. Prediction scores range from a theoretical low of 0.00, which means there is no relationship between the component and the outcome, and 1.00, which would mean that the component perfectly predicts the relevant customer behaviors. The larger the number (the closer it is to 1.00), the more strongly this factor predicts these behaviors. We see that brand admiration is strongly associated with both brand loyalty (.90 is close to 1.00) and brand advocacy behaviors (.91 is again very close to 1.00).[8] This information validates our model, which suggests that the more people admire a brand, the more they are loyal to it and the more they advocate on its behalf.

When we dig a bit deeper, we find that the brand is mediocre on brand admiration (score of 45.72 out of 100) and its component measures of brand-self connection (43.33 out of 100) and TOM recall (46.89 out of 100). Moreover, we see that brand-self connection has a

Table 12.2   Brand Admiration, Brand Loyalty, and Brand Advocacy Behavior Scores: Supermarket Brand

Grocery Supermarket Brand Data	Absolute Score[9]	Contribution to Brand Loyalty Behaviors B*; (p+)	Contribution to Brand Advocacy Behaviors B; (p)
Brand Admiration	45.72	.90; (.001)	.91; (.001)
Brand-Self Connection	43.33	.84; (.001)	.85; (.001)
TOM Brand Recall	46.89	.59; (.001)	.57; (.001)
Brand Loyalty Behaviors	41.44		
Brand Advocacy Behaviors	29.33		

*B = the strength of the relationship; −1.00 means a perfect negative relationship among the variables (the greater the X, the less the Y); 0 = no relationship between the variables; 1.00 means a perfect positive relationship between the variables (the greater the X the greater the Y).

+p = significance of the relationship; a p-value of <.05 means that the relationship between the variables is statistically significant.

strong effect on willingness to engage in brand loyalty (.84 out of 1.00) and advocacy behaviors (.85 out of 1.00). Its effect is also stronger than that of brand recall on brand loyalty (.59) and advocacy (.57) behaviors. The fact that it is not just brand admiration, but also its components (brand-self connection and TOM brand recall) that affect brand loyalty and advocacy behaviors also validates our thinking. The finding that brand-self connection has a stronger effect on loyalty and advocacy behaviors than brand recall means that the supermarket brand might have more success by investing in efforts to foster brand-self connections as opposed to those that foster TOM brand recall. Consumers are probably familiar with the store. So, added efforts in building TOM recall may not pay out as much as efforts to enhance brand-self connections would.

Why does the brand not score higher on brand admiration and its key components (brand-self connection and TOM brand recall)? What should the supermarket brand do next to improve on these key metrics? This is where we need to examine the brand's ability to capture customer brand trust, love, and respect. The reason for this is that these three variables together determine the components of brand admiration and its strength.

Brand Admiration: Brand Love, Brand Trust, and Brand Respect

Table 12.3 shows how well the brand scores on love, trust, and respect, the key drivers of brand admiration and its components. The first column shows the brand does relatively well on brand love (a score of 65.44) but does not do as well on brand trust (42.56) or brand respect (41.66). However, the second column shows that brand respect is the strongest predictor of brand admiration (.86) followed by brand trust (.25). Brand love's impact on brand admiration is relatively weak (.15 out of 1.00). This means that *the company is weakest in providing the most important driver of brand admiration (and brand-self connection), namely, brand respect.* Why is this so?

The 3Es

Looking at the 3Es we see that the brand is better in providing enticement benefits (63.67 out of 100) than in providing enablement benefits (56.26 out of 100) or enrichment benefits (48.11 out of 100). But enrichment benefits contribute more strongly to brand admiration (.72), brand self-connection (.82), and TOM brand recall (.70) than enticement benefits or enablement benefits do (for brand admiration, brand self-connection, and TOM brand recall the model's scores are .27, .41, and .62, respectively, for enticement benefits. They are .26, .36, and .67 for enablement benefits, respectively).

The implications are clear. The company can generate the greatest change in brand admiration, brand loyalty, and brand advocacy behaviors if it focuses on doing a better job on providing enrichment benefits.

Let's zoom in and take a closer look at the subbenefits associated with the 3Es in Table 12.3. We see that the benefits associated with reflecting one's personal beliefs and hopes (.72, .84, and .70 for brand admiration, brand self-connection, and TOM Brand recall, respectively) and those that foster belongingness and distinctiveness strongly relate to brand admiration and its components (.68, .78, and .69 for

Table 12.3 Scores on the 3Es, and Love, Trust, and Respect: Supermarket Brand

Grocery Supermarket Brand Data	Absolute Score	Contribution to Brand Admiration B; (p)	Contribution to Brand-Self Connection B; (p)	Contribution to TOM Brand Recall B; (p)
Enticement Benefits	63.67	.27 (.01)	.41 (.001)	.62 (.001)
Provide gratifying sensory experiences	68.33	.24 (.01)	.38 (.001)	.57 (.001)
Provide heart-warming benefits	59.00	.28 (.001)	.41 (.001)	.60 (.001)
Enablement Benefits	56.26	.26 (.01)	.36 (.001)	.67 (.001)
Solve customers' prob-lems/keep customers safe	53.11	.26 (.01)	.35 (.001)	.68 (.001)
Conserve customers' resources	58.56	.24 (.01)	.32 (.001)	.62 (.001)
Enrichment Benefits	48.11	.72 (.001)	.82 (.001)	.70 (.001)
Reflect personal beliefs and hopes	46.66	.72 (.001)	.84 (.001)	.70 (.001)
Foster belong-ingness and distinctive-ness	49.56	.68 (.001)	.78 (.001)	.69 (.001)
Brand Love	65.44	.15 (.05)	.23 (.01)	.56 (.001)
Brand Trust	42.56	.25 (.001)	.34 (.001)	.74 (.001)
Brand Respect	41.66	.86 (.001)	.93 (.001)	.71 (.001)

brand admiration, brand self-connection, and TOM brand recall, respectively). But the brand's performance on these benefits is not only mediocre in an absolute sense; it's even lower than the brand's performance on the enticement and enablement subbenefits. Clearly working on strengthening enrichment benefits should be a priority.

Brand Heart Share, Mind Share, and Spirit Share

We also gain insight by looking at how much customers love, trust, and respect the supermarket brand relative to other supermarket brands. We do so by using the love, trust, and respect share measures shown in Table 12.4. There, we see that the *heart* share (relative love) score is only 55.84 (out of 100), suggesting that almost half of customers' love goes to competing brands. Worse still are the brand's mind (relative trust) and spirit (relative respect) shares. Table 12.4 shows that only about one-third of the trust (32.58) and respect (36.37) customers have for brands in the category go to the tested supermarket brand. The rest goes to competing brands. The score for respect share is particularly problematic because Table 12.4 shows that spirit share is the strongest predictor of brand admiration (.90), particularly the brand-self connection component of brand admiration (.96).

Facilitating an Action Plan: What Does the Brand Need to Focus on Next to Reach Its Goals?

Now that we know the brand's status, let's see how brand managers and others in the organization can use these metrics to detect the

Table 12.4   Scores for Heart Share, Mind Share, and Spirit Share: Supermarket Brand

Grocery Supermarket Brand Data	Absolute Score	Contribution to Brand Admiration	Contribution to Brand-Self Connection	Contribution to TOM Brand Recall
Heart Share	55.84	.16 (.05)	.19 (.05)	.55 (.001)
Mind Share	32.58	.26 (.01)	.35 (.001)	.77 (.001)
Spirit Share	36.37	.90 (.001)	.96 (.001)	.72 (.001)

underlying cause of lackluster performance and decide what to do next (see Table 12.1).

Briefly, the brand does relatively well on TOM recall, one component of brand admiration. This result is not surprising since the brand spends a lot of money on advertising and promotion campaigns to keep TOM brand recall strong. However, the brand may have to invest more in efforts to foster strong brand-self connections, another component of brand admiration. The most strategic move would be to focus on (1) enhancing enrichment benefits to build brand respect, followed by (2) enablement benefits that build brand trust, and then (3) enticement benefits that build brand love. How? Some possible recommendations are noted below, purely for illustration purposes.

Enrichment Benefit Ideas

First, brand managers and others involved in the brand consider how enrichment benefits can be enhanced. The brand has a successful loyalty membership club card that might have a marginal effect in making loyal users feel like special customers. But perhaps the brand could challenge customers to become better citizens, encouraging donations to food drives or promoting support for local farmers. Perhaps they could give customers the chance to take part in local community events (e.g., fighting poverty, making the local community safer, etc.). The supermarket might develop affiliation groups of people who share similar dietary preferences or constraints (e.g., Asian cooking; gluten-free diets; weight-loss diet enthusiasts) who could contribute recipes, offer brand reviews, or offer other types of support. Perhaps marketing communications could highlight how the brand contributes to charitable causes and what difference it makes to the environment or struggling people's lives. Inspirational quotes related to healthy eating and living could also be shown inside the store, on shopping carts, on the walls of the store, and at the exit.

Enablement Benefit Ideas

Competing on price has helped customers conserve resources, but the real driver of enablement benefits is the brand's ability to solve customers' problems and making them feel safe. One option would be to offer a range of organic products and clearly labeled signs that certify the quality and safety of the foods the brand sells with some short background stories about the farmers or producers. Parking lots could be lit more brightly, the checkout service could be made more efficient, and online ordering could ensure the safety of credit card data. Clearly, input from employees, brand managers, and customers could yield some significant and relevant marketing actions.

Enticement Benefit Ideas

To enhance heartwarming benefits, the store might encourage staff training to facilitate more pleasant customer interactions. The store design; decoration of the walls with friendly, comforting images; and the sincere and welcoming smile of employees can all be used to enhance the warming the heart benefits for customers. Cashiers might use information from the loyalty card to address customers by name, making the shopping experience more personal. Special areas of the supermarket (e.g., the baking section) could be designed in such a way as to create a nostalgic vibe (e.g., cookies like grandma used to make). Scents from baked bread or cookies could augment the sensory appeal of the area.

Taking the consistency and complementarity principles into account, it is through the accumulation of many small things, such as the ones described here, that the grocery supermarket brand can make a big difference to boosting brand admiration over time.

What Else Needs to Be Done?

The brand admiration dashboard data can also be used for the other purposes shown in Table 12.1.

Tracking Progress, Enhancing Performance Accountability, and Internal Knowledge Sharing

To track progress, brand admiration assessments should be made over time. Online dashboards could be set to create alerts when brand performance on a particular metric deviates from stated goals. Such data help managers see where additional work is needed and which of the

3Es the brand needs to focus on next. Tracking also lets managers know if investments to date are paying off. To create a sense of urgency and ownership, dashboards data should be shared regularly. When a milestone is achieved, it should be celebrated to enhance the feeling of success and camaraderie among employees and teams in the company.

Comparing Performance to Previous Years and Competitors

When the company collects the dashboard data regularly, it can compare the current state of its brand to its status in a previous period at any time. Comparisons over time can show whether the situation is improving or worsening, and hence whether priorities need to change and where adjustments need to be made. In addition to direct competitors (such as other grocery supermarket brands), there may be other competing brands (such as Amazon, fast-food delivery, and restaurant chains) that the brand can include in its dashboard assessments. The data that pertains to these potential competitor brands can complement the data shown in Tables 12.2 through 12.4.

KEY TAKEAWAYS

1. Effective dashboards help brand managers, employees, and CEOs assess a brand's current status and performance, facilitate action planning to reach strategic objectives, and track progress toward such goals.

2. Dashboard data should be collected routinely to facilitate brand team members' accountability for achieving the brand's strategic goals.

3. Brand dashboards must be accessible and shared across units in the organization. They should be assessed over time, to ensure a brand remains relevant to customers as the environment changes.

4. Brand admiration (and brand-self connection and TOM brand recall) drives brand loyalty and brand advocacy behaviors. The major drivers behind brand admiration are brand love, brand trust, and brand respect—and in turn the drivers behind these are the 3Es. Each of these elements needs to be captured in the brand admiration dashboard.

5. Enticement benefits (1) please the mind and senses, and (2) warm the heart.

6. Enablement benefits (1) solve customers' problems and make them feel safe, and (2) conserve customers' limited resources.

7. Enrichment benefits (1) reflect customers' beliefs and hopes, and (2) foster belongingness and distinctiveness.

8. While brand love, brand trust, and brand respect capture the extent to which customers love, trust, and respect a brand in an absolute sense, the heart share, mind share, and spirit share dashboards of a brand give important insights about the extent to which such love, trust, and respect is exclusively limited to one brand or spread across different competing brands.

WHAT ABOUT YOUR BRAND?

1. To what extent have you been using nonfinancial indicators to assess the health of your brand? Are these non-financial indicators linked to an overarching integrative model like the brand admiration framework? Have you started to think about how the brand dashboard data can be used to assess the current status of the brand and facilitate action plans to reach desired goals effectively?

2. To what extent are you sharing dashboard data with employees and teams in your organization? How can the dashboard findings be used to create a sense of ownership and urgency such that employees and teams want to act on the insights that the brand dashboards offer?

3. Have you started to capture customer brand loyalty and brand advocacy behaviors?

4. How much admiration does your brand command?

5. To what extent does your brand build strong self-connections and capture TOM brand recall?

6. Have you examined how well or poorly your brand does on the 3Es, brand love (heart share), brand trust (mind share),

and brand respect (spirit share) to better understand where your brand needs to improve next? How could you go about exploring these?

7. Which E is your brand particularly doing well on? How can you strengthen it further? Which E does your brand need to improve on the most?

APPENDIX

Table 12.5   Examples of Measures

• Think about brand X and indicate the extent to which it provides each of the benefits below to you. Brand X has benefits that ...

Enticement Benefits

Provide Gratifying Sensory Experiences	Not at All	Completely
Arouse pleasant visual; auditory; gustatory (taste); tactile (touch); and/or olfactory (smell) sensations or experiences; gratify my visual; auditory; gustatory (taste); tactile (touch); and/or olfactory (smell) senses; are fun to look at; taste; touch; smell; experience; or consume.	1 2 3 4 5 6 7 8 9	
Provide heartwarming benefits		
Are heartwarming; make me feel grateful; touch me emotionally.	1 2 3 4 5 6 7 8 9	

Enablement Benefits

Solve customers' problems/keeping customers safe		
Help me feel secure; make me feel safe; make me feel protected.	1 2 3 4 5 6 7 8 9	
Conserve customers' resources		
Make my daily life easier; fill my needs without wasted time; help me manage my life with less hassle; help me save money or spend less money.	1 2 3 4 5 6 7 8 9	

Table 12.5 (*continued*)

Enrichment Benefits	
Reflect personal beliefs and hopes	
Help me truly appreciate my own heritage and who I am; help me understand who I am and where I am from; express my identity.	1 2 3 4 5 6 7 8 9
Foster belongingness and distinctiveness	
Help me feel connected to others; help me feel part of a bonded group; enhance my relationships with the people I am close to.	1 2 3 4 5 6 7 8 9

- With brand X in mind, how much do you agree with each of the statements below?

Brand Love	Not at All	Completely
I have great affection toward the brand; I love the brand very much; I have warm feelings toward the brand.	1 2 3 4 5 6 7 8 9	

Brand Trust	
I strongly believe in the brand; I have great faith in the brand; the brand is very trustworthy; the brand cares about the well-being of its customers; the brand can be relied upon to consistently deliver high-quality products and services.	1 2 3 4 5 6 7 8 9

Brand Respect	
I greatly respect the brand; I hold the brand in high esteem.	1 2 3 4 5 6 7 8 9

Heart Share/Mind Share/Spirit Share	
Assume you have 100 points that you can allocate to a brand (X) on the one hand versus all of the other brands that you consider to compete with brand X.	

(*continued*)

Table 12.5 *(continued)*

Think about these points as points of love (trust/respect). You have 100
points that you can allocate to either brand X or to the other brands
that it competes with. For example, if you think brand X competes with
four other brands, and you love (trust/respect) these brands equally, you
would give brand X 20 points and the other brands 80 points. If you
only love (trust/respect) brand X, you would give brand X 100 points
and give 0 points to the rest of the brands.

How many points of love (trust/respect) out of 100 do you allocate to
brand X (the rest of the points are allocated to the competitor brands):

Brand Love (Trust/Respect) Points

Brand X	( )
All Other Brands	( )
Total Points	100

Brand-Self Connection

I feel personally disconnected from the brand.					I feel personally connected to the brand.			
−4	−3	−2	−1	0	1	2	3	4

The brand is *not* part of me and who I am.					The brand is part of me and who I am.			
−4	−3	−2	−1	0	1	2	3	4

TOM Brand Recall

	Not at All Completely
To what extent are your thoughts toward the brand often automatic, coming to mind seemingly on their own?	1 2 3 4 5 6 7 8 9
To what extent do your thoughts toward the brand come to your mind naturally and instantly?	1 2 3 4 5 6 7 8 9

NOTES

1. Peter C. Verhoef and Peter Leeflang, "Understanding the Marketing
   Department's Influence within the Firm," *Journal of Marketing* 73, no. 2
   (2009): 14–37.

2. Don O'Sullivan and Andrew V. Abela, "Marketing Performance Measurement Ability and Firm Performance," *Journal of Marketing* 71, no. 2 (2007): 79–93.

3. Park et al. "Brand Attachment and Strong Positive Brand Attitude"; Park et al. "Attachment-Aversion (AA) Model of Customer-Brand Relationships".

4. For an overview and discussion, see Dawn Iacobucci, "Structural Equations Modeling: Fit Indices, Sample Size, and Advanced Topics," *Journal of Consumer Psychology* 20, no. 1 (2010): 90–98.

5. When the model's fit is poor, meaning that it does not reflect customers' actual responses to each variable in the model, managers must consider multiple possibilities for what's causing low fit (e.g., low-model fit could be due to poor-quality customer responses, as might happen when customers don't spend much time in responding, or it could be due to poor measures of the variables in the model, as might happen when translation issues compromise the quality of the data collected).

6. For example, CFI (comparative fit index) = .99 (see Li-Tze Hu and Peter M. Bentler, "Cutoff Criteria for Fit Indexes in Covariance Structure Analysis: Conventional Criteria Versus New Alternatives," *Structural Equation Modeling* 6, no. 1 (1999): 1–55); TLI (Tucker-Lewis index) = .99; RMSEA (root mean square error of approximation) = .042.

7. Meaning that the individual metrics (measures) are linked within the network of related metrics (measures) as we predicted; for example, if a brand scores very high on the enablement benefit but it is not at all trusted by customers, then the metrics are not linked as we argued.

8. Correlation scores are reported for the contribution to brand loyalty and brand advocacy behaviors. The correlation score shows us how strongly two variables are related. The closer the correlation score is to 1.00, the stronger and statistically significant the relationship between the two variables is.

9. Scores on a 100-point scale are converted from a 9-point scale. Remember that the brand admiration score is obtained by multiplying the brand-self connection score with the TOM brand recall score; thus, Brand Admiration = Brand-Self connection × TOM brand recall.

AFTERWORD: CONCLUDING THOUGHTS

We started our book with the company's end game—creating brand equity—in mind. Our brand admiration framework offers unique causal insights into how brand managers can strengthen the equity of a brand, regardless of where in the company's business hierarchy the brand resides (e.g., a branded product variant, a branded product, a branded business unit, or a branded company). We show that admired brands induce brand loyalty and brand advocacy behaviors, creating opportunities for efficient profit and growth. We conclude by reminding readers of a few key points:

1. Brand managers should focus on building, strengthening, and leveraging brand admiration because it (1) represents the most desired brand-customer relationship state, and (2) it has enormous payoffs for a brand and a company (Chapter 1).

2. Building, strengthening, and leveraging brand admiration is relevant to all types of brands—regardless of whether they are in a B2B or a B2C market, or whether they are products or services, celebrity brands, place brands, or entertainment brands (Chapter 2). Some markets (such as B2B markets) will have the most to gain by thinking through the 3Es and identifying opportunities to drive brand admiration, since many are blind to the critical role of enticing and enriching benefits in building and sustaining brand admiration over time.

3. Marketers control the extent to which they build, strengthen, and leverage the admiration of their brand by the extent to which their brand offers benefits that are known to underlie human happiness; that is, the extent to which the brand enables, entices, and enriches customers (Chapter 3).

4. Building brand admiration is not limited to external customers. It starts with building brand admiration from

within. Given companies' ongoing efforts to attract and retain talent, internal brand admiration building efforts are critical (Chapter 4).

5. Brand managers need to think carefully about customers' need profiles and how to offer enabling, enticing, and enriching benefits in a consistent and complementary way (Chapter 5). These activities build the two foundational components of brand admiration: brand-self connections (Chapter 3) and top-of-mind recall of a brand (Chapter 6).

6. Brand admiration ranges on a continuum from high to low, with some brands being more admired than others. But even the most highly admired brands can use a set of value-enhancement strategies to continually enhance admiration for their brand (Chapter 7).

7. Once a brand is admired, companies have the opportunity to leverage brand admiration using product and brand extensions for efficient growth. Good extensions reinforce the brand's core identity, broaden it to include other associations, and facilitate future growth options (Chapters 8 and 9).

8. Brand managers have a variety of brand-naming choices when extending their brands. Ideally, brand-naming decisions will be made within the context of the company's entire brand architecture (Chapter 10).

9. It is possible to measure brand equity. Our novel brand equity measure has powerful conceptual and measurement advantages over other financial measures of brand equity (Chapter 11).

10. Finally, companies can and should construct a brand admiration dashboard to map brand health over time and identify and prioritize areas in which continued efforts at improvement should be made (Chapter 12).

We hope this book has been a good companion along the way, offering guidance and encouragement to help you reach that precious goal of building and strengthening brand admiration, fostering brand advocacy and loyalty behaviors, and enhancing the financial value of the brand to your organization.

INDEX

Note: Page references in *italics* refer to figures and tables.